Praise for

The Light from a Thousand Wounds

"Many mothers who face difficulties raising an autistic child will really relate to this book."

—TEMPLE GRANDIN, author of *Thinking in Pictures*

"Rarely have I encountered such a stunningly poetic memoir. Corey Hatfield has managed to spin pure gold out of darkness. This is a *must-read* for any hurting parent looking for insight, inspiration, faith, and a best friend in the trenches."

—LINDA SIVERTSEN, *New York Times* best-selling coauthor and host of the *Beautiful Writers Podcast*

"With vulnerability, bone-marrow honesty, and un-self-conscious prose, Corey Hatfield has gifted her readers with a challenging, inspiring, and illuminating testimony of the power of suffering to open the deep heart. In the midst of a relentless, unremitting roller coaster of challenges, she confirms the truth Elder Alexander of Gethsemane observed—that the amount of suffering the soul can accommodate is also how much it can accommodate the grace of God. Through sleepless nights, emergency room visits, repeated public embarrassment, and frantic efforts to protect her children from themselves, as well as from uncomprehending teachers and public officials, Corey found, as she navigated the inner landscape of religious conversion, powerful epiphanies and experiences of divine grace: 'Little by little, and completely without realizing it, I was gradually learning to pray from my heart—from the deepest, darkest, most jagged crevices.' Her memoir is a testimony of faith, of grateful surrender and thanksgiving to the power of grace to uphold us and refine us through the darkest times, of crossing a spiritual desert we would never desire or approach willingly on our own but for the love and faith that draws us forward in ways we could never do on our own. Glory to God. Don't miss this book."

—FR. STEPHEN MUSE, PhD, trauma therapist
and author of *Being Bread*

"Although Corey's memoir has excellent insight into having a child with special needs, it has much more to offer. This book shows the power of resilience, emotional integrity, and consistency—particularly in gold-plated devotion to family and making hard choices."

—BRANDON J. ROTH, licensed professional counselor and
co-owner of BA Counseling, Consultation, and Education

"Corey's ability to share the insights of a mother's heart is breathtaking. Her honesty will envelop you in a journey of restoration and healing."

—FR. EVAN ARMATAS, author of *Toolkit for
Spiritual Growth* and *Reclaiming the Great Commission*
and host of the *Orthodoxy Live* podcast

"The work uncovers unspoken and universal feelings of parents who strive to do the best they can for their children. An earnest, sorrowful, and relatable remembrance."

—*KIRKUS REVIEWS*

"A mesmerizing memoir of a family's unconditional love for one another, even while navigating extreme difficulties."

—*PW BOOKLIFE*

"Corey Hatfield's *Light from a Thousand Wounds* is a testament to the resilience of the human spirit and the transformative power of finding meaning in the midst of life's most challenging trials. This beautifully written memoir chronicles Corey's journey through motherhood as she grapples with autism, trauma, and moments of profound struggle, all while discovering unexpected grace and beauty along the way.

What Corey has created with this memoir is nothing short of remarkable. Her raw honesty and poetic prose invite readers to walk alongside her through the highs and lows of parenting and self-discovery. Each chapter is an offering, rich with insight and brimming with compassion, that shines a light for others navigating similar struggles.

At its heart, this book is a love letter to the mothers and caregivers who feel unseen and overwhelmed, showing them that their brokenness can be a fertile ground for beauty and redemption. Corey's reflections on her journey are deeply inspiring, and her ability to find beauty in the shattered pieces of her life will resonate with anyone who has faced adversity.

The memoir is not only a personal healing process but also a gift to the world. It will undoubtedly help countless others who are struggling to make sense of their own hardships, offering solace, understanding, and the courage to keep moving forward. Through her story, Corey demonstrates that even in the darkest moments, there is potential for growth, love, and a profound sense of purpose.

The Light from a Thousand Wounds will leave you moved, inspired, and more compassionate—not only toward others but also toward yourself. It is a must-read for anyone seeking to find meaning and beauty in the midst of life's challenges."

—SUZANNE BLAISING, PhD, psychotherapist
at the Wholeness Center

"Author Corey Hatfield's narrative is raw and filled with emotions, taking the reader into the depths of her experiences while also offering moments of amazing inspiration. Her ability to find light amid darkness makes this memoir both heartbreaking and uplifting. . . . *The Light from a Thousand Wounds* is a powerful and unforgettable story of finding grace and beauty in the most unlikely places."

—READERS' FAVORITE

"An emotional and powerful memoir inside the life of a young mother, with five children under the age of five, a crisis of faith, a marriage on the brink, and a child diagnosed with autism. With each page, you feel the depth of her journey—her fears, frustrations, and setbacks. She confronts these challenges with a startling strength of character. Corey Hatfield's book is not just about coping; it's about courage, patience, and the fierce advocacy that comes with loving a child whose needs are as complex as they are unique. This book is a must-read for anyone touched by autism, including parents, families, and practitioners."

—CORI ANN STEPEK, PhD, owner of
Rocky Mountain Neurobehavioral Health

The Light

from a

Thousand
Wounds

A Mother's Memoir of Finding
Beauty in Life's Darkest Moments

COREY HATFIELD

RIVER GROVE
BOOKS

The names and identifying characteristics of some persons referenced in this book have been changed to protect their privacy.

Published by River Grove Books
Austin, TX
www.rivergrovebooks.com

Distributed by River Grove Books

Design and composition by Greenleaf Book Group and Mimi Bark
Cover design by Greenleaf Book Group and Mimi Bark
Cover image used under license from ©Shutterstock.com

Publisher's Cataloging-in-Publication data is available.

Print ISBN: 978-1-63299-925-2

eBook ISBN: 978-1-63299-926-9

First Edition

To Carol, my *anam cara*,

— and —

to Arin, my soulmate, the love of my life,
and my *kalyana mitra*

The wound is the place where the Light enters you.

—RUMI, *The Masnavi*

Contents

PART TWO: PAINFUL BEAUTY

PART THREE: BROKEN WHOLENESS

Introduction

I came here to study hard things—
rock mountain and salt sea—
and to temper my spirit on their edges.

—ANNIE DILLARD, *Holy the Firm*

Unlike Annie Dillard, I did not set out to study hard things—autism and police restraints, cocaine and car crashes—nor did I wish to temper my spirit on their edges. Yet that's precisely what happened. The jagged crags split me open and spilled my guts. They unraveled everything I knew to be true. Annihilated the woman I believed myself to be. I cried out in protest, cursed their Creator. And all the while, my spirit grew soft and lithe.

In the end, I built an altar at the foot of hard things, and from bent knee, I made a burnt offering of my brokenness and pain. For in my destruction, I found my salvation.

Now I come willingly to study hard things.

PART ONE

———— ❖ ————

Joyful Sorrow

1

Cracking

Man has places in his heart which do not yet exist, and into them enters suffering in order that they might have existence.

—ATTRIBUTED TO LÉON BLOY

October 27, 2011—Grayson's sixth birthday. I have always heard that good things come in small packages. No one ever told me huge, mind-boggling challenges could arrive the same way.

What started off as a tiny, seven-pound, four-ounce baby—initially no different from my other four children—had grown into a strong and violent six-year-old thrashing madly about in my arms. Headbutting, foaming at the mouth, clawing, and biting—he appeared more feral than a cornered wildcat. The middle-aged nurse to my right desperately strove to keep the blood-draw needle in his tiny vein as I tried to manage the rest of his turbulent body with all my might. She kept up with Grayson's pace momentarily and then called for reserves. The second nurse restrained his arms while the first attempted to collect a sample. Bobbing and ducking, they dodged his flailing, out-of-control legs, and their rhythmic movement felt oddly choreographed. Chaotic but somehow functional.

And then, it all fell apart.

The first nurse missed her cue. She bobbed right instead of left, and Grayson's well-placed kick caught her square in the gut. The next few seconds are a blur. But when I close my eyes, I can still see the airborne, splattering blood. I can still feel the weight and pull of his stocky body whipping from side to side. I can still hear their irate voices echoing in my ears.

Suddenly, my son went limp, dead asleep, as he was prone to do when life grew overwhelming. An icy silence froze the room as I, through cringing eyes, apprehensively assessed the damage. The first nurse was breathing hard, still doubled over from Grayson's kick, while the second stood statue-like to my left, hands covering her mouth in shock. Blood streaked their gloves, their faces, my son. Had the earth opened and swallowed us whole, I would have considered it a blessed reprieve.

Finally, after what seemed like an eternity, the first nurse peeled her hands from her knees and stood, meeting my mortified gaze with her steely glare. Without a word, she slowly spun to exit the room and then paused. As if an afterthought, she looked back over her shoulder, almost maliciously, and spat—through tight-pressed lips—the fiery words that would remain forever seared in my brain: "Next time, don't bring a kid like that in here. We don't do violence."

I recoiled in stunned silence as her words reverberated through my body. A viscous mixture of shame and anger began filling my lungs, drowning me from the inside out. Where else was I supposed to bring him? I had yet to discover a blood draw lab that catered explicitly to "kids like that." Kids who were having a hard time in life and whose parents had no idea how to help them. Kids who screamed for hours on end for no apparent reason. Kids whose mothers took them to the pediatrician in search of answers, only to hear their child just needed a good spanking. I thought the medical community *was* the place for "kids like that," but so far, it had been one continuous letdown. Dead end after dead end.

At that moment, something inside me ruptured—punctured by mere words—and began to deflate, permeating the room with my perceived putrid stench. I fumbled for an apology to adequately express my remorse—not only for my son's behavior but also for my very existence.

Back then, I didn't know I could repudiate shame. I simply spread my hands wide and beggarly, indiscriminately accepting any rotten scraps hurled my way. I unquestioningly tolerated the nurse's words. Assumed I rightfully deserved them. Truly, there was something wrong with my son and, therefore, with me. We were not welcome. This much, I understood.

I propped his limp body between my hip and the counter as I fumbled around my purse for my wallet. Regrouping Grayson's dangling limbs, I awkwardly paid and then lumbered sideways through the door while the nurses watched. They stared, hawkeyed and accusing, till I was seated in my car as if they suspected me of shoplifting their last shreds of decency.

2

Encountering

You looked with love upon me
and deep within your eyes imprinted grace;
this mercy set me free,
held in your love's embrace,
to lift my eyes adoring to your face.
—St. John of the Cross, *Spiritual Canticle*

Grayson Andrew slid into this world like the plunge of a double-edged sword. His birth was clean and effortless. Still, it left its mark, carving an indelible groove that would forever compartmentalize my life into two: pre-Grayson and post. In my mind's eye, I see his birth as a vertical slicing, longitudinal in nature, that divided my life into opposing hemispheres: east and west. All northbound travel eventually turns south, but never will eastbound travel turn west. Such is the separation I feel when considering life before Grayson. Although lost to hazy and distant memories, I know with certainty that I was once young and carefree.

Still, there is one link that connects my severed halves.

If Grayson's birth represents a line of divide, Arin's enduring presence would be the ever-uniting equator. Spanning the breadth of my disjointed life hemispheres, he binds them together beneath the spread of his arms. He has known me in both stages and sees none of the partitioning I feel. When I am with him, I feel whole. That's how it has always been. I am most fully *me* when I am with *him*.

For long before the darkness, there was light. In the beginning, there was a love story. Not the larger-than-life, oversexed, front-page kind of story that blows in and back out like a tornado, but the quiet, intimate, deep-rooted type that comes only once and stays forever. The kind that is only fully known by the two who are in love.

I was eighteen the first time I saw him. It was the second semester of my freshman year, and I had just completed my first volleyball season at California Baptist University. It was a gorgeous winter day, and I was basking in the slower pace of the off-season. The air was crisp and the sky finally blue, revealing a new-to-me mountain range previously shrouded in smog. I reveled in my good fortune. It was February, and I was not in Colorado. I laughed as I envisioned my family battling the early morning ice crystals on their windshields.

En route to my first class of the day, I was in no particular hurry to arrive. Lost in my own little world, I passed beneath my favorite tree on campus—a California pepper tree. I loved the way its branches draped like lacy fingers, gathering me beneath its canopy as I grew further sequestered and blessing me with a moment of solitude before merging with the busyness of my day. Under the fullness of its arc, I glanced up to notice a handsome young man headed straight toward me. His backpack was casually slung over one shoulder, and he moved with the telltale jaunty strides of a basketball player. We locked eyes, sheltered by the privacy of my tree, and he cast an easy smile—confident but lacking the typical dose of athletic cockiness. Something in my heart perked up and told me to pay attention. To what, I didn't know. Here was a stranger, a rarity on a small campus. How was it possible I had never seen him? Yet, from that point on, I began noticing him everywhere.

❦

February 16, 1998. El Niño had unleashed its fury. Rainwater stood ankle-deep on sidewalks, and the grassy lawn leading up to our dorm had become a miniature pond. Teetering between youth and adulthood, my teammates and I had succumbed to a good old-fashioned mud fight. Dripping wet and covered in muck, we turned our deviant attention to the boys' dormitories. As we plastered first-story windows with palms full of mud, one cautiously creaked open. Through the widening crack, I saw *him*. He stood silently while his animated roommate leaned out the window to introduce himself. We invited them to the lobby for pizza in a gracious act of surrender. But Arin never showed up. He would later shrug and offhandedly explain, "I never thought a girl like you would actually meet a guy like me for pizza, so I figured I'd save you the trouble."

February 18, 1998. My nineteenth birthday, my first away from home. Apparently, my mother believed that my introverted self would prefer the shame of public humiliation over the discreet care packages sent by other, more normal parents. I was quietly eating lunch, just minding my own business, when suddenly, an absurdly dressed lunatic burst through the double doors of the cafeteria as if it were a saloon. Pitching rolls of unraveling toilet paper, he wove his way through the tables while shouting my name. After my teammates happily betrayed me, the ruthless intruder demanded everyone's full attention before bellowing his screeching rendition of "Happy Birthday to You." I buried my burning cheeks in my hands, and when I finally emerged, I saw only one face. Of course, it was his. Dark-haired and unfairly good-looking, he sat one table to my right, more than slightly bemused.

I noticed him days later, once again, in the cafeteria. Tray in hand, I heard the scene before I saw it. The walls reverberated with the "beats" being drummed on the back table by the men's basketball team. A physically impressive group, their broad shoulders connected one teammate to another, and they thumped to the rhythm in a unified mass—laughing, slightly obnoxious, and very loud. But there was one gap in the solid wall of shoulders. There he sat, casually tipping in his chair, smiling and enjoying the camaraderie, yet separate and self-contained. Somehow, he evaded the limelight without appearing aloof.

Although I knew nothing about Arin Hatfield besides his name and the fact that he played basketball, something about him completely undid me. I spent many moments wondering when I'd next see him.

Thankfully, I didn't have to wait long. That Friday evening, our volleyball team breezed into the boys' lobby, laughing and squawking like a gaggle of geese, where we had planned to meet the men's soccer team and carpool to a party. I trailed behind, less self-assured than the others, but I perked up the second I entered the door.

Off to the right sat Arin. He was casually perched on the arm of a sofa—one leg stretched long and lanky, the other tucked comfortably beneath. Despite the heavily perfumed young women that had just flounced their way across his path, his softly rounded spine did not stiffen with attention; nor did his chiseled jawline swivel to stare, and this minor observation encouraged me to no end.

Yet, when I passed by, his head spun as if alerted by some invisible force, and our eyes locked once more. With a short, upward jerk of his chin, he simultaneously greeted and beckoned me near.

As if in a dream, my legs mechanically bore me across the crowded lobby and deposited me before a young man whose inner flame sucked the oxygen from the room in the very best way possible. Face-to-face, he searched my eyes through his—narrowed, hazel, and thoughtful—and I felt horribly exposed. Even so, it felt quite wonderful to be *seen*. There was something about his eyes—although pure and without guile, they were intoxicatingly intense. They lured me into their speckled pools, made me want to blow off the birthday party, my team—the whole world, for that matter—and stare into their depths all night long.

Suddenly, his pensive look evaporated, and he bolted decisively upright as if he'd resolved an unsettled matter. Leaning forward, he spoke in a low, steady voice meant only for me. "I want you to know I see God in you."

Shocked, I stepped backward, inwardly reeling. Never in a million years could I have predicted such words. None of the boys I knew would ever allow God's name to pass their lips unless they were cursing. But this twenty-year-old near-stranger, who hardly knew my name, had the guts—no, the *audacity*—to peer into my soul, a place unfamiliar even to me, and report on his findings.

My face flushed, whether with delight or embarrassment, I didn't know, and my tongue awkwardly fumbled over what I intended to be a grateful response. Snapping from my stupor, I suddenly realized we were alone in the lobby. Abruptly excusing myself, I hurried to rejoin my team, who, by that point, had already started cramming too many bodies into too few cars.

I spent the rest of the night in a fog-like haze, detachedly tailing my excited teammates with the enthusiasm of a limp fish. Thoughts flashed through my brain as rapidly as the pulsating arcade lights at the local Dave & Buster's: *Who is this Arin guy anyway, and what did he even mean? What can he possibly see in me, and when could he have even noticed? How come I've never seen him before, and why is he now suddenly everywhere?*

I replayed the lobby scene over and over in my mind until I finally remembered my bumbling departure. I then spent the rest of the evening inwardly cringing.

The second I returned to my room, I scribbled a painfully girlish and bubbly note, and slipped it into mailbox 308. "Arin, I just wanted to say thanks for your words of encouragement. What you said stuck with me all night. It was one of the nicest things anyone has ever said. I felt bad because I was kinda rushed and brushed you off, but I'd really like to get to know you better. I'm interested in your story. Well, thanks again for your encouragement. Have a good day!"

Days turned into a week, and I received no response. Finally, after a home basketball game, I descended the bleachers to congratulate Arin on a game well played. But what I intended as a high five turned into the interlacing of fingers and him drawing me close. Close enough to feel the heat radiating off his body and his soft breath grazing my cheek. Close enough to confirm, young and innocent as we were, that our chemistry would never lack.

Gaining courage from his intentional gesture, I offhandedly inquired whether he had received my note. That night, he attempted to break into the campus post office. Suddenly, his mailbox held much more allure than the standard bill receptacle he had previously avoided.

During that week, my friend Becky had been visiting from Colorado. On the day of her arrival, I had asked Arin for directions to the airport, nervous about my inaugural drive to Los Angeles. Thanks to his exceptional instructions, I ended up at the Rose Bowl Stadium in Pasadena, thirty minutes *away* from my intended destination. The day Becky departed, I graciously allowed Arin to regain my confidence by inviting him to accompany us back to the airport.

After successfully dropping Becky off for her flight, I offered to buy Arin dinner in exchange for his time and (finally) good directions. I was thinking of fast food. He was not. Saying he knew of an excellent restaurant, he directed me away from the downtown skyline toward the Pacific coast. A steep, declining exit abruptly dropped us off at sea level, where the ocean unfolded, panoramic and sparkling. We parked at a metered lot and ascended the nearest stairs. As we crested the top step, I was instantly awash in the sights and smells of my first boardwalk experience. Everything vied for my attention, from the brightly clothed vendors to the rip-roaring roller coaster and fleeting screams passing by overhead. We ambled down the lengthy boardwalk to a Mexican restaurant at the tip of the Santa Monica Pier. The waitress seated us in a window booth overlooking the ocean. Outside, the sun was barely sinking into the water, and a light rain had begun to fall.

It would be nice if I could remember any further details, but they've since disappeared like sand through a sieve, as did the four hours that elapsed effortlessly that night. We sat across the table, dissecting our uneaten burritos, and talked about anything and everything that came to our minds. He was more intriguing than anyone I'd ever known yet somehow familiar as a broken-in pair of jeans. After dinner, we meandered back down the pier, where he bought me two red roses from a vendor's plastic bucket.

Arin was silent on the drive back to campus. I can still remember his oversized frame filling the corner of my black Honda Civic and his cheek piled high atop his fisted arm, contemplatively propped on my window. His thoughts crackled tangibly through the car like static energy, escaping through the narrow slits I now know as his "thinking eyes."

Finally, he spoke, with the directness I've always loved and admired. "I like you. I do. But if you don't like me, just let me know so I don't waste your time." I laughed at his boldness and said he was "cool." Later he told me he spent the rest of the night in a quandary, wondering what *exactly* I meant by "cool."

The next night, unaware of his puzzled state, I jotted a Bible verse and clipped it to his door: "Whatever is true, whatever is noble, whatever is right, whatever is pure, whatever is lovely, whatever is admirable . . . think about such things."[1] At the bottom, I added a few words of my own: "Thinking of you."

From then on, we ceased to exist in any form of separateness and simply became *us*. I never had to worry if I should call him or vice versa. We just did what we wanted, and what we wanted was to be together. He woke me up Saturday mornings with the cliché pebble thrown against my window, and we spent the rest of the weekend lost to the world. We could be found lounging on the lawn on Sunday afternoons, strolling hand in hand among the magnolias at dusk, or seated hip-to-hip beneath the wooden gazebo late into the night. We made a rule that if we were together, we simply had to be touching; we had already endured most of our young lives apart. I wanted to know everything about Arin, and he about me. We talked as if the world were ending and we were the last humans on Earth.

After hours of conversation, I slowly began piecing together the mysterious Arin Hatfield. Little by little, I began to understand why I had never seen him before and why he was so content to linger in the background.

3

Uniting

It seems to her that he is now always gazing upon her.
It is a moment of exposure, as she finds herself
a factor in another's life and heart.

—FATHER IAIN MATTHEW, *The Impact of God*

Arin Hatfield grew up on a ranch in Maricopa, California—not so much a rolling-green-hills-kind of ranch as a sandy desert, armpit-of-the-state-type ranch. He always joked that the toothbrush was invented in Maricopa, for had it been designed anywhere else, it would have been called a "teethbrush."

Sandwiched between an older brother and a younger sister, he grew up in a double-wide trailer twelve miles from town. His father raised cattle and grew hay for a living, and Arin was more than happy to wrangle calves, brand cows, and skip school to haul hay. He had BB guns for shooting, rain barrels for bathing, and aqueducts for swimming. It was the perfect, carefree life for a boy—until the day his father died.

Baby Arin and his father

In life, Jay Hatfield was a hardworking, old-school cowboy—government-hating, land-owning, and self-sufficient. He was known to punch a horse for kicking him and once shot a dog for biting his daughter. Not so much out of spite for the hound but more for the love of his child. He was a tougher-than-nails, kindhearted family man—the type a twelve-year-old boy couldn't help but idolize.

One afternoon, while returning from hauling hay, Jay's semitruck blew a front tire. The truck jackknifed, causing one of its two trailers to flip and land on top of the cab. Arin's father died in the ambulance before ever reaching the hospital.

The ranch breathed its last breath along with Jay. It ceased to function and simply became a double-wide trailer on 160 acres. There was no running water, and electricity was limited to anything that could be run off a small generator. Animals were sent to auction, and the abandoned land grew wild. Arin, his mother, and his siblings, lived rudimentary lives with few modern conveniences. Waking and sleeping in cycles with the sun, they relied on kerosene lanterns, propane heaters, outdoor bathroom facilities (i.e., a hole in the ground), and weekly showers at their aunt's house. During the summer, they slept on the trampoline to stay cool. The soaring desert heat made for an even hotter house. In wintertime, they piled together on one bed, shivering beneath mounds of blankets to get warm.

I could hardly believe Arin's stories. He was like a time traveler visiting from a bygone era. I had never met anyone like him who lived the way he did in such modern times. Yet never once did I hear him complain about his father's death or the way he was raised. Rather, he spoke of it as if it were a grand adventure. He loved his childhood and was refreshingly grateful for everything I took for granted—hot showers, running water, flushing toilets, and lights that toggled on and off with the flick of a wrist.

But, tough as Arin's father raised him, nearly every time I visited him, I found him curled in a massive ball, cradling the phone to his ear, a goofy smile on his face, and laughing at inside jokes with his sister or telling his sweet southern mama how much he loved her. He was tender and unperturbed by the thoughts and emotions of women. And as much as he looked the part of a hip, young athlete in his slightly sagging britches, the first time I saw him around a horse, his face softened like aged and worn leather, and I recognized him for what he truly was—an old soul in a young body, simple and good to the bone.

He was full of such incongruities, as untamed and fancy-free as the wind—boldly passionate, spontaneous, and visionary. Everything that I was not. At the same time, there was something solid and oak-like within him that grounded a latent wildness within me. Because of our manifestly different personalities, one might have been tempted to label us a classic case of attracting opposites. Initially, I might have agreed. But the more I learned about him, the more I came to believe that we were actually the same person beneath our outside appearances or, at the very least, that we shared the same roots. We were tethered deeply and profoundly from the start.

Before we met, I never felt like I belonged anywhere. Afterward, there was nowhere left for me to belong.

Yet, as I learned more of his story, one discrepancy stood out. While talking in my car late one night, I asked how he could be so tender and sensitive when his father was so rough around the edges. By then, I had already heard the story of how his dad refused to tell his mom "I love you" more than once. He had gruffly retorted, "I said I loved you once, Lilla Gay. I don't need to say it again."

Arin spoke slowly, pausing thoughtfully between sentences as if considering the question for the first time. "My dad taught me to be a man. My mom taught me to love and be soft." He shocked me by quietly adding, "I'm actually thankful my dad died. It ended up being a blessing. If he hadn't, I would have hauled hay with him my whole life. I would never have left home or gone to school. . . . I would never have met you."

Nine months after our first date, Arin proposed to me in a candlelit room of his mother's apartment. He led me upstairs by the hand, where a basin of warm water awaited. On bended knee, he symbolically washed my feet in silence. Only the sound of sloshing water filled the air. When he finished, he asked in a hoarse whisper if I would allow him the privilege of serving and caring for me all the days of my life.

In true Arin fashion, he remembered (after the fact) that he had forgotten to consult with my dad and promptly called to beseech his belated blessing. Afterward, we went to a movie. There was no fanfare, no engagement party, no friends with bottles of champagne. It was just Arin and me—the way we both preferred. He was all I ever wanted and everything I never knew I needed.

We married on July 30, 1999, after approximately a year and a half of dating. I was twenty. He was twenty-one. Our wedding was humorous and carefree, meaningful and rich, and its tone mirrored our relationship. There was no stress in blending families, no overbearing mothers or dramatic bridesmaids, no pre-wedding arguments, no nerves. I bought the first dress I tried on. It cost three hundred dollars.

At one point during our reception dinner, my uncle suddenly stood and made his way to the DJ's table, where he hijacked the microphone. Arin and I exchanged nervous glances as he cleared his throat.

"Marriage is a time for new beginnings," he began austerely. "It is a time to let go of the past and walk forward in the newness of life. At this time, we would like to request that all young men with keys to Corey's dorm room please come forward and relinquish them in this basket."

Our wedding day, July 30, 1999

Nearly every young man in attendance rose from his seat. With feigned, remorseful waves of goodbye, each deposited their key, which my family had planted beforehand.

Then, my uncle made the same request of any female possessing a key to Arin's dorm. The room went deathly silent until, finally, an eighty-five-year-old woman popped up from her seat. Blushing and giggling like a schoolgirl, she pitter-pattered toward the basket with narrow, wobbling steps, her too-tight skirt preventing a full stride. She blew an exaggerated kiss in Arin's direction and then reluctantly surrendered her key.

After our honeymoon in the Bahamas, we loaded a rental van with wedding gifts and returned to California to finish school. Arin served as an associate pastor at a local church and coached girls' basketball on the side. Since we were just as poor as we were in love, our first year of marriage was highlighted not so much by our activities as by the characters we met. There was Pastor Phil, the leather-clad, goateed biker-preacher who got in knife fights and turned Led Zeppelin songs into praise music. Tim, the church parishioner, came to dinner on multiple nights without ever bothering to remove his motorcycle helmet. He sat—helmet-clad—for hours on end, squinting through thick coke-bottle glasses and sharing story after story of his failed suicide attempts and rampant drug usage. Then there were Candace, Tommy, and Safron, the beloved trio of hilarious high school basketball players who gifted Arin with a softly filtered photograph of themselves on the last day of the season, with the affectionate, handwritten inscription, "2 our favorite coach this season. I know you likes us so I don't have to ask. Much love from da homies on well-fare."

Although I initially believed Arin to be mild and reserved, in reality, he was a swirling flurry of ambition. There was a restlessness that pulsed through his veins, propelling him forward at warp speed. Perhaps his father's untimely death had bestowed an acute awareness of his own mortality. Nevertheless, he was constantly chasing, searching, for something—but that *something* always existed just beyond his reach. He longed to be the next Billy Graham, circling the world teaching and preaching, and there was nothing he wouldn't do to succeed.

We traveled anywhere he was invited to speak—motorcycle rallies, retirement homes, Korean churches, and mountain chapels. None of that would have seemed extraordinary had my upbringing been ever-so-slightly more adventuresome. But Arin was the introduction of color to my world, so normally black and white.

I grew up in a sheltered and protected suburb—exactly how I preferred. I lived within one block of the same house my whole life and attended the same schools as my mom. Downtown Denver and homeless people scared me, and the rugged unpredictability of nature made me queasy. Sundays were for church, followed by lunch at McDonald's. Friday nights were for pizza and movies, and summers were for reading and riding bikes. My mom, who stayed home to raise my two younger sisters and me, read *Little Women* aloud over home-cooked breakfasts, while my dad, who ran the family sod farm, played catch with us in the cul-de-sac after dinner. Life was idyllic, dependable, and safe, and we blended in perfectly with every other middle-class, midwestern family I knew.

Still, I possessed *one* distinguishing feature.

I was a "mixed baby." My dad is Japanese, my mom Caucasian, and I, the final by-product, am naturally half of each. As a child, my ethnicity was constantly spoken of as if it were my key selling feature. But it was rarely expounded on and, practically, meant less than nothing to me—that is, until one dusky summer evening when a neighborhood boy pedaled by on his bike. Using his fingers to pull his eyes taut, he chanted, "Chinese, Japanese, dirty knees, look at these!"

I puzzled over his taunt for some time, churning his words over and around in my fourth-grade mind. I couldn't grasp their meaning, but the look on his face informed me that whatever mixed-up version I was obviously wasn't good. Perhaps I should have told my parents, but I was too ashamed to repeat his words. I never told anyone about that brief but life-changing drive-by. Yet from that night on, I began to wish so badly it hurt that I looked more like my beautiful, blonde-haired, light-skinned best friend.

In hindsight, I realize my growing-up years were imperceptibly but unquestionably tainted with an underlying sense of non-belonging, which I carried with me always like identification papers. Therefore, I never thought it odd when people asked, "What *are* you?" I always understood their meaning and dutifully obliged them by respectfully answering, "I'm half-Japanese."

Even as a child, I understood they weren't asking about my half-white part.

Grown-ups thought my sisters and I were exotic. I just wanted to feel normal and make it through dinner at a restaurant without some well-intentioned adult interrupting our meal to inquire, "Excuse me, but I just have to ask . . . what *are* they?"

This subtle half-distinction unknowingly defined me and made me half-different from all the other girls—not different enough to tease but not similar enough to befriend. I drifted solo, lost in the nondescript land of "neither-nor." My first elementary school friends were Korean, Vietnamese, and Thai, and although they welcomed me as a fellow Asian, I still felt half-fraudulent.

Me and my sisters, Jenna and Dani

By middle school, I subconsciously began studying people alongside my textbooks—namely, other girls. I wondered what they knew that I didn't that allowed them to move effortlessly through life—laughing, conversing, casually tossing their hair, and claiming their God-given right to exist. For me, every interaction with people felt awkward and challenging, and everywhere I turned, I sensed the universe whispering, constantly reminding me that I only halfway belonged.

Still, I was astute enough, and eventually, I learned to fit in by blending in, to disappear by standing out. By high school, my titles were sufficient to mask my insecurities, and I hid behind them like an iron-forged shield: honor student, annual homecoming royalty nominee, four-year varsity setter on the volleyball team, three-year captain, all-state player . . .

On and on, the list grew. But my confidence did not.

In my mind, although I was part of the homecoming court, I never actually won. And despite my academic and athletic accomplishments, I was never smart or talented enough to secure a "real" scholarship at a big college like my other teammates. I excelled enough but never overachieved; I did what I was supposed to but never with flair. More of the same: "neither-nor."

Father Iain Matthew, a Catholic priest, once quoted a Spanish mystic, saying, "'A person is enlightened,' not 'when they get an idea,' but 'when someone looks at them.' A person is enlightened when another loves them. The eyes are the window on to the heart; they search the person out and have the power to elicit life."[1]

So it was when I met Arin. Like Lazarus summoned from his tomb, Arin's gaze called me into being. In his eyes, I saw parts of myself reflected that I never knew existed.

He stared long and hard as though I were the first human he had ever encountered. I always dropped my eyes in embarrassment and (somewhat) jokingly ordered him to look away. Even then, he refused. He continued to stare unabashedly and unapologetically. When I finally glanced up, I would encounter his eyes—gentle, undeterred, still gazing. They overflowed with unadulterated devotion, and this alone was enough to terrify me.

For in my heart, behind the shallow titles and whatever he *thought* he saw in me, I knew the truth. I was a "neither-nor" and was not, and would never be, enough. I knew with certainty that one day the scales would fall from his eyes, and the diamond-in-the-rough that I had fallen so desperately in love with would finally see me for all I was not. And when that happened—and I knew that it *would*—he would have no other choice but to move on to greener pastures.

Twenty-three years later, I am still waiting for the scales to fall. Still, Arin stares adoringly as if I hung the moon. He stubbornly refuses to see anything but good in me and believes I can do anything I desire.

And still, I have no idea why.

4

Beginning

Every morning was a cheerful invitation to make my life of equal
simplicity, and I may say innocence, with Nature herself.

—HENRY DAVID THOREAU, *Walden*

It was Arin's increasing restlessness that uprooted us after our first year of
marriage and drove us back to my home state of Colorado. My grandparents owned a small house in the country that sat vacant on the family
farm, atop six hundred acres of perfectly manicured, emerald-green sod,
and they were more than happy for us to live there rent-free.

We drove straight through from California, and when we finally exited
the freeway, I began to view the old, familiar landmarks through Arin's
country-born eyes. Off to the right, the Pepper Pod restaurant stood alone,
while a mom-and-pop grocery store and the slightest hint of a main street
ran briefly to the left. There were no stoplights, and what little traffic passed
through did so under the sleepy watch of a worn and solitary stop sign.

Within seconds, we crossed over the heart of town, which was marked
by a double set of rickety old railroad tracks running straight through its

center. The back half of town consisted of a small library, a smattering of dilapidated houses in tidy rows, an elementary school, and a white clapboard church. Then, as quickly as it came into view, the town vanished, swallowed whole by swaying stalks of corn.

Ahead to the east, black pavement pointed long and straight as an arrow, stretching infinitely onward—or at least to Kansas. To the north and south, long furrows of corn clawed through earth and soil to kiss the horizon, and exactly three-and-a-half miles past town stood a crooked metal signpost, half-heartedly showing the way home. It was plainly labeled "CR 49½" and served as our oft-missed cue to turn from the main road onto a tapering dirt lane. Instantly, towering corn engulfed our car, and as the world narrowed to a singular focal point, I felt once again like a child, wrapped in the comfort of my family's farm.

Eventually, the field on the right gave way to a pond, and the road curved to follow its shoreline. When, in time, the left field opened up, we were spat out at the end of a long dirt driveway—*our* dirt driveway. Straight ahead was a mechanic's shop, and to the left, a cluster of trailers where the migrant workers lived. A smattering of chickens and peacocks roamed free, and freshly washed laundry hung limply from clotheslines.

Slightly uphill from the other trailers sat a modest cream-colored house surrounded by newly planted geraniums and petunias and nestled in an endless ocean of green. A lone, archaic oak rose high above the house, and its majestic presence never ceased to remind me of the smallness and brevity of human life.

It was in this home that we began our second year of marriage.

Immediately, the countryside implanted itself in my soul. Over time, its gestational seed took root and claimed me for one of its own. Although a city girl by birth, in the wide-openness of the country, my roaming spirit found its home. I felt infused with an insatiable longing that refused to be quenched by anything other than beauty.

But in all our days there, I never once thirsted.

During the summer months, the first sight my eyes beheld upon awakening was a plush, green carpet of grass that lay unrolled as far as the eye could see. Only the lilting melodies of early morning songbirds could be heard, and our bedroom curtains danced along to their tunes, lifting and twirling on a cool morning breeze. The slightest waft of manure floated in through open windows, but to me, it was the fragrance of home.

Every evening after dinner, we went on long, rambling walks—not on any carved or trodden path made by man, but straight as the crow flies— wherever we pleased. Our Weimaraner puppies romped and raced their way beneath irrigation sprinklers while we wobbled foot-over-foot across the rusty railroad tracks that demarcated the farm's edge. Both we and the puppies were equally carefree and happy.

It was only when the heat of day finally collided with the settling cool of night and sent opposing temperatures swirling like miniature tornadoes around our ankles that we finally turned to head toward home. Tucked away in our cozy house, we read and discussed our findings. Oftentimes, we read aloud. When, at last, the conversation waned, and eyelids drooped heavy, we climbed into bed as one and drifted off to sleep, serenaded by the haunting yet comforting lullabies of passing train whistles and transient coyotes. Part of me wishes we could have stayed there forever. I sometimes wonder what life would have looked like had we never left.

Still, there was something about the tranquility and endless physical space that created room for new growth. I found parts of myself unfolding, breathing, and awakening. I was calm, I was happy, and I was in love.

I was also with child.

Caleb Jordan Hatfield burst forth into the world on July 17, 2001, two weeks before our second anniversary. Both of our families were present, ears pressed tight to the door, and at the sound of his first cry, not a dry eye was to be found. He was the first grandchild on either side, and one would be hard-pressed to find a child more doted on and adored.

I spent countless hours staring over the rails of his crib—following the rhythmic rise and fall of his chest and smiling softly at his wheezing breath. I scrutinized every inch of his dark skin, long eyelashes, full lips, and those slender fingers with their contrasting, stumpy nail beds. I constantly fought the urge to reach out, stroke his silky hair, and kiss his squishy cheeks. But as a new mother, I deeply understood the value of sleep—both his and mine—and so resigned myself to being a passive observer, choosing instead

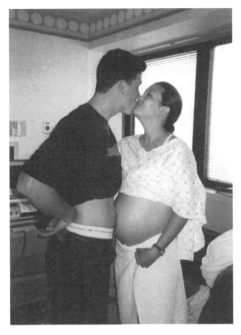

Getting ready to deliver baby Caleb, July 17, 2001

to speculate in silence: *What will his first words be? When will he take his first steps? When will he wake up so we can play?*

Little did I know that eighteen years later, I would find myself staring at that same son over a new set of bedrails. Unyielding metal bars would replace the wooden slats of his crib, the warmth of his nursery exchanged for the cold sterility of a hospital. I would clutch his calloused, man-sized hand in mine and once again study his features for hours on end—the gash above his right eyebrow, the swelling of his broken nose, the bright red stream that trickled from somewhere deep inside his ear, and those same stumpy nail beds, now caked in dried blood the color of earth. I would synchronize my breath to his, artificially induced, and would grow immune to the steady whine of the machines that kept him alive.

But at his bedside eighteen years later, I would show far less restraint. I would endlessly stroke his coarsened hair, smother him in the kisses I had been missing for so long, curl up in the bed beside him—my hand on his faintly beating heart. And while my sandpaper eyes would once again yearn for sleep like those of a new mother, my son would slumber on for days in his medically induced coma. Once more, I would ask the old questions, but with a slightly different twist: *Will he ever speak? What will his first words be? Will he be able to move, to walk? Will he ever wake up?*

Six stories below, Arin would pace circles around the hospital parking lot, head hung low in desperate prayer, hands firmly clasped behind his back, rambling aimlessly as we once did on the farm. A shrouded veil of suffering would separate us then, and the world would lose its color.

But in all our days on the farm, I never once thirsted.

Shortly before Caleb's birth, Arin accepted a pastorate at a small country church, where kindhearted parishioners still helped one another harvest crops and slaughter pigs. Women rose early to cook breakfast and gather eggs and then routinely convened on Main Street to scour the Saturday morning craft fair.

News of Arin's hearty appetite spread quickly. Therefore, we never lacked a Sunday-supper invitation. No proper country-bred woman could bypass the opportunity to showcase her skills. Each had a specialty—their gramma's pot roast or mama's apple pie, cherry cake with butter-rum sauce, or a hash brown casserole served in vintage wedding crockery. Much to their delight, Arin always helped himself to seconds and then thirds, and his profuse stuffed-mouth compliments made their plump cheeks glow with pride.

At the ripe old age of twenty-three, the parishioners loved Arin and the new life he breathed into their stagnating community. There were a few old-timers who resisted change of any kind, but even they agreed—Arin's voice was loud, and it carried. Finally, they could hear a preacher from the back of the church.

Occasionally Arin filled in at neighboring churches that couldn't afford to hire their own full-time pastor, and it was at one such church that we met Bob. Bob was a chaplain at a maximum-security prison, one hundred miles away, and like everyone, he and his wife, Connie, invited us to supper one Sunday evening.

The experience, however, proved to be anything other than normal.

Their home was well-decorated, slightly Victorian. Pewter pitchers replaced the typical ceramic roosters, and a pressed linen tablecloth supplanted the oh-so-practical vinyl. Glistening china sparkled in flickering candlelight, and upon being seated, we were served a multicourse meal by their young daughters in plaid holiday dresses. Salmon, still on the skin, was passed on a platter in sharp juxtaposition to the standard Sunday roast.

Bob and his wife had six or seven children, maybe even eight, all of whom were homeschooled and impeccably polite. After dinner, the girls cleared the table and washed the dishes while the boys were excused to play.

I had never witnessed such a family. They functioned smoothly as a well-oiled machine—perhaps a little too smoothly for my liking. But Arin, who had long been interested in homeschooling, was intrigued to learn more.

Bob and his family were *Calvinists*, Arin later explained—a word that easily slipped from my brain. In time, Bob invited Arin to preach at the prison, and the two-hour drive provided ample opportunity for conversation. Whenever Arin met with Bob, he came home with a new stack of books. He perused each one cover to cover, and gradually our times of evening reading evolved into theological discussions and the occasional debate.

Our first day in Florida. Caleb, Arin, me, and baby Rylee

Just twenty-two and fresh out of college, I found theology, by and large, uninteresting. Much of the information Arin conveyed sounded foreign, if not slightly absurd. But his appetite had been whet, and an undiscovered love of learning unearthed. He voraciously devoured any literature Bob provided and then later regurgitated it—for my sake—in small, digestible chunks.

Several months later, Bob's agency offered Arin a full-time chaplaincy. We had our pick of several states, and in the end, we accepted a position at the Pinellas County Jail in Clearwater, Florida—the twenty-eighth largest in the nation.

In March 2003, Arin loaded our meager possessions into a moving van and headed east in search of a new adventure. I followed behind days later by plane, with twenty-month-old Caleb in tow, and our latest addition, sweet and spunky Rylee Blythe, not even two months old. My last memory of Colorado was Caleb's little hand sticking out the window waving goodbye to my mom, his gramma, and wondering—through streaming tears—what in the world we were doing.

5

Shrinking

History, including the history of Christianity,
is littered with caricatures of God, like so many mental idols
which have led people either to cruelty or to atheism.

—OLIVIER CLÉMENT, *The Roots of Christian Mysticism*

Once in Florida, my husband was absent more than not for the first
time in our marriage, and our lives diverged onto freshly forked
paths. Arin was thriving in his new career, with chapel services soaring
from 10 or 15 inmates to waiting lists of more than 250. He consoled
the broken and desolate, wept with gang members when their children
were killed in drive-by shootings, and then woefully informed them
they were ineligible to attend the funerals. Sometimes, he received death
notifications in the middle of the night, like when a prisoner's father
wearied of his multiple sclerosis and rolled his wheelchair in front of a
semitruck, thus ending his pain. On those nights, Arin slipped silently
from our bed into his slacks and tie and then drove over an hour to
deliver the heartbreaking news; he never felt right making anyone wait.

He returned before sunrise the following morning, peaceful and happy beyond comprehension.

Despite being the frequent bearer of bad news, Arin quickly became a sought-out favorite. The officers snagged him for lunch while the inmates constantly solicited his presence, especially the lonely women for whom he eventually requested a female chaplain.

While his naïveté amused the irreverent inmates and made him the butt end of many jokes, his good-natured optimism allowed him to see through their crimes into their souls. He treated everyone the same—a sinner like a saint—and eventually, even the most reclusive hearts extended their undying loyalty, like one hardened Italian mobster known to Arin as "Tag." Allegedly, a well-known gangster movie was based on the life of Tag's infamous uncle. Upon his release, Tag made it abundantly clear that if Arin needed *anything* (and he meant anything), Tag would be there in a heartbeat. No one, he stressed, would ever mess with his friend "The Chap."

Meanwhile, I was back in our tiny apartment changing diaper after diaper, feeding babies, and cleaning messes, only to start anew the next day and the next. Although I loved motherhood more than life itself, I missed my family in Colorado and was struggling to find meaning among the mundane.

So I sought comfort where I normally did—between the covers of a book. After leaving Colorado, I'd acquired my own pile, compliments of Connie, Bob's wife. The books contained lessons on holy living—how to be a good wife, mother, and Calvinist. Everything I supposedly needed to learn.

I immediately noticed how every author resembled the other, each looking as if they just stepped off the cover of *The Little House on the Prairie*. They all had long hair with longer dresses; their faces were plain, their bodies unadorned. None of them worked outside the home, choosing instead to homeschool their enormous broods of children, grind their own wheat, and bake their own bread. Without ever declaring it directly, each page seemed to imply, "*This* is what godly women do. *This* and nothing else."

Imperceptibly, as if by osmosis, I slowly began fashioning myself into a robotic replica of the woman I thought I should become—a little less makeup, slightly longer hemlines, a few more opinions kept silent.

We joined a reformed church that espoused Calvin's doctrines and began absorbing the lingo, adopting it as our own. I committed to memory their summary of faith, which, in a nutshell, asserts that we are born entirely wicked, incapable of choosing good. Therefore, in His infinite wisdom, God "elected" some of His created beings for Heaven; the rest He damned to Hell. And just like a toy in a quarter-operated claw game, once you've been *picked*, that's it. *No one* can resist God's will.

It is here that words fail me. This chapter of life, this version of me, has emerged as a black, gaping hole. I recoil at its death-stench and look left and then right for an alternative path to traverse its expansive perimeter. There is one way; it's called avoidance. I can bypass the next few years as if they never existed. But in my heart, I already know—if I detour, my story collapses.

From the edge of my memory, I wrestle with resistance. Our religious choices were irrelevant. No one will even know what's missing. But, after several days of internal warfare, I wave the white flag. In the spirit of authenticity, I will descend the darkness, revisit the intentionally forgotten.

I already know how it will sound—like fringe religious fanaticism. People will judge, shake their heads, and wonder how anyone could have believed such things to be true. Even I still wonder the same. But an innocent heart that desires to please both God and man can be convinced of anything, no matter how ridiculous it may seem.

Besides, it's not like we joined a Kool-Aid cult. We only became Reformed Presbyterians, and almost all the members we encountered were wonderfully kind, well-intentioned truth-seekers, as were we.

Still, the annals of history are filled with gross examples of religious abuse. Many crimes have been committed in Christ's name, and beautiful lives have been marred by ugly theology. Such was certainly the case for me.

Fully embracing our new theology, Arin and I began attending conferences led by well-known speakers who taught that wives should obey their husbands as slaves once obeyed their masters. If a husband commanded his wife to blow their entire life savings on Twinkies, not only should she comply *immediately* but also sweetly and lovingly, with a smile on her face.

It became quickly apparent how wholeheartedly the speaker embodied his belief. When he once caught his wife whispering in the back of the room, he abruptly stopped his monologue to address her out loud. "Mrs. S., it's my turn now. Stop talking." She obliged him with a demure smile, but as she lowered her head, I caught the color rising in her cheeks.

Bible verses were quoted, such as "Children are a heritage from the Lord," and "Blessed is the man whose quiver is full of them."[1] Who, in their right mind, the speaker questioned, would willingly refuse a gift? Children, then, were to be received with gratitude as often as the good Lord supplied. Even attempting to space a baby's birth could indicate a wavering faith. Desirous of being a godly woman, I stopped preventing pregnancy on July 5, 2003—of course, with my husband's blessing. I labeled it in my journal as *The day I surrendered my will and control.* I had never experienced such difficult obedience. More forced than offered, it seemingly consigned me to a life of inevitable misery and insanity.

Several weeks later, six-month-old Rylee suddenly stopped breastfeeding. Although I knew her to be hungry, every time I nursed her, she would suckle and then angrily refuse to eat. Befuddled, I wracked my brain for answers as a vague memory swelled like my rising anxiety. Was it something I'd read or a friend who'd experienced the same? Somehow, I recalled that a fluctuation in hormones could change the taste of my milk.

In a flash, I understood—I was pregnant with baby number three.

I shook my head repeatedly, willing the truth away. Large, overwhelmed teardrops crashed and shattered against the hard surface of my engorged breasts. Somewhere in the background, a starving, red-faced infant wailed.

Numb with shock, I gave up trying to force-feed Rylee and rendered her instead to my lap. I studied her floundering body through a helpless blur of tears. In just eight short months, there would be another child, fully dependent on my incompetent self. Doing the "right thing" had never felt so wrong.

How could I ever please a God so seemingly unwilling to be pleased?

Me with baby Jacob, 2004

I began ascribing to the belief that I was good for nothing more than cooking, cleaning, and childbearing. After doing the math, I figured that, without intervention, I could feasibly birth at least twelve children more. I felt pressured and conflicted—as though I had to choose between my health and sanity or my faith in God. A dark corner of my heart secretly hoped for a miscarriage until the day my son was born. I had surrendered all control of my body and the ability to think for myself. Freedom had been usurped by duty.

And still, I smiled sweetly.

To add insult to injury, Jacob Emery was at once the sweetest, most even-tempered baby that ever lived. For years, I carried the guilt of wasting my pregnancy by wishing it away. Indeed, I concluded, I was assuredly wicked.

It was then, with three children under the age of three and a husband so fulfilled and jovial it hurt, that I slipped past the gray mundaneness into a pit of endless darkness.

Slowly but surely, I began morphing into a walking manifestation of poor theology. I became genuinely convinced that my existence as a woman served first to glorify God and then my husband. Lest such claims seem exaggerated, my journal serves as proof. On the last page in slanted cursive is a long list of dutiful aspirations as recorded by my right hand: *A Biblical Woman is the glory of man, created for the sake of man, modest, discreet, and a worker at home. She receives instruction with entire submission, is not to teach or exercise authority over a man, is subject to her husband and does him good and not evil.*

The remainder of the page continues with similar mandates, and even when the allotted lines expire, still my list twists and turns insidiously up the side margin like a winding, choking vine.

As a human, I believed myself evil to the core. But as a woman, my thoughts had been deemed illogical, my perceptions unreliable, my opinions unimportant, and my hormonal emotions as shifting as the tide. As one with little to offer and nothing to lose, I began extinguishing my already waning light so God and my husband could shine even brighter.

Over time, Arin grew unnaturally dominant, while I receded in feigned submission. We began fighting more than ever, each of us playing a role unsuited to our personalities. Over the next few months, our experiment failed miserably, and in the end, we finally refused to coexist in such a way. Discarding our expected roles, we called a truce and instead returned to being best friends.

Yet despite abandoning our "traditional" roles, there were others who vigorously pursued them.

One Sunday afternoon, we visited the home of an older couple for lunch. We admired them for staying faithfully married and raising four godly adult children. When it came time to eat, Arin followed the wife into the dining room to sit with the other adults. I meant to follow, but a protruding arm across the doorway stopped me dead in my tracks. The husband redirected me to a small table in the kitchen, where one plate of food was waiting with four forks.

"This is for you and your children to share," he explained.

Apparently, I did not deserve my own meal; nor was I worthy of dining with the other adults.

Perhaps I misinterpreted his behavior, or maybe they didn't prefer small children in their dining room. But I think not. Years later, I came to learn of a time that same man took his wife shopping, purchased her dream ring for their fortieth anniversary, and then placed it high on a closet shelf, telling her she could have it when she earned it—after she finally learned to be a good wife.

In all fairness, that man did not represent the whole of the Reformed faith. We met many wonderful people along our journey. Still, the church's faulty theology did nothing to challenge his beliefs and, most likely, exacerbated his unfathomable actions.

Approximately one year into his chaplaincy, Arin enrolled part-time in seminary to pursue his master of divinity degree. The school was two hours away in cooperating traffic, so he occasionally stayed with the parents of a police officer, who'd grown quite fond of Arin. On one such occasion, I was awakened by an early morning phone call. My husband's voice came through weak and strained. He was calling to let me know that his head was pounding and that he was driving himself to the hospital. I clucked my appropriate sympathies as, rolling my eyes, I mentally scoffed, *Pffff! Typical man. Can't even handle a headache.*

I was mortified when a nurse called hours later. Arin had been diagnosed with bacterial meningitis and was, in her words, "very, very ill." Immediately, his mom flew in from California. A lifelong nurse, she was the perfect bedside companion. Besides, we knew of no one to stay with our kids.

The first night of Arin's illness, his respirations dropped to three breaths per minute.

Death hovered throughout the night, kept at bay by three feeble breaths.

After a lengthy recovery, Arin developed a newfound zest for life. He enrolled in spin classes, bought a Trek road bike, and took short rides after work and longer ones on the weekends. He always came home with funny stories, like when he couldn't unclamp his shoes while braking for an unloading school bus. As his momentum waned, the bike started tipping, and he landed hard on his side, right in front of all the waiting parents. When another time, he grew mesmerized by a low-flying crane, he suddenly found himself upside down in a ditch, shoes still clamped to his pedals.

Grateful to witness the life in his eyes, I belly-laughed at his stories and happily stayed home with our children as he cycled his way back to health. Eventually, his Saturday morning rides gave way to sprint triathlons, and he began traveling around the state to compete in weekend races. His sister rooted him on in person while I did my cheering back home.

One evening, while lying in bed, I caught sight of Arin's shirtless body sticking out from the covers. For the first time, I took note of his changing frame. Two collarbones protruded sharply, rising like bridges to span the hollow pools at the base of his neck, now gaunt and sinewy. His shoulders, however, had grown broad and striated from swimming, and his chest muscles rolled like foothills emerging from the flat plains of his abs.

Turning my attention toward myself for the first time in a long while, I became acutely aware of the sagging folds of flesh that buried my once athletic body. The tiny hole that once housed an impulsive collegiate belly button ring now harbored a massive scar, which undulated across the swells of my belly in the shape of a watery "X." Like a recycled balloon, I'd been stretched taut then released, repeatedly inflated and deflated three back-to-back times. Any life that once existed had been suckled from my chest. And half my hair seemed to fall out with every passing birth.

Arin appeared to me as a stranger then, as did I to myself. Here he was, flourishing before me, while I was struggling just to find time for a shower.

While I once found solace in my love for God, I realized that lately He'd grown aloof and evasive, moody and unreliable. My husband, on the other hand, was brimming with life and happier than I'd ever known. I couldn't tell whether it was his happiness that separated him from me or my emptiness that isolated me from him.

Nine months after moving to Florida, I wrote in my journal:

> *My life is characterized by anger and frustration, which I*
> *spend my days trying to conceal. I no longer see clearly.*
> *Everything is blurred and buried so deep that I cannot even*

pretend to understand what's wrong. All I know is that I'm rotten on the inside and know nothing. I am nothing. I have nothing. And anything I try to achieve ends in failure. "Christianity" and "God" seem more distant than ever. I know God is faithful and "sovereign," but I question—what hope there is for a heart so hard as mine, for a mind so lost, a spirit so unwilling? I strive yet remain internally unchanged. What makes faith real? Homeschooling, submission, spanking, reading the Bible? I attempt to glorify God; still, my heart is His enemy, opposing all that He loves. Nothing in me is pure. I am ugly, undone, lost, and unsure—not knowing how to get on the right path, not sure I've ever known.

I never considered my anger might be holy, a flashing signpost of righteous indignation urging me to jump ship and swim for solid ground. It never occurred to me that my constant barrage of self-deprecating language might be the source of my angst.

By then, I had fully concluded that the thoughts and feelings of women—and now additionally, their health—really didn't matter.

6

Unraveling

Transformation isn't sweet and bright. It's a dark and murky,
painful pushing. An unraveling of the untruths you've carried
in your body. A practice in facing your own demons.
A complete uprooting before becoming.

—Victoria Erickson, *Edge of Wonder*

Grayson Andrew was born October 27, 2005, in Jackson, Mississippi,
where we had moved one month prior. That home was our sixth in
seven years of marriage, and Grayson, our fourth baby in approximately
four years of childbearing.

After tiring of his two-hour commute to seminary, Arin had discovered
a sister campus in Mississippi, where the cost of living was significantly
lower. Thanks to a housing boom, we sold our Florida house for double its
purchase price and paid cash for a new one up north. The leftover funds
enabled Arin to work part-time by night and attend classes full-time by day.

We became like passing ships in the night. He worked while I slept and
then drove straight to school without even a nap. In his scant spare time,

he studied, rode his bike, and dozed (in that order) and then started all over again.

Our weekly schedule left us exhausted—him more than me—and desperately missing each other. Therefore, Friday nights organically evolved as a necessary time of reconnection, and Logan's emerged as the perfect location to celebrate.

Week after week, our waiter-turned-friend, Red, welcomed us to the local restaurant. Sweeping up Rylee, his little sweetheart, into his arms, he seated us near the fire. Mounds of steaming buttery rolls materialized like magic; then, three chubby hands made them vanish into thin air. Shirley Temples with extra cherries were delivered on a wobbling tray, while Red—with Rylee still in tow—poured Arin's tall IPA.

Rules did not exist at Logan's. The kids could get refills, gorge themselves on bread, order anything they wanted (even dessert), and the same held true for us. We sat for as long as we wanted, ate whatever we wanted (even appetizers), and leisurely reconvened. Caleb, Rylee, and Jacob—respectively ages four, two, and one—were angelically content to color their never-ending supply of kids' menus. Grayson, still a newborn, slept peacefully in his carrier.

Back home after dinner, Caleb and Rylee ripped off their clothes as they raced up the stairs, only to emerge seconds later as Spiderman and Snow White. Jacob waddled in shortly after wearing Star Wars underwear and a random purple cape, his flashing light-saber trailing limply behind. Arin, the villainous Doc Ock, repeatedly flung Spiderman across the room onto a giant beanbag, where our pint-sized superhero valiantly fought his way back again and again to protect his princess sister. Occasionally, Jacob half-heartedly waved his sword in a lame attempt to fend off Doc Ock, but by and large, he was content to linger in the crook of my arm, silently observing through his laughing, half-moon eyes. Sweet Grayson slept soundly in my other arm, and I soaked it all in, relishing every moment with my perfect little family.

Soon enough, we found a new church to call home. Still Presbyterian, it was additionally seasoned with the Bible-Belt flavor of the deep South.

Every Sunday, a handful of fathers showed up to church with twelve-inch glue sticks poking straight up from their back pockets. Weekly, without fail, several children shared the sad misfortune of being hoisted over their fathers' shoulders or tucked like a football beneath their arms and whisked away to the bathroom at the back of the church. Buffered by only a thin, hollow-core door, the *whack, whack, whacks* could be easily heard, followed at once by loud, unhappy tears. I never fully understood what those kids did to deserve their spankings. Mostly they wiggled, I think.

Certain Presbyterian literature likened children to donkeys and wild beasts. Their strong wills, the authors argued, required being broken unto total compliance. Only then could they truly be happy and free. But it always seemed to me that those who spent the most time in the back bathroom were the ones least happy and free.

Our Mississippi church observed the Sabbath, which ideally meant no work was to be done from sundown to sundown, Saturday to Sunday. Many congregants, including the pastor, Grady, refrained from eating at restaurants to avoid creating work for others. Still, hospitality being what it was in the South, Sunday suppers were a pretty big deal.

The church women worked hard to prepare meals the night before. Even so, there were dishes to wash and food to put away.

One morning in Sunday school, I hesitantly raised my hand and asked a pointed question that had long been weighing on my mind. "Since hospitality is of such great importance, and women end up doing all the work, when do *they* get *their* Sabbath?"

Visibly caught off guard, Pastor Grady stammered his choppy response, "Well, erm, that's when, uh, the husbands should really, like, er, help out their wives, so they can, ya know . . . get some rest."

I never replied to his unsatisfactory answer. But inside, I silently wondered, *Which husbands are those—the ones watching football in the living room or the others smoking cigars and drinking home-brewed beer out back? Or perhaps the ones loudly talking over one another and debating theology on the front porch?* In all our church gatherings, I never once saw a man lift a finger to help in the kitchen—the pastor included.

That day after church, I squeezed by Pastor Grady into the painted cinder block hall. He was standing at his stationary post in the doorway, shaking hands and greeting his flock. As I edged past him, I caught a whiff of his cologne. It smelled old and musky, just like I imagined a white-haired, southern gentleman might smell. He kindly smiled as I passed, and his twinkling, crinkled eyes softened his face and my heart. Something about his short, stubby frame and jovial movements reminded me of a robotic Santa at the mall. He looked so endearing, I had to resist planting a peck on his weathered, wrinkly cheek.

Full of imagined holiday cheer, and perhaps slightly remorseful for putting him on the spot, I extended an olive branch. "You look nice today, Pastor Grady."

Instantly, the twinkle departed from his eyes, and his jolly crows' feet stretched taut as two eyebrows shot straight for his receding hairline. He shrunk back, pressing himself against the cold metal door. Bewildered, I stepped further into the hallway as he sputtered his attempted gratitude like an old car on its last lick of gas.

His embarrassment morphed into my shame; I had obviously said something wrong. Did he not understand I considered him like a grandpa?

I lowered my eyes—a harlot caught in sin—and swiftly retreated down the hall.

Back in those days, the best part of Sunday mornings had nothing to do with church but rather an old, dead tree trunk. Blindingly white, it sat in a barren field off a back road we took to church, and it became one of the few Mississippi friends I ever had.

I once made Arin pull over so I could traipse through the field in my long skirt to snap a photo. I enlarged it and hung it over our mantle. I even wrote it a poem:

Branches stripped smooth and bare, shaven of all pretense
Stark simplicity, uncommon beauty, creation in its purest form
Alone but not lonely, it abides in silence
An obvious misfit, unwilling to conform
White, jagged limbs reach stiffly toward Heaven, and long for
the warmth of the sun
I close my eyes, and it is me
Stripped and bare, simple and free
Content to wander, yet restless for Home
Sometimes, I see the same tree in a different season
No longer brilliant and white
No longer warmed by the sun
Now dull and gray, freezing and forsaken
Doing all it can just to stand
I fear that impending change and wonder
Will I withstand or wither limb by limb
Till I am nothing more than a dried-up, old stump?
Will I be able to endure the numbness
Until feelings return with the spring?

I've never written words more eerily foretelling.

As soon as Grayson could sit on his own, Friday nights at Logan's assumed a much different tone. Whenever we placed him in his high chair, we had a brief moment of peace while he scarfed down his food. But the second he finished, the screaming commenced. He'd fling himself backward and let loose with a wail. That was our cue. One of us would whisk him from the restaurant and walk him around to calm him down, while the other remained inside with the kids. Our celebratory evenings of reconnection quickly deteriorated into ones of frustration and chaotic separateness, and we found ourselves rushing through dinner just to hurry and return home. As much as we wanted to hold on to them, Friday nights at Logan's gradually dwindled and then eventually ceased.

Meals at home were no better. One afternoon, I invited a church acquaintance for lunch. She was the embodiment of a southern belle—well-dressed, flawless makeup, not a hair out of place. Besides that, she homeschooled her four children, who *always* answered, "Yes, ma'am" or "No, sir," and never failed to refer to adults as Mr. or Mrs. so-and-so, unlike my children, who had a Midwesterner for a mother and were constantly saying things like "yeah" or "nope" and brashly calling adults by their first names.

Already insecure, I had prepared lunch ahead of time to ensure a smooth visit. But the one thing I'd neglected to consider was Grayson.

As soon as I placed him in his high chair, he slammed his head against the seat and screamed. I smiled and spoke in my nice, level mommy voice, but the second I turned around, he climbed out and stood teetering on the tray. I sat him back down, still unruffled, and proceeded to help him eat. But when another child required my attention, he popped right back up on his tray. That time, the chair wobbled, Grayson toppled, and I had to lunge to catch him. Collecting myself, I took a deep breath, brushed the hair from my eyes, and then plopped him down a bit more firmly, with lips pressed a little more tightly, and strapped him down snugly in his seat. He thrashed in defiance, threw his food against the window, and howled.

My southern-belle friend politely diverted her eyes, but the damage was already done.

The embarrassment was minor in light of events still to come. But someone, far wiser than I, knew my ego needed to be wounded gently, little by little in ever-increasing doses. One knuckle at a time, my fingers were being gingerly pried back, and any semblance of control slowly dissolved.

The rest of the afternoon followed suit, and by the time my friend left with *her* perfect children, *I* was completely exhausted. Flopping down on the couch, I wracked my brain for answers.

Grayson had been such an easy baby. True, he was two weeks premature and had spent his first week in the neonatal intensive care unit (NICU) for

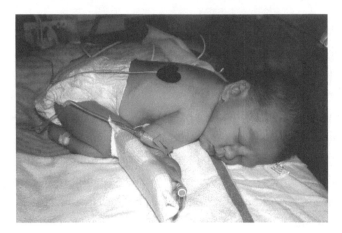

Grayson in the NICU, October 2005

underdeveloped lungs, and yes, I'd tested positive for group B strep, which had gone untreated because of the hospital's negligence. Yet all that seemed irrelevant now. Grayson appeared no worse for the wear. He had smiled and cooed like his older siblings and so far had passed all his milestones right on cue.

But everything started changing right around his six-month birthday when we began introducing solid foods. Practically overnight, he evolved from a good-natured baby into an angry, inconsolable mess. He'd point to food and then cast it to the ground, act tired, and refuse to sleep. He'd wail for hours on end, and although I fed him, changed his diaper, and tried gas medicine, nothing seemed to help. Even our doctor could find nothing wrong, but instead very technically diagnosed him as "fussy."

Getting Grayson to nap became my new dreaded chore. After all my ordinarily dependable tricks of the trade failed me, I'd eventually resign and lay him in his crib to cry. Sometimes he fell asleep; more often he didn't. Meanwhile, I plopped down on the stair outside his door, where I could at least observe the rest of my family.

If Arin was home, he was studying, and from my post, I had a straight line of sight to his office. It was his haven, the breeding grounds of new knowledge, but to me, it was a husband-gobbling cave. Already sleep-deprived and half crazy, I envisioned shoots sprouting from the ground, winding their way round his ankles and holding him firm until he calcified into a statue. I felt sure that one day I'd look down to behold the built-in bookshelves, the scored concrete floors, and my fossilized husband. He'd be frozen exactly how I remember him—legs crossed atop his desk and deeply reclined in his chair. A book would remain perpetually open in the crevice of his thighs, and wire-rimmed glasses would cling to his nose. It would be impossible to determine whether he was reading or staring *through* the pages in puzzled consternation, and an ink pen would inevitably dangle from a sagging corner of his mouth—the seminarian version of a Cuban cigar.

I never resented Arin for studying, but I *did* miss him. I grew tired of loving him through glass doors and fighting the constant urge to intrude.

As Arin endlessly studied and Grayson constantly cried, our other children played happily in the upstairs bonus room. Their innocent peals of laughter danced lightly across the air, gracefully maneuvering around the deafening shrieks emanating from the nursery.

On my left were three content children, and on my right, a screaming infant who refused to be consoled. As for me, I remained firmly affixed and overwhelmed in the middle, where my top step became a crumbling drop-off. I perceived the creep of rising water and tasted the panic of being ill-prepared. Sand began slipping between my tightly clenched toes. It eroded my ledge, and I had the foreboding sensation that if my feet did not quickly connect with solid ground, I would most certainly drown.

Rylee, Caleb, Reagan, a very tired me, Grayson, and Jacob in Mississippi, 2007

In time, I discovered that Grayson would sleep in my arms with minimal effort, so I began napping with him in my bed for efficiency's sake. Upon awakening, I held perfectly still so as not to rouse him and instead spent many silent moments examining his unique features. His face was thinner and longer than his siblings'—theirs were more heart-shaped and chubby—and baby acne sprinkled the bridge of his turned-up nose while the corners of his eyes slanted downward. A faint grouping of pinprick holes flanked his left nostril, forming a nearly-invisible birthmark, and although untried by life, dark half-circles drooped from his eyes.

Like a cartographer, I was subconsciously charting a mental map of the child I'd one day need to know better than the back of my hand. As Grayson lay sleeping in my arms, an unbreakable bond was being forged with the one who would require more than I'd ever feel capable of giving.

Although I felt pleased with my nap-time solution, Arin was less than enthused. He hinted, and then outright suggested, that I was causing, or at the very least exacerbating, Grayson's behavior by spoiling him and not scheduling his sleep, as I'd done before.

I bristled at his words. Whatever was wrong with Grayson had nothing to do with sleep schedules or being spoiled.

I'm sure Arin had more to say on the subject, but I didn't care to listen. He was busy all the time anyway. How could *he* possibly know what was wrong with *my* son?

For the first time in our marriage, an unidentifiable tension sprung up between us. Sometimes it was quite palpable and other times nearly undetectable. Still, it arrived shortly after Grayson's half-birthday and would linger for years to come.

While Arin was in seminary, he commonly invited fellow seminarians to our house for Friday-night beers. On one such night, I was attempting to rock ten-month-old Grayson to sleep as heated arguments drifted up from downstairs. I listened to their fragmented strains and then placed Grayson in his crib and sat down to journal.

From the kitchen, a loud voice bellowed, "God is spirit, infinite and eternal!"

I picked up a pen and jotted my silent response: *But what is God, really? What is an infinite spirit, and what does eternal even* mean? *Why do we pray, and to* whom? *In my heart, I don't believe prayer changes a thing.*

As the men grew drunker and their voices more boisterous, I heard them berate those who believed differently and wondered about the basic commandment to "love your neighbor as yourself." Next, their words grew increasingly hostile toward other Christians who embraced one nuanced doctrine over another. Exasperated, I let my head fall back against the rocking chair and dispassionately exhaled my renunciation of faith: *If this is Christianity, I want nothing to do with it. If these educated men can't agree on the Bible, what hope is there for someone like me?*

I determined then and there to be done with the Bible, done with trying to understand it, and less assertively, done with God. I closed my eyes in defeat, my initial question still reverberating in my head: *What is God, really?*

Almost immediately, I opened my eyes to behold the kids' Bible timeline encircling the room like a wallpaper border. Crayon-scribbled pictures depicted the God of Abraham, Isaac, and Jacob, the God of history, the God of eternity.

Suddenly, like the surging tide, came a whispered response: *I am that I am. I am that I am. I am that I am.*

These words were inaudible and yet crystal clear. Although I didn't understand them, they made me weep with relief, and as the sounds of men droned on below, I wrote one more thought in my journal: *God needs no definition. He simply* is.

That night, none of my questions were answered, and true to my word, I wouldn't pick up a Bible for years.

I penned one last poem that night and then slept the deep slumber of peace:

Gestating words
Churning, nearing discovery
Microscopic in utero

Still unspoken
I am conscious of a nameless something
A nothingness, really, as its presence is yet unconfirmed
But I am aware of its growing essence, its unsettled restlessness/
Rising within me
A babbling brook long dammed to silence
Then . . . something
Something seen, something said
It resonates, confirms, evokes, and calls forth
Unknown knowledge breathes its first
Summoned by its articulated echo
Like a longing fulfilled, words are born when spoken into existence.

I closed my entry with the poem "A Word" by Emily Dickinson:

A word is dead, when it is said
Some say—
I say it just begins to live
That day[1]

7

Spinning

Tears are a tangible way of addressing our pain
and our panic. . . . Tears confirm our readiness to allow our
life to fall apart in the dark night of the soul.

—JOHN CHRYSSAVGIS, *In the Heart of the Desert*

My dad stood frozen before a beverage dispenser, streams of orange juice cascading down his middle part like a rain gutter in a deluge. Chunks of pulp clung to the ends of his salt-and-pepper hair, his eyelashes, and his round, unblinking face.

True, Grayson *had* pointed to the juice. But with more than twelve hundred miles between us, my dad was largely unacquainted with the quirky habits of his two-year-old grandson. I should have seen it coming; I should have warned him. I knew how Grayson motioned for things and then threw them to the ground.

But I didn't.

And now, my dad, who abhorred public attention more than anything, was dripping wet with the literal fruit of Grayson's anger, smack-dab in the middle of a hotel lobby in Columbia, Missouri.

For a split second, nobody moved. Then Grayson jarred us back to life with an angry shriek. He flailed backward, my dad fumbled to catch him, and I flew from my seat to rescue not my son but my father. Meanwhile, Arin scurried for paper towels, and my mom remained seated with the other kids.

In the end, we made it to my sister's volleyball tournament—our whole reason for convening—frazzled and sticky but on time.

As our kids piled from the van, I pulled our newest addition from her car seat. Anxious to make the game on time, I quickly swaddled Reagan McKenna, just two months old, in a pink, fuzzy blanket, inadvertently omitting a tiny foot and five even smaller toes. They dangled bare and exposed, right at Grayson's eye-level.

Inside the gym, I kept his hand firmly grasped in mine while scanning the bleachers for gaps. Sick with a bad cold, Grayson's red-rimmed eyes matched his flushed, scaly cheeks. Sniffling and hacking, he wriggled and hopped from foot to foot—more hyper than ever because of his prednisone prescription. My arm bounced along like a leash on a high-strung dog.

I didn't take note when my arm fell slack, never recognized Grayson's movements growing still. But, suddenly, Reagan's body stiffened, and her silvery eyes flew open in surprise. She pulled for air in short, jerky bursts and then let loose with an ear-piercing scream.

I released Grayson's hand to unravel her blanket, frantically seeking the source of her cries. As I assessed her newborn body, I felt a light tap on my hip. My eyes traveled downward toward Grayson's impish face. It was glowing with pride, and his body squirmed excitedly as if suppressing a fat, bulging secret.

As I puzzled over his expression, my mom sharply inhaled my name in one ear, while in the other, Grayson exclaimed two of his few-known words, "Baby bite! Baby bite!" Swiveling my head to match my mom's gaze, I finally noticed the bright red blood dripping from Reagan's dangling toes. Beneath her, the gym floor looked like the beginnings of a Jackson Pollock painting, with splatters of baby blood proclaiming my maternal neglect to the world.

Sadly, *that* is my first vivid memory of Reagan—a split-second of her pain before returning my focus to Grayson. I couldn't have known then just how normative that pattern would become.

Arin and I argued the whole drive back to Mississippi. He sided with our pediatrician, who, one month prior, had diagnosed Grayson with a serious case of the terrible twos. I needn't worry about his delayed speech, I was told—it was inevitable with three older siblings speaking on his behalf. Grayson would talk when he was ready. And as for his tantrums, they were nothing a firm hand and good spanking couldn't fix—doctorly advice that could only be shared in Mississippi, where corporal punishment was still legal in schools.

My husband couldn't have agreed more. He (and his backside) had grown up well-acquainted with his father's belt, and with only fond memories of both his childhood and his deceased father, Arin wholeheartedly concurred—there was nothing a firm hand and good spanking couldn't fix.

But as staunchly as Arin planted his heels on the matter, I rooted mine just as deeply. I knew in my gut something was wrong with Grayson and couldn't fathom punishing him for behaviors potentially beyond his control.

Before long, conversations about Grayson became taboo. They always ended in sharp disagreements that were rarely resolved. Consequently, Arin parented his way when my back was turned, and I did what I wanted in his absence, which was almost always. In this way, we were able to remain—by and large—happily and peacefully married.

By the time Arin graduated from seminary that December, we'd already decided to move back to Colorado. With five children under the age of six, the thought of living near my parents and two sisters (i.e., built-in babysitters) was quite alluring.

Arin had intended to pursue his PhD at the University of Denver. But after his initial interview, the sobering reality of five to seven more years of rigorous classes, endless studying, bleary-eyed night shifts, and intermittent winks of sleep quickly led to a disheartened and disillusioned husband.

As his long-term career path crumbled before his eyes, Arin reluctantly but gratefully accepted any available job, desperate to support his growing family of seven. He began serving banquets at a ritzy hotel in Denver and then walked several blocks to his second job, where he worked as a bouncer. His burly, six-foot-four, 280-pound frame was a natural fit for kicking inebriated college kids out of bars but not so much for weaving through swanky crowds while balancing trays of delicately plated beef Wellington. He sustained frequent scoldings from wealthy, demeaning women at the hotel. Then he transitioned to the bar, where he dealt with obnoxious drunks who amused themselves by defecating in urinals, urinating in trash cans, and then ridiculing Arin as he cleaned up their messes. Late-night stragglers pointed and smirked as Arin swept littered sidewalks after hours. It mattered not that he had a master's level of education and a wife and five kids at home who adored him. To them, he was a poop-scooping trashman, a moving target for their stinging darts.

It broke my heart to hear his stories and watch the embarrassment flicker briefly across his face. This, too, I knew, would be added to a growing mound of safeguarded emotions, kept strictly off-limits to me.

Arin crawled into bed around 3:30 a.m., where, for three hours, he anxiously tossed and turned before rising to start his day job as a social worker. He left the county office by 3:00 p.m. every day and then hit the gym for a quick workout before heading straight to the hotel and back to the bar. He kept this schedule six days every week for three very long years.

Meanwhile, Grayson had developed a strange set of phobias. They took me a while to identify, but in time, I categorized four:

1. Costumed characters: Grayson was on high alert in his car seat, scanning the anticipated street corners for the dreaded Chick-fil-A cow. I came to *hate* that stupid bovine and the panic it induced— the thrashing, the head-smashing, the gut-wrenching screams. Eventually, I altered my route to avoid the spotted cow, but it would be *years* before Grayson could walk into a Chick-fil-A without first sending me inside to scout.

2. Things that could *potentially* blow in the wind: Picnics at the park mutated from leisurely to nerve-wracking. Grayson clung to my chest like a baby sloth, quivering with fear over a grocery bag lying in the sand twenty yards away. The slightest breeze sent the bag

fluttering and Grayson clambering for the top of my head. We stopped going to the park if there was a single cloud in the sky.

3. People who might *possibly* steal his food: If anyone besides me was present while he ate, Grayson eyed them suspiciously as he protectively encircled his plate with his arms. Should they get too close, he'd leap at them from his booster into thin air. Fortunately, I was always close enough to catch him. But when my sister once absentmindedly popped a bite of his waffle into her mouth, he flew from his seat, and wrapping limbs around her head, proceeded to pry her mouth open to recover his waffle. After that, he ate with two hands covering his mouth—just in case anyone tried to pry *his* mouth open and steal the food from *his* mouth.

4. Anything that could *conceivably* knock his toys out of line: Grayson became obsessed with anything containing wheels: cars, monster trucks, tractors, school buses, tricycles, knee-high plastic horses, and rolling dishwasher racks. These *loooong* lines of "toys" wound their way from room to room, and may God have mercy on the soul of anyone who even contemplated stepping over his serpentine creation. Grayson turned into the Tasmanian devil at the mere prospect of a single item being knocked from formation, and we all quickly learned to walk the long way around, or at least quickly step over his toys when he wasn't looking.

As Grayson's vocabulary slowly increased, so did his ability to pinpoint his frustrations. Grass, sand, water, buttons, zippers, back pockets, and seams were all equally intolerable. He wore one pair of shoes and shunned the rest. Clothes were handpicked by their level of fuzziness, and if a tag even dared to graze his skin's surface, he stopped, dropped, and rolled as if on fire, howling and writhing in agony.

Despite his heightened sensory awareness, Grayson was impervious to heat, cold, and pain. He strolled barefoot through the snow as if on a warm, powdery beach and sweated through fleece pajamas in ninety-degree weather. Once, in an angered frenzy, he smashed his head against the corner of a dresser. He rose without even a cry of pain—his good sense seemingly knocked back into him—then brushed his fingers across the emerging goose egg as if shooing a fly and calmly walked out of the room.

From the moment Grayson learned to walk, he has been the perpetual bearer of head-to-toe bruises and scabs.

Although the small things drove him mad, like seams and buttons, he couldn't get enough of the big stuff. A daredevil from the start, he grew instantly fascinated by water slides and roller coasters. In his broken little language, he memorized the names and locations of the biggest in the world. There was the Kilimanjaro in Rio de Janeiro, the Insano in Fortaleza, Brazil, and the Kingda Ka in New Jersey, to name a few. His bucket list was more expansive than mine, though his geographical knowledge most certainly was not. He *incessantly* asked to visit Germany for one day to ride the drop slide. Just once. Could we *pleeaaase*?

To appease my son (and preserve my sanity), my dad printed several photographs of Grayson's favorite rides, binding them in a three-ring notebook. Forgoing the usual teddy bear or blanket, Grayson cuddled his notebook at night—his standard Ziplock bag of ham resting limply on the headboard *in case* he grew hungry mid-sleep. The child would have ridden every slide and roller coaster in the world—if only he could have figured out how to grow tall enough.

I dismissed Grayson's phobias as infantile fears, rolled my eyes at his sensory issues, and tolerated the inconvenience. I assured myself he'd grow out of them all. But deep down, I knew these were all flimsy attempts to muffle my gnawing sense of concern.

I briefly wondered whether he might be autistic, although Grayson didn't match the stereotype in my uneducated mind. He spoke well enough to communicate, made adequate eye contact, gestured and pointed, and had no stimming behaviors like hand-flapping or spinning.

Perhaps Arin was right, I conceded. Maybe I *was* the problem. Maybe I *had* spoiled Grayson. Had I let him get away with murder in my wearied, postnatal state? But nobody else seemed concerned, and besides, who was I to know?

I was only a mom.

One Sunday, on Arin's single day off, he decided it would be fun to try a new church. Recently, he'd grown infatuated with something called Eastern Orthodoxy, which, to me, seemed no different than Catholicism. I paid his excitement little attention, chalking it up to another passing phase. I reminded myself that I was through with religion, and less certainly, finished with God. I was just happy the church wasn't Reformed.

Consequently, I found myself sitting on a pew beneath a massively decorated dome in the Assumption of the Theotokos Greek Orthodox Metropolis Cathedral—a mouthful, even by Greek standards. The church was culturally Greek but theologically Orthodox, and it took me a while to understand that an Eastern Orthodox Church could be Serbian, Russian, Romanian, or Greek—differing in languages and culture but united in beliefs.

I'd never been inside such an ornate church. Gleaming marble floors refracted the morning sun streaming in through warbled leaded glass, and each inch of every wall was covered in scrolling details, framing the paintings I now know as icons. The depicted men and women were arrayed in long and colorful robes, their names printed indecipherably above in triangulated Greek. Although some wore crowns and others carried crosses, their faces bore the same expressionless stares that made me squirm beneath their scrutiny.

I uncomfortably shifted my gaze toward the dome, which was at least two times the height of the nave (sanctuary) where we sat. Sky blue, its edges stretched earthward like a canvas from Heaven, and its gradient shading added dimension, as though the dome extended infinitely beyond itself and we in the pews were only privy to its surface.

Suddenly, the priest began chanting loud and clear. Bouncing off the marble floors and rounding the dome, his voice landed in my ears cold and cavernous, unlike the rich, inviting tones as perceived by my husband. Immediately, our kids perked up and started giggling, while I felt more awkward by the minute. The priest's words were incomprehensible—literally "all Greek to me."

For the first time, I understood what it felt like to be a minority—and not just a half.

After stomaching all I could handle, I escaped through the back doors to head for my safe place—the bathroom. On the way, I passed an old Greek *yia-yia* (grandmother). Smiling, I greeted her warmly. In return, she scowled, looked me up and down, and in her thick accent, asked if I was "Gdeek."

Confused, I shook my head no. Clearly, I was half-Japanese.

By the time I reached the restroom, I had gone from uncomfortable to agitated, and by the end of the service, I was full-on fuming. I cried a good portion of the drive home, told Arin we might as well move to Israel—or any other foreign country, for that matter. He allowed me to monologue and patiently listened, and then he asked if I'd be willing to try one more church.

The following week, we tried a new, smaller church. Father Evan, the priest, was Greek but seemingly unfazed by our non-Greekness. The service was chanted (and spoken) in English, and by the time it ended, Father Evan had memorized all five of our children's names, as indicated on the visitor's card. Unlike the stairwell yia-yia, he greeted us warmly, and his welcoming smile lowered my guard—if only a bit.

Six months later, we converted to Eastern Orthodoxy. I didn't really want to, but I also didn't care to protest. Besides, Arin had enough passion for us both. I spent my first six months internally stewing and spitting mad. Everyone around me seemed so happy it made me sick. The whole thing grated on my nerves, from the icons to the wafting incense to the obviously futile chanting. Even so, I took the kids to church alone when Arin felt too tired and brought them to the midweek service while he worked.

So it came to pass that I found myself sitting outside our new church one dusky summer eve, watching Grayson twirl in circles. I had dropped him off in the fellowship hall to play with the other children, but as I sat in the church, an out-of-breath teenager came running to fetch me. Grayson had snuck out the door to find me and was now roaming the neighborhood. Could I help?

I tracked him down and brought him inside to sit with me, but he quickly grew restless and pitched an angry fit. So I rushed him outside, where he calmed immediately, and we slowly made our way to the lawn behind the church. I sat down heavily on the splintered wooden steps and then buried my head in my hands and sighed. It was becoming harder and harder to take Grayson anywhere.

Through parted fingers, I watched him start spinning. Round and round. Faster and faster. One minute turned into five and then ten. Now happy as a lark, he flapped his arms up and down on the airwaves. His loud, high-pitched squeals echoed through the summer night, ebbing and flowing as he pirouetted toward me and then away.

What I once perceived as a foreboding fear on a Mississippi step now emerged as truth on a rotting Colorado stair. My life was spiraling out of control, in faster and faster circles like my son. I watched his arms flail, and they became mine—slapping the water, grasping for land, reaching for something not there. No longer could I sense the encroaching water, for I was looking up at its luminous surface from below. The drop-off had crumbled, abandoning me to the water now high above my head. It was unavoidable; I was officially drowning.

Huge teardrops careened recklessly down my nose, bailing from the tip as if even *they* recognized I was a sinking ship.

Finally, after gathering my composure, I collected my children and loaded them in the car. There was no point in staying. I closed the van door to the sound of Grayson's on-again screams, and as I trudged around to the driver's side, I allowed myself the indulgence of one more honest admission. I no longer had the energy to keep it stuffed away. It seemed so obvious; I couldn't believe I hadn't spoken it sooner.

Despite God's allegedly inerrant wisdom, He had plainly made a mistake. He had chosen the wrong woman to be Grayson's mother.

My frazzled emotions agreed, so I accepted the statement as true. Heaving myself into the van, I placed my hands on the steering wheel and braced myself for the long drive home.

8

Undressing

For a seed to come fully into its own it must become wholly undone. The shell must break open, its insides must come out and everything must change. If you don't understand what life looks like, you might mistake it for complete destruction.

—ANN VOSKAMP, *The Broken Way*

*N*ovember 13, 2021. I am watching old home movies. Hours of them. Lately, I've been feeling deeply troubled by my current retelling of past events. They feel disconnected, like they happened somewhere outside of time to a girl I once knew, or like twenty lives have passed since their alleged occurrence. I wonder doubtfully, *Was life really as I've depicted, or has it been warped and exaggerated by my aging forty-two-year-old brain?*

So I pull out our old camcorder to either prove or disprove my own life.

What I witness astonishes me. These are the times I vaguely recall—the good ones, paradisiacal as the Garden of Eden.

There, in our Mississippi house, basking in the sunlit streams of morning, are my three oldest children, freshly bathed, damp hair neatly combed, and dressed in clean, adorable clothing. It's Friday, or "piggy-stick" morning, as proclaimed by two-year-old Jacob, when the kids recite their homeschooling memory work and get rewarded with Pixy Stix. One at a time, they reel off long passages of Scripture, each according to their abilities, while the other two quietly thumb through pages of their picture Bibles. Grayson crawls from child to child, trying to steal their books but calm. After their recitations, Caleb, Rylee, and Jacob sing Christmas songs in Latin—another part of our curriculum. I'm surprised by my voice. It's patient and serene, much kinder than I remember. No trace of the beast I've since created in my mind.

In the next video, Caleb and Rylee roll around under our counter-height table in the dumping beds of yellow Tonka trucks as Jacob rams them in his pink Little Tykes car. Shrieks of laughter epitomize child-hood glee.

The camera cuts out and then reopens to Spiderman defending Snow White from Doc Ock. It's obviously Friday night after Logan's. Arin is so fun and full of life; the kids can't get enough of him, and Caleb's eyes sparkle with adoration.

I pause the video, amazed at what good parents we *were*, and then grow saddened by the erosion I know is forthcoming.

I press Play, and it's Christmas. Kids with rumpled hair open gifts in their pajamas while Grayson toddles about inspecting balled-up wrap-ping paper. So far, no signs of the pandemonium I've depicted. Then Arin remarks, "I might be crazy, but Grayson's been good all morning; he's played alone without crying once." His statement is jinxing, for moments later, Grayson unwraps a fuzzy red Elmo. Throwing the Sesame Street character to the ground in a panic, he collapses closely behind, screaming. I pick him up, laughing, as Arin mutters under his breath, "Here we go again." In other snippets, he lightheartedly refers to Grayson as a "monster" and a "nut job." My icy silence is revealing.

In the last video, I'm breastfeeding seven-week-old Reagan, sur-rounded by our three oldest children, who are gazing lovingly at their new sibling. Grayson is on the couch behind me—manic, screeching, and bouncing—flopping from one end of the sofa to the other. Arin's voice narrates loudly behind the camera, "Grayson, when we're all watching this video fifteen years from now, I want you to know, this is how you always were. Crazy. All the time." I smile and affectionately press into Grayson, trapping him behind my back. He giggles and worms his way out and then grabs for a glass on the end table. Arin rebukes him sharply, and my eyes shoot daggers as I start to correct him and then stop short when I notice him filming.

"Go ahead, Corey," he says sarcastically. "Say what you need to say on camera."

Dropping my eyes to fixate on Reagan, I snarl in a low voice, "Just tell him *no*. You don't have to *fuss* at him like that."

An uncomfortable feeling arises, making me squirm in my seat, cringing.

Back on the screen, irritated by Arin's scolding, Grayson plants his face on my leg, and I push it away with a firm "No bite." He tries again repeatedly before moving on to Caleb's toes, and I hold his head back, scolding, "Don't bite toes." Then he points to Reagan, asking, "Bite baby?"

Seven weeks later, he bit her toes until they bled.

It's all on film—Grayson's developing phobias, his sensory desire to bite, the mounting tension between Arin and me.

After that, there are no more videos. They just stop. Abruptly. Like a drop-off.

My heart sinks. I know what comes next; I can still feel the chaos in my body.

I stood at the stove in our new Colorado home, stirring pots and pans, mechanically nodding and smiling at all the right times. Greg, my sister's boyfriend, who lived with us while attending law school, sat hungrily anticipating dinner with his elbows propped on our kitchen table.

Upstairs, Grayson's heels slammed against his locked door, rattling the house and my head. He'd pulled the original door off its hinges, ripping from the bottom with eight little fingers, and had already littered his new solid-core door with copious, heel-sized holes.

Damaged drywall had begun popping up everywhere—lovely souvenirs left by flying candlesticks and golf clubs, baseball bats, and butcher knives. For the most part, I'd managed to duck, leaving the drywall to fend for itself, save the one time a metal curtain rod connected with the unsuspecting bridge of my nose.

At just three years old, Grayson's fits were growing right alongside him, and I needed a way to safely contain his rage. So I shot from the hip for a desperate solution. I reversed his doorknob. That way, I could peel his out-of-control body from my leg, fling him into his room, and then quickly slam and lock the door from outside.

I was certain that one day men in black suits with briefcases would show up at our door to charge me with neglect. Some days, I secretly prayed they'd arrive.

Back in the kitchen, outwardly calm, I peppered the conversation with polite, get-to-know-you questions. If Greg might be part of our family, it was important that he like me, or at the very least respect me. But Grayson was making it hard to respect myself. He had been screaming for two solid hours, and his voice had turned hoarse and raspy. Somewhere in the distance, Greg monologued about becoming a tribal lawyer, followed by anecdotes of life on the reservation.

Upstairs, Grayson's rage had dissolved into tears. He pleaded with me to open his door, and the sound of his pitiful cries was a fork shredding my heart. I longed to run up the stairs two at a time and comfort him in my arms, but there was dinner to cook, laundry to fold, other kids who needed me, and a potential brother-in-law to entertain. Besides, I knew from experience, if I opened his door before a fit ran its course, his rage would reignite, and we'd have to start from square one. If only I could get dinner on the table. . . .

Meanwhile, golf ball-sized accusations pelted my already hurting brain: *Who locks their child in his room? When are you going to figure out his problems? Who are you going to consult for help? Why can't you fix him? Terrible mother! Terrible mother! Terrible mother!*

Massaging my brow to soothe the voices, I choked back hot tears and poured myself into cooking. I mixed and stirred with all my might, embarrassed that a non-family member was witnessing our discord and then further ashamed of my embarrassment.

Later that night, I slipped into my closet, where I turned for privacy. Clothes hung all around, muffling any sounds that came from without and obscuring any cries from within.

I slid to the floor in dread, landing cross-legged before an icon of Christ, which sat on my bottom shelf, surrounded by shoes. I was neither ready nor willing to display such public objects of faith, though Arin was eager to fill every room. I had come dutifully to perform my nightly prayers. In my heart of hearts, I genuinely *wanted* to pray; I *needed* to pray. I longed to unburden my cares. But nothing inside me felt right.

Since converting, I had learned that the preferred posture of prayer was either standing or kneeling. But by the end of my days with Grayson, all I could do was sit—a blatantly lazy and rebellious act in my rigid, ex-Reformed mind.

Even so, I sat.

Obstinately flipping through my little blue prayer book, I guiltily eyeballed the icon that seemed to be eyeballing me.

That small object, so revered by the church, so foreign to me. What had I to do with it? To me, Christ looked stoic, even angry, and his dark eyes stared back cold, beady, and condemning. *Terrible mother . . . terrible mother . . . terrible mother*, they chided.

I expected nothing better. I deserved nothing more.

The God of my upbringing had become as strange and distant as that painted icon. I sat in my closet at an impasse. Newly Orthodox, I felt unable to go back and seemingly incapable of moving forward.

I testily challenged the wooden Christ to a staring contest, dared Him to look away first. He didn't blink, never even wavered, so I reluctantly lowered my eyes in defeat.

I tried to pray the words in my prayer book but couldn't make them my own. Irritated, I punitively shoved the book beneath a pile of high heels, where it would remain, banished, until I declared otherwise.

Laying my discouraged head on the shelf, nose-to-nose with the icon, I scrutinized the One yet so unknown to me. I scoured my soul for the slightest hint of recognition, but my search turned up empty. The austere Christ neither confirmed nor denied whether I appeared familiar to Him.

I spent all my days trying to stay one step ahead of Grayson. After enough sessions in his room, he eventually learned that he could not come out unless calm. Therefore, he converted his angry energy into concocting devious escape plans. Rather than screams, his silence became my new alarm.

His first successful getaway began with an urgent plea to use the bathroom. The second I opened the door, he slipped past me—stark naked—and bolted straight through the front door down the street. The next time he asked to use the restroom, I told him he'd have to wait. He threatened to use his floor as a toilet. I called his bluff—then he called mine. When I cracked open his door, a little brown log was laid out like a decoy in the middle of his room, coaxing me to leave my post unattended. A bare-bottomed Grayson sat on his bed, squiggling boastfully, where I left him for the next hour until he agreed to dispose of his handiwork.

He never pulled that stunt again.

Yet another time, a passing neighborhood child rang our doorbell and informed me that Grayson was standing in his bedroom window at the front of the house, once again, naked. I had no earthly idea why I couldn't keep clothes on the child. I now understand his sensory issues made clothing unbearable. Regardless, I opened his door to find him standing on the sill, lifting his window to make his escape on the roof. He flashed an ear-to-ear grin as his body twitched with excitement, already anticipating the thrill of the chase. I had never bothered to permanently lock his window since it sat high above his head, and his room, which housed only a plastic race car bed opposite the window, possessed nothing else on which to climb. Still, he had managed to grab hold of the sill with his strong little fingertips and shimmy his toes up the wall till he could elbow his way onto the narrow three-inch ledge.

One day, Father Evan came to visit, having graciously offered to make a house call since Grayson was so difficult to manage in public. We sat in my office while Grayson played upstairs, my heart pounding at the prospect of being alone with a man. After my compliment toward Pastor Grady had been so ill-received, I couldn't fathom how pouring out my feminine heart might be perceived. So I spoke cautiously, *briefly* touching on my struggles with Grayson and *glazing over* my disgruntled thoughts on prayer. I mentioned that I *might* be sitting during prayers and then braced myself for the ensuing lightning bolt.

I expected to encounter condemnation, cold and beady eyes, like my icon. Instead, our priest smiled broadly and said, "That's okay."

His answer silenced me. How could a priest be *okay* with prayers said *improperly*?

He asked how I preferred to pray, and I was physically unable to respond. Since when did my womanly preferences matter, especially regarding religion? There was right, and there was wrong—and I was clearly wrong. I sat, wordlessly mulling over his trick question.

Father Evan tried again. "How do you best connect with God?"

Biting my lip, I hesitantly replied, and my answer came out more like a question. "Over early-morning coffee? While sitting on my porch listening to birds?"

He beamed. "Great! Sounds perfect!"

My consternation doubled. I was accustomed to rules, parameters, and boundaries, and this extended freedom felt more terrifying than their sum.

As I shifted in my seat, mystified, I heard Grayson on the stairs. First his feet, then his knees, and finally, his whole body came into view. My stomach lurched. Of course, he was naked. Mortified, I quickly dressed him; he undressed himself even quicker. His agitation mounted, and I knew that insisting on clothing would cause a scene. Sensing my dilemma, Father Evan laughed and told me not to worry. He, too, had a wife and three young daughters and could identify with the challenges of child-rearing.

A married priest with children? Being affirmed as *okay*? Coffee on the porch for prayer? The morning had blown my mind, and despite having a pleasant visit, I breathed a sigh of relief when Father Evan stood to leave.

❧

If containing Grayson in the house felt *nearly* impossible, controlling him in the car was *actually* impossible. When upset, which was often, he unfastened his car seat, bolted to the front of the van, and grabbed my hair. Buckling his knees, he hung like Rapunzel's prince, suspended by only my hair. Bound like a hostage to the headrest, I had to rely on my older children to disentangle or contain his hands until I could pull over.

When Grayson wasn't in the mood to fight, he resorted to flight. He randomly lurched for the door handle, intent on leaping from the car. I had illegally moved his booster to the front, where I could better monitor his behavior. Out of the corner of my eye, I kept constant vigil for the slightest twitch of his arm. I felt his eyes furtively glancing my way in preparation and preemptively wrapped his shirt round my fist—just in case. When he made his move, I was ready. Yanking his shirt, I held him away from the handle as I pulled off the road, where I remained until he was calm enough for me to resume driving.

My right arm still bears the scars from his nails and teeth, and car trips almost always took twice as long as they should.

Finally, someone mentioned that the Children's Hospital sold customized harnesses that zipped from behind and tethered to a metal clip on the car's floorboard. The harness was guaranteed to keep him constrained, I was told. But within minutes of our first industrial-strength outing, Grayson had wriggled free.

One day, in a rare stretch of peace, we were driving along a frontage road, where a farmer was plowing his fields. Grayson calmly observed rows of sharp-toothed blades overturning crusty soil. Completely out of the blue, he turned to his baby sister and suggested, "Reagan, you play in that field. Tractor cut you, make you die." He smiled innocently and returned to staring out the window as Arin and I exchanged worried glances. Grayson rarely watched TV and had never before said anything violent. Perhaps it was a fluke. But while I was cooking dinner several nights later, he watched the boiling water from his stool, mesmerized, and then cheerfully invited Reagan—as if to a game of hide-and-seek—to climb in the pot and "cook off her skin." He suggested something similar at a later date, while observing fire dancing in the fireplace.

Such suggestions were uttered more and more frequently, and I felt sure Grayson was a future sociopath in the making. Our new doctor was baffled and referred us to a pediatric psychiatrist at the Children's Hospital, the largest hospital in Colorado. Unfortunately, their first available appointment was a daunting seven months away. Without a better option, I hurriedly gave the receptionist our information and settled in to wait.

As Grayson's behavior intensified, I grew increasingly desperate for something, anything, to make sense of our unraveling life. I was searching for meaning, purpose, and answers—not in a curious, poking-around-under-rocks kind of way, but more like a foaming-at-mouth mama bear, overturning boulders, demanding-justice-for-her-cub kind of way.

With clenched fists, I railed, *Why does my innocent child have to struggle? What has he ever done to deserve such torment? For that matter, what have I ever done? Why him? Why me? Why us? Why, God, why?*

Little by little, through reading and Father Evan's gentle nurturing, I uncovered the true gem of the Orthodox Church: its beautiful theology on suffering.

Rather than a punishment for sin, as I'd come to believe, suffering was honored as a sacred gift to be held with tender compassion. "Sin" was not a wrongdoing deserving of punishment but a festering wound in need of divine healing. Suffering, the church affirmed, was merely the instrument that exposed such wounds. Deep-rooted heartaches were likened to portals. If acknowledged and held open long enough, light would enter, flushing and sanitizing. Sores would be free to properly mend.

Our previous church had subtly suggested that I mask my imperfections and certainly never expose them. Owning my brokenness felt like stepping naked-souled into the open air—scary, vulnerable . . . and liberating.

Already, my sufferings with Grayson were unearthing so many buried wounds—my need for control, my pride, my perfectionism, my self-hatred, my fear of never being *enough*. His behavior exposed my wounds in humiliating ways, and similar to my son, I couldn't seem to keep my private parts hidden and dressed. Dissimilarly, I was not yet brave enough to flaunt my naked soul.

Very slowly, I began to embrace my brokenness and cradle the incongruities that resided within my heart. In August 2009, I wrote:

> *Love/hate, chaos/stillness, rage/peace, gentleness/aggravation, trust/anxiety, wrestling/resting . . . me. Some days it's a fight to wake up, to put one foot in front of the other, to not hate my life. But herein lies the irony—my suffering is my "cross," and on it lies my salvation. In the midst of the struggle, I find unexpected peace.*

The next time I returned to my closet, I sat down to study my icon once more. Surprisingly, Christ's gaze didn't look quite so fierce. I remembered my previous admission, that God had wrongly chosen me for Grayson's mother. I was not yet convinced otherwise.

Still, a new option entered my mind. Perhaps He had rightly chosen Grayson for me.

9

Quieting

I have always loved the desert. One sits down on a
desert sand dune, sees nothing, hears nothing. Yet through
the silence something throbs, and gleams.

—ANTOINE DE SAINT-EXUPÉRY, *The Little Prince*

The modest, cabin-like room was dark, save the glow of tiered bees-
wax candles. Flickering flames cast shadows up walls to dance on the
ceiling, wild and looming as a bonfire. I shifted awkwardly from foot to
foot, skeptically questioning my presence. Suddenly, a back door opened,
followed by waves of swishing robes that wrapped and flapped around
swift-striding ankles. Shrouded figures filed in with soundless footsteps,
filling either side of the makeshift chapel. A dead hush fell over the room
followed by a sound I'd never before heard—a smooth vibration, nearly
undetectable. It swelled and surged as if gathering breath and then gracefully erupted in a dignified exhale. The hair on the back of my neck stood
on end as angelic voices filled the air. Perfectly on pitch, the nuns har-
monized so synchronously that it was impossible to distinguish one voice

from another or even the direction from where they came. Somehow, their crystalline voices filled every pore of the room without consuming or overwhelming it. They were softly feminine, pure, and uncomplicated. Yet there was an essence of strength that could have pierced steel. Time melted away, and I joined the flow of an eternal stream.

The irony of it all—that my parched soul would first be quenched in a dusty Arizona desert.

I sat alone on a bench later that morning, the sun barely having crested the horizon. The barren land was haphazardly scattered with hostile, arthritic plants and would have stretched on indefinitely save the abrupt interruption of jagged, protruding peaks. Behind me, brick dormitories and flourishing gardens speckled the monastery grounds, where Father Evan annually brought groups to retreat.

I had come seeking and empty.

I had not come expecting to be filled.

From my post on the bench, the first thing I noticed was an *absence.* The crisp morning air did not move. Nothing rustled, nothing breathed, and aside from the occasional bleating goat or calling bird, not a sound could be heard.

In contrast, energy radiated through my body like jittery waves of electricity. The chaos from home clung to me like a needy toddler, but the untamed desert welcomed it to roam, seemingly unbothered by our discord. I hesitantly turned it loose, and as it ran about exploring and scattering, the desert likewise invited me to bare my soul-wounds to the rising sun.

For the first time in ages, no one clambered for my attention. There was no screaming, no battles to be won; no one needed a thing. I leaned back on the bench and breathed a blissful sigh of relief.

But the bliss was short-lived, for hiding in the solitude was a trickster. Extending peace and silence with one hand, it stripped me of my meager titles with the other, thus fully exposing me. Out there, I was not Arin's wife, Grayson's mother, or my father's daughter but simply *me,* a little lost soul fidgeting on a bench in the vast desert.

Uncomfortable in my stripped-down presence, I diverted my focus to the unread book in my hands—a gift from Father Evan the day prior. I had zipped it up without looking as I loaded my suitcase into his car. But now, the title stared up at me with a crooked grin. In lieu of my children, the desert was vying for my attention.

The title of my new book was *In the Heart of the Desert.*

"'Desert' . . . literally means 'abandonment,'" the book read. "[There] you will find no one and no thing. In the desert, you can only face up to yourself . . . to your temptations, and to your reality. . . . [It] is a place of spiritual revolution, not of personal retreat. It is a place of inner protest, not outward peace."[1]

Already, I knew these words to be true.

Intrigued, I continued, "One does not have to move to the geographical location of the wilderness in order to find God. Yet, if you do not have to *go to the desert*, you do have to *go through the desert.*"[2]

I scribbled in the margin: *Grayson = my desert.*

Now fully absorbed, I poured through the chapters, reading and rereading Chapter 7, "Silence and Tears." Thirteen years later, this well-worn chapter has been dog-eared, underlined, and asterisked in every shade of ink. Like the paper version of the Velveteen Rabbit, it has grown tattered and shabby, made "real" through love.

"We come to self-knowledge through stillness and silence," I read, "through attentiveness and watchfulness. When words are abandoned, a new awareness arrives. . . . Silence is *a way of waiting, a way of watching, and a way of listening* to what is going on within and around us . . . a way of entering within, so that we do not ultimately go without. Silence is never merely a cessation of words; that would be too restrictive and too negative. . . . Rather, it is the pause that holds together . . . all the words, both spoken and unspoken. . . . Silence is fullness, not emptiness; it is not an absence, but the awareness of a presence."[3]

My body relaxed at these words. What was it about them that gave my own words the right to breathe, to think, to *exist?* They said everything without saying anything overly specific, like rambling ellipses trailing off in the desert, freed from the tyranny of closed punctuation. They encouraged abstract contemplation rather than commandeering my thoughts and reminded me of my own words, recently written: *I am unconsciously conscious of a nameless something, a nothingness really, as its presence is still unconfirmed.*

Would this presence reveal itself if I slowed my jittery energy, muted the golf ball-sized accusations that so often pelted my brain? What if I stilled my body, waited in silence? Would I hear anything other than my own critical voice?

For five days, I returned to the log chapel at 3:30 a.m.—the stars still dangling high in the night sky—where the nuns' voices floated across flickering darkness to soothe my aching soul.

During daylight hours, I followed dirt trails alone and in silence. They snaked their way through the desert to the monastery cemetery, where I encountered a gaping, expectant hole. A five-year-old girl was soon to be buried, and it seemed apropos to pause at her grave, pondering death and the words I'd been reading: "And then, when we allow our heart to be broken, when we allow our life, as we know it, to fall apart, we are free to be reborn and—quite simply—to be more and more. The ultimate form of renunciation in the desert is letting go of life. As we shall see below, what is far more important than learning to live is, in fact learning to die."[4]

I stared into the black void that awaits us all and envisioned a wheat seed as held forth by the church—cracked and broken with spilled guts, already shooting green sprouts of life through the damp soil of its tomb.

What if my brokenness was part of something greater? What if my struggles with Grayson were a death leading to life? If I genuinely believed this, could I lean into the suffering, possibly even *embrace* it?

My quizzical musings straggled off into the desert, open-ended as trailing ellipses.

A common theme was emerging, one I felt destined to understand.

By then, the energy from home had dissipated, and my head felt clear. But I had yet to address my internal chaos, the discomfort of being in my own skin.

My whole life, words were hard to come by, so I was called shy, and because I enjoyed being alone, other girls considered me snobbish. I felt constantly pressured to be *more* outgoing, *more* confident, *more* bubbly—more of *anything* than what I already was. What I gathered, again and again, was that *I* was not *enough*.

But out in the desert, I could breathe. No one pressured me to change, to be different or better, and for once, my silence was met with more silence—two negatives equaling a positive—and my imagined deficiencies were absorbed in the desert's indifference—two absences forming one peaceful presence.

Some Orthodox Christians believe if a person has lived humbly with love—whether Hindu, Muslim, Buddhist, or Christian—upon death, they will meet their Creator and, beholding Love Incarnate, will proclaim, "*You* are the One I've known and loved. I just didn't know what to call you."

So it was with silence and solitude. I had known and craved them from a young age but had blindly accepted others' wrongly appointed titles. "Shyness" and "snobbery" were obvious vices, not virtues, so I spent my young life working feverishly to overcome my embarrassing malfunctions.

But the desert rightly introduced us, and in proper naming, I correctly identified the attributes I'd so desperately strived to eradicate.

And for the first time ever, I beheld them as lovely—both in the desert and in myself.

In the silence and solitude of the desert, I uncovered aspects of my personality I never knew existed, though I'd long desired them.

They say every human has a doppelgänger, or twin, somewhere in the world. Perhaps the same is true for our souls. Maybe our fragmented soul-pieces abound in the created world, and we must travel through life collecting our missing parts like a scavenger hunt, all while becoming increasingly whole.

In hindsight, it's clear: Everything we need lies within. Nevertheless, we must journey. We must trust the crazy, quiet voice that insists, "I have to go to a monastery in the middle of the desert because . . . because . . . I don't *know* why. Even so, I must."

For, as I would read many years later in a book by Beldon Lane, "The physician of souls heals by abandoning us. . . . The desert becomes a good place for distinguishing between what is indeed a threat and what is actually another way of being loved."[5]

When I returned from the monastery, one phrase echoed continuously in my head: *Teach me to be more silent.* Unlike the words in my blue prayer book that refused to become my own, these words sprung forth like an endless fountain—an outer expression of my heart's inner inscription, and perhaps, my first genuine prayer.

While I once felt ashamed of my silence, like a broken girl with nothing to say, after the monastery, it became my refuge of comfort and tranquility.

Once again immersed in the chaos of daily life, I longed for a physical space to practice my newfound silence. So I emptied our office—a catchall for clutter—and repurposed it into a room of my own. I painted the walls "Paris Rain," the calmest grayish-green I could find. It made me feel as if I was swaddled in cashmere on a stormy day and nothing inside could go wrong. I replaced our imposing executive desk with two overstuffed leather chairs and a fuzzy sheepskin rug and then scoured the basement for photos, still in boxes from our move.

I unpacked a framed black-and-white portrait of Caleb, where his profile, still round with baby fat, was tipped back and giggling over Saturday morning cartoons. Next came Rylee in her yellow cotton dress atop a hillside of white dandelions; then Jacob in a sagging diaper, bent-necked and somersaulting; and Reagan crying through parted fingers over the terrifying petting-zoo billy goats. The last picture made me laugh out loud. Grayson sat in his car seat—lips pursed and calmly "reading" his handpicked library book. Besides being upside down, *Curioso Jorge* was also written in Spanish.

My eyes filled with tears as my finger gently traced the resurfaced memories I'd inadvertently forgotten to cherish. I hung the photos in my room as a bittersweet reminder to savor the fleeting moments.

With this space of my own, always orderly and clean, I began waking earlier and easier in anticipation of a quiet house. Some mornings I read; others, I stared out the window in silence. All mornings, I drank coffee.

These times grew quickly sacred. My room, my chair, and the first light of dawn became meeting places, tangible points of intersection like the desert, where Heaven stooped low to touch Earth. There was the dark liquid that warmed me from the inside out, the steam that rose like wafts of incense, and the smoothness of the ceramic mug encircled by my wrinkly, calloused hands. All were commonplace items made holy, nurturing both body and soul.

Initially, my chaos had dissipated into the desert's disarray. But in my room, it was simply absorbed by the softness of an overstuffed chair, a fuzzy sheepskin rug, and the soothing Paris Rain walls.

Sometimes, the wilderness is necessary to make our own wildness appear less severe.

But perhaps, more often than not, we just need a soft place to rest and a piping hot cup of coffee.

10

Clinging

Our afflictions drag us into a fresh and vivid awareness that
we are not in control of our circumstances, that we are not
quite whole. . . . If we care to acknowledge these truths and are
faithful enough to lean into them, then the particular ache of
that waking can initiate an emptying, an efficacious hollowing
that can lead us into something of a hallowing as well.

—SCOTT CAIRNS, *Short Trip to the Edge*

Grayson's new game started the same every time, with an urgent cry
from one of my kids: "Mom, it's Grayson! Come quick!"

I always knew what they meant by the tone of their voice and immediately dropped whatever I was doing to scurry to the scene. Grayson
typically preferred to play when I was least prepared, so I normally arrived
dripping wet and wrapped in a towel, covered in greasy soap suds, or partially dressed.

Regardless, I invariably knew what to expect.

My three-year-old son would be standing *outside* our second-story railing, which he'd proudly climbed up and over. Then, hand over hand and foot over foot, he'd swing out sideways from the thin wooden spindles like they were vertical monkey bars, giggling and racing their span like an aerial version of tag.

Occasionally, he'd pause and stretch out as stiff as a five-pointed starfish—dangling one foot over the twenty-foot abyss and holding on with a single hand. I'd catch my breath but stifle my expressions, for by then I had learned that Grayson was a showman at heart, a pint-sized Houdini, and any reaction on my end would only add fuel to his fire. Slowly, I'd make my way toward him, and he'd scoot the other direction. I'd back off; then he'd edge closer.

There was never any question as to who controlled his game.

Pressing his back to the spindles, he'd grab one in each fist. Then, leaning out as far as his little arms would allow, he'd raise one eyebrow, furrow the other, and curl his lips back in a devilish smirk.

Come and get me, his expression would dare, and my heart would sink, dreading what came next.

With that one look, time comes screeching to a halt. Like in an out-of-body experience, my head seems to detach and bob along the ceiling like a helium balloon, assessing the situation while rationally directing my steps from above. Down below, my body slips effortlessly into crisis mode. An unnatural blanket of calm settles heavily across my shoulders, and the house falls silent, save the whoosh of pumping blood in my ears. My breath slows to a shallow ebb and flow, and my other children fade away like a blackening vignette, where only Grayson and I remain in its center.

Our eyes lock, and he lets go.

My gut wrenches and calls for my immediate reaction, but my floating head counters coolly, reminding me to stay calm. It speaks in a smooth voice that is my own but also not, and its question is always the same: "How will you handle it when this happens?"

Now, cruel images roll through my head in slow motion, as if a preview of coming attractions might somehow better prepare me. In my mind's eye, I watch. How could I not?

Grayson twists as he falls—his fingers raking for the spindles just beyond his reach, his sparkling, devious eyes now round and wild with fear. His arms flail for me, but I am not there. There is only blackness and the deafening silence of my son falling through endless layers of space. Somewhere far away, I hear the sickening thud of his body breaking against thinly carpeted concrete, and I watch myself grip the handrail, white-knuckled, to peer fearfully over the edge. I know what I'll find—it's the same every time: his tiny body—contorted and mangled, twitching and splayed.

My head repeats its question one last time: "How will you handle it when this happens?"

A split second later, Grayson would recapture the spindles.

The moment would pass in the blink of an eye, but I would have endured a tormented eternity.

Back in the present reality of one of these instances, Grayson was still standing outside the railing—alive and well, taunting and teasing. But now, fearful adrenaline pulsed through my veins and throbbed through my temples at a rip-roaring speed.

My floating head reminded me that fear was a costly emotion. One that I could not afford. Although I longed to indulge in the panic, rush toward my child, and gather him in my arms, I was more worried that any sudden movement might cause his fatal slip. So I swallowed my fear and forced it down deep with a gulp. I shoved my hands in my pockets alongside my screaming maternal instincts, stuffing them down wherever thwarted instincts get stuffed.

I casually strolled toward Grayson one slow shuffle at a time while fake smiling and distracting him with promises of roller coasters and water slides. I inched closer and closer until he was finally within an arm's reach, and then and only then did I lunge to snatch his shirt and haul him over the railing to safety.

Crisis averted, the kids breathed a sigh of relief, and the world resumed its busy pace, as did I. But a new level of chaos had invaded my body and taken up residence. Although life moved on, something inside me could not.

How many times would I brace myself to witness Grayson's death?

Nearly ten years later, an eye movement desensitization and reprocessing (EMDR) therapist would ask me to envision that same scene once more. With a deep breath, I would allow myself to descend and permit my body to feel, for the first time, the fear my mind once strictly forbade. I would turn cold, and my muscles would tremor. My chest would grow tight, and a physical panic would rise in my throat—a regurgitation of swallowed emotions.

After the body sensations had passed, my therapist would press me— what else could I see?—and the blackened vignette would gradually expand beyond my once narrowed scope of vision. There, just over Grayson's shoulder, less than two feet to the right, Rylee would emerge with incredible clarity. She stood, trapped in time, below the rusted horseshoe that hung above her childhood bedroom door. Still round-faced, shorter than the railing, and no more than six years old, her fingers were clenched between her teeth as she anxiously gnawed her already shredded nails. Many years too late, I would finally notice her terrified eyes brimming and then spilling over with tears.

On the therapist's couch, my sobs would instantly erupt in short, jerky bursts. *How could I have missed Rylee? I had rescued one of my children but failed to save another.*

After regaining my composure, the therapist would then ask me to reenvision that same scene but with someone of support standing behind me. Could I reimagine that day with Arin's strong frame looming large in the background? *No,* I would reply, *it could not have been Arin. He would have been too angry, and the situation would have ended in a fight—or something worse.* Years later, I would still prefer to go it alone.

Back then, my choices seemed bleak. If I told Arin of the daily occurrences, the regularity and intensity with which they occurred, I risked turning his anger toward the one I felt a burning need to protect. But if I didn't, the weight of the world was mine to bear alone.

To be fair, there was a purity to Arin's anger that was rooted in the sacred hollow of love. I knew that even then. For what man in his right mind could stand to come home from work only to find the beloved bride of his youth, once joyful and vivacious, now bleeding and bruised, now curled like a fetus in a puddle of her tears? What man's righteous indignation would not be stoked to rise and fight, protect and preserve?

But matters are always complicated when protecting one of your own from another who is also your own. For I, too, had become aware of the fierceness that arises somewhere deep within a mother when summoned to protect her young—even when protecting her own from one of her own.

Such powerful ferocities arose from the same hallowed root. Arin and I were waging a holy war, fighting savagely on behalf of our family. Unfortunately, amid the confusion, we would find ourselves at a standoff, weapons drawn, pointed straight toward each other. Fully immersed in the battle, we'd fail to remember we were fighting the same war.

During Grayson's third year of life, the atmosphere at home grew prickly. Innocuous conversations quickly fanned into full-blown flames. Therefore, whenever Grayson's behavior started flaring, Arin resorted to retreating, muttering angrily under his breath the whole way, "I can't do this anymore. We can't keep doing this. We've got to protect the other kids. There has to be something."

By and large, I disregarded his venting, not caring to understand its source. Suffering has a strange way of turning our focus inward, where the only relevant pain is our own.

Finally, one afternoon, Arin's intentions became clear, though I don't remember quite how. I do know that he was sitting on our brown leather sofa, one leg crossed over the other. The wooden blinds were slanted behind him, casting the light downward in a dull, moody haze. It irritated me to no end—the way he always turned down the blinds—and the gloomy dimness of the living room stands out more than anything else on that day. He was scrolling through his laptop with razor-sharp focus, and maybe I asked, or perhaps he offered, but somehow, I came to understand that he was searching for group homes for Grayson.

I recall only one phrase that day. Arin tossed it out casually without even glancing up from his screen. "Well, we obviously can't keep him here," he flatly intoned, as if Grayson were a stray dog and not my beloved son. There was no hesitation, no question implied, no discussion desired.

I don't remember whether I replied out loud or not, and if I did, I can't recall whether I spoke out of anger or sadness. Although my heart was splintering, I stiffened my spine and hardened my resolve. Whether or not I declared it aloud, what I promised myself was this: *If Grayson goes, I go, and I will never, ever forgive my husband.*

In a long line of arguments that have since been forgotten, that one remains burned in my brain.

Several weeks later, Arin and I sat on a weathered wooden park bench, watching our children play. Already on edge, we sat a full body's width apart, ignoring our old rule that if we were together, we simply had to be touching.

Perhaps the wind changed directions and ruffled his hair—God only knows what went wrong—but in an instant, Grayson dissolved on the basketball court, and Arin stormed over to fetch him.

"I'm so sick of this," he fumed, thrusting Grayson roughly in his car seat. "We can't do anything with this kid! It's not fair to everyone else!" He gruffly strapped Grayson in while he raged. His sparking anger ignited mine.

Barreling my way between husband and child, I shoved Arin backward with two hands, seething and foaming at the mouth like a wild she-bear. We tussled for a moment, him pressing toward Grayson and me struggling to force him aside. Then we caught ourselves acting barbarically and stepped back—four eyes all ablaze with disdain.

"I hate you," I hissed.

"You're such a bitch," he spat back.

The moment deflated me, left me panting and breathless, internally contorted and mangled, twitching and splayed—as I'd so often envisioned Grayson at the bottom of our stairs.

What was this child doing to us?

I had piously read phrases in the stillness of the monastery, such as "let your life fall apart" and "learn to die." I could even assent to their value. But my marriage? This fighting? *That* seemed cruel, torturous even. And *that* I refused to accept.

We rode home livid and speechless, and our mutual silence lasted all night and into the next day, when I finally caved and called Father Evan to ask—in a trembling voice—for his help. He agreed to see us the next morning, although it was Pascha, the Orthodox Easter.

Seated in his office, Arin and I stared stiffly ahead, our skin crawling in each other's presence. We took turns civilly presenting our positions, constraining our normative screaming in the company of our priest. When we finished, Father Evan leaned back in his chair, pensively stroking his chin.

"Corey," he slowly began, "do you believe that your husband is—at the core—well-intentioned and good?"

I forced myself to look at the stubborn ass on my right. He infuriated me to no end, but he had also loved me ardently and unconditionally for nearly eleven years. My icy heart began melting, and I allowed myself to respond earnestly, like a promise I once made, "I do."

Turning to Arin, Father Evan asked the same thing—as if we were officially renewing our vows. I glanced out the corner of my eye to witness my groom set his jaw. Looking down at the table, he resolutely confessed, "I do not."

I broke down and cried, disgusted by my vulnerability, and shocked that Arin no longer saw anything good in me. His answer confirmed my suspicions. Our problems had grown too large to be solved; we were too ragged to be patched.

But Father Evan rose to the challenge, gently confronting Arin priest to man. "Resentment is building in your heart toward your wife," he admonished. "You need to forgive her before bitterness takes root."

Arin hesitated before responding and then slowly exhaled, his body softening imperceptibly. "You're right," he evenly conceded. "What you're saying is true, and although it might take some time, I'll work toward that end."

We finished the morning by offering what the other needed. Arin swore to not lay a hand on Grayson except to restrain him when he was endangering himself or someone else, and I promised to give Arin breathing room to learn and grow as a parent without constantly henpecking his style.

So it was that we found ourselves seated at a cafe one sunny afternoon, intent on peaceably sifting through our differences. The foul air between us had been cleared, and we felt ready to talk as well as listen.

Arin spoke passionately of how powerless he felt to aid and defend me while at work. He had seen my emotional pain and physical scars and was worried about the well-being of our other four children. Our lives had been overturned, and the lack of control—coupled with a complete inability to protect his family—felt overwhelming. He had been wracking his brain for ways to make life more manageable, hence the group home. Although his attempted solution would have led to my undoing, I was able to see through his actions to his good intentions.

Viewing Arin as a struggling man and not a monster helped me feel compassionate and to share openly instead of defensively. Still, I chose my words carefully and spoke slowly, "Sometimes, I feel like my only worth stems from the suffering I've experienced with Grayson. It's real and substantive, and it's changing me—despite my resistance. If such times humble and refine me, why would you desire to alleviate or remove them? If you truly believed this suffering was a gift, could you learn to embrace it, recognizing that within my pain lies my very salvation?"

Arin paused, chewing on his sandwich and my words. "I've never really considered it that way," he mused aloud. "I'd have to think about it. But it does make it easier, hearing it's helping and not harming you."

We finished our lunch in contented silence. None of our problems had been fully resolved; nor did we understand how to parent a child like Grayson. But somehow, our time with Father Evan and our cafe conversation provided a common ground, a point of agreement—modest as it was—that would form a meager foundation.

Like an inverted pyramid, every year would grow increasingly weighty and more difficult to balance. Yet that unsteady, meager, triangulated foundation would somehow manage to support our massive load that initially seemed so unbearable. No parent ever begins their journey with a special needs child feeling capable and prepared. One simply starts with the common tools at hand and builds illogically from the ground up, larger layers topping the smaller, while fervently praying their insufficient foundation will not topple.

That day in the cafe, for the first time in a long while, I felt truly seen and heard. Perhaps it was the warm winter sun streaming through the window that thawed our hearts and enlightened our eyes, or maybe we'd just grown weary of fighting. Regardless, I saw Grayson through Arin's point of view, and he through mine. Arin's gaze grew soft in once again beholding my goodness, and my eyes shone anew with respect for the good residing in him.

We finished our lunch then walked hand in hand to the car—cradled in the hand of Another.

11

Conceding

What is called resignation is confirmed desperation.

—HENRY DAVID THOREAU, *Walden*

*M*ay 13, 2010—the long-awaited day of Grayson's psychological exam.
Arin and I walked single-file into the largest pediatric hospital in
Colorado, followed by Grayson and our secret weapon—Gramma. My
mom could entertain Grayson in an empty room on a rainy day, and her
specialized skill set would allow Arin and me to visit with the psychologist
alone and in peace.

As we entered the sunlit atrium, the pinging sound of a metallic marble
display and the brightly colored tile floors made it easy to imagine we
were entering a children's museum and not a hospital. But the bald cancer
patients being wheeled around in miniature gowns kept me firmly bound
to reality. I dropped my eyes as we passed. The parents behind the wheel-
chairs were fatigued although smiling, fighting for their kids in a way I'd
never known. I felt ashamed of taking up space with our petty problems.

Once in the waiting room, Grayson sat on a wooden chair, pumping his legs and munching on the snacks he'd prematurely fished from his bulging backpack. I felt oddly excited. Finally, we would receive an explanation, and hopefully a cure—ideally in an easy-to-swallow capsule. Next to me, Arin shifted nervously, the appointment more my idea than his.

Shortly, the door opened, and a woman in a white coat strode briskly into the room. Introducing herself, she gave each adult a no-nonsense handshake and a quick once-over, as if insinuating that we were under as much scrutiny, if not more, than Grayson. Bending low to greet him—her face far too close for his comfort—her curt tone scaled a few octaves to mimic the lilting intonations of a preschool teacher.

"Hi, Grayson," she squeaked, slowly enunciating every syllable. "I'm Dr. Keller, and we're going to play some fun games today. M'kay?"

Grayson responded by swinging a fist in my direction and then releasing a spring-loaded leg toward her face. Fortunately, Dr. Keller had quick reflexes. She caught him by the shin and then rose to her full height—leg still in hand—somehow assuming the shape and hulk of a linebacker. Grayson froze, as did we, and then watched wide-eyed as Dr. Keller lowered her face to meet his.

"*No!*" she growled, instantly forgetting her preschool teacher voice. "We do *not* act like that in here!"

Arin and I shrunk back, vicariously reprimanded, while my mom's head swiveled in shock. Grayson's flickering eyes calculated the cost of a tantrum but was sufficiently deterred by the solid wall before him. He sullenly acquiesced as everyone froze in an awkward silence.

Before the first test ever began, already we seemed to be failing.

After several long hours, Arin and I had met with multiple specialists, rehashed Grayson's history from birth to present, and shared our every concern. Blood had been drawn for genetic testing, and Grayson had undergone a battery of exams, including IQ, verbal and nonverbal reasoning, and behavioral and cognitive functioning. At one point, Grayson let out a long sigh, laid his head on the table in frustration, and softly mumbled, "I just want to get my prize and go home."

The ride home was long and quiet, and by the time we pulled into the driveway, my feet were as heavy as concrete blocks. Wearily, I dragged them across the threshold of our door. The day had been strangely discomforting, certainly not revelatory as I'd hoped. I still knew nothing and felt entirely unsure of our next move.

Grayson, on the other hand, marched swiftly into the kitchen as if on a mission. I watched, curiously cemented in place, as he grabbed a large glass vase off the counter and then calmly opened the back sliding door and tossed it onto the patio—where it naturally shattered into a million tiny slivers. Clearly bemused, he turned on his heels and disappeared into his room, slamming the door behind him.

I stepped out onto the patio, completely bewildered, and plunked down amid shards of glass. Burying my head in my arms, I ugly cried—dripping snot, heaving shoulders, and all. I wept not for the day or our uncertain future but for the mess. Should I vacuum the glass? Sweep it? Blow it into the grass and bandage cut feet later? No solution seemed right to my throbbing head.

Those shards remained for I don't know how long. It seemed easier to simply avoid going outside. More than anything else that day, it was the shattered glass that felt unbearable.

After three long months, we returned to the hospital to discuss Grayson's results. Dr. Keller's recorded observations began: "Grayson was joined by his parents for this evaluation. Greeting was difficult, and he did not make eye contact and seemed upset to meet me. When introduced, he became agitated and hit at his mother. When a limit was set, he hit and kicked at me." She added, "Grayson's parents have used a broad range of appropriate parenting strategies. They are experienced, nurturing parents."

Perhaps we hadn't failed our exam after all.

After seven pages of test results and observations, Dr. Keller presented her final diagnosis, the enlightenment I'd been anxiously awaiting: "Grayson is a handsome but complex little boy with very significant mood and behavioral concerns. His emotional and behavioral functioning is significant for significant mood and behavioral dysregulation. Pediatric onset bipolar disorder seems the most appropriate and important consideration at this point."

At the time, bipolar disorder was not technically diagnosable in children, as the *DSM-IV* listed symptoms only for adults.[1] Juvenile cases had not been adequately studied, so Grayson's diagnosis was not actual but merely tentative and descriptive. He was *officially* diagnosed with an MD-NOS, a Mood Disorder—Not Otherwise Specified, which seemed a fancy way of admitting that nobody really knew what was wrong.

Dr. Keller sent us home with a script for Risperdal, an antipsychotic medication used for schizophrenia. We promised to research the drug and then update her should we choose to try it.

It was another long ride home. Something about our four-and-a-half-year-old son ingesting antipsychotic pills made *us* feel queasy. But what else could we do? We had just left the best pediatric hospital in the state, after having waited ten months for a tentative diagnosis from their leading psychologist. Where else could we go?

After a depressing internet search, I journaled on August 2, 2010:

> *Much sadness today. Read reviews on Risperdal and Bipolar Disorder. "Symptoms worsen when taken off meds. Oftentimes multiple medications must be layered. Increased substance abuse in bipolar teens—a 30–60 percent spike in suicide rates." I had hoped Grayson might function normally on meds. But it seems like such a long, bleak road. Another level, another call to acceptance, another fight against hopelessness, despair, and depression. My goal = joy and gratitude.*

Very slowly, the potential longevity of Grayson's situation was penetrating my thick skull one small drop at a time. Horrified, I wondered, *What if he never becomes "normal?"* But I quickly dismissed the thought. We lived in America, and there was nothing modern-day medicine couldn't resolve. I just had to find the right one.

After several months of Risperdal, along with weekly speech and occupational therapy sessions, we still had not witnessed any changes in Grayson's behavior. So Dr. Keller suggested lithium, a heftier antipsychotic drug specifically used for bipolar disorder. It *might* help, she tossed out flatly while staring at her notes, but the potential side effects could be serious. Blood would be drawn monthly to test for lithium toxicity, of which symptoms could include muscle weakness, twitching, mood changes, blurred vision, irregular heartbeats, confusion, slurred speech, trouble breathing, or seizures—to name a few. These the doctor listed as if reading off a grocery list.

It's not that lithium seemed wrong per se; it just never felt right. Besides, how could we entrust such a weighty decision to hands so calloused and brusque? We left Dr. Keller's office that afternoon and never looked back.

Eventually, I discovered the Wholeness Center, a newly opened holistic clinic in Northern Colorado. Doctors Steve and Mary were a husband-and-wife team. Warm, down-to-earth, and inviting, their soothing presence put me instantly at ease. They spoke to Grayson like a child, not a caseload, and they addressed me like a hurting parent, not his case manager. Then they compassionately and patiently proceeded to assess his body and mind—*holistically.*

In time, a colonoscopy and endoscopy revealed a hernia at the top of Grayson's stomach. A steady dose of bile had been seeping into his esophagus, which was lined with oozing, bleeding ulcers. Bloodwork exposed more than thirty different food sensitivities, including dairy, gluten, eggs, nuts, oats, soy, melons, mushrooms, and yeast. After years of consumption, such irritating foods had resulted in a "leaky gut" that allowed partially digested food and toxins to leak from his intestines, causing systemic inflammation and a worsening of acid reflux. Finally, a stool sample revealed a thriving clostridium infection in his intestines—the root of his chronic and bloody diarrhea. Dr. Steve later shared his first impression of Grayson, stating that he appeared to be writhing with discomfort, trying to find a way to crawl out of his own skin.

Vancomycin was prescribed for Grayson's clostridium infection, along with an antifungal medication to eradicate an overgrowth of yeast. The psychiatrist at the Wholeness Center prescribed Abilify for his aggressive behavior, and Dr. Mary set about preparing an elimination diet to calm Grayson's raging belly.

No one suggested lithium.

For the longest while, every change or new medication aroused an expectant hope within. I became like the child who wakes at the crack of dawn every Christmas, secretly hoping *this* will be the year for a new puppy. I silently wished and earnestly believed that with one magic pill, I might awaken as if on Christmas morning to find a new boy beneath the tree—still Grayson, but Grayson 2.0—the calmer, happier version. With each remedy, I watched his every move like a hawk, scanning his behavior for less volatility and better responses, all while growing wildly optimistic over the smallest of signs. *Did you see how calmly he waited in line?*

Many years passed before I stopped doing this. I had to learn for myself that there was no Santa. There wasn't going to be a new boy. There would be no magic pill.

I suppose we all have to grow up some time.

12

Purging

I am a forest, and a night of dark trees: but
he who is not afraid of my darkness, will find banks full
of roses under my cypresses.

—FRIEDRICH NIETZSCHE, *Thus Spoke Zarathustra*

My emotional purge began the day they left.

Aware of Grayson's upcoming dietary overhaul, my mom and sister had graciously offered to take Grayson and Reagan to Disneyland—a last hurrah of sorts—thereby granting me five glorious days of freedom to plan menus, shop for new foods, and rest.

Wednesday morning started with a big Individualized Education Program (IEP) meeting to discuss Grayson's transition to kindergarten. There were seven teachers or specialists present, and the meeting lasted nearly three hours. By the end, I could have crawled back into bed and slept just as long, but I'd stockpiled my February 18 birthday celebrations for my week without Grayson.

First on the agenda was a date with my best friend, Carol, who had grown up near my grandparents' farm. Although I was thirty-two years her junior, our bosom old souls shared a natural affinity for cornfields, dirt roads, and open plains uncluttered by cookie-cutter subdivisions. I had planned to show her the sod farm and then eat lunch at the Pepper Pod, where Arin and I once frequented and patrons and waitstaff still knew one another by name.

However, a small problem arose when I couldn't find the farm.

Driving east out of town, I'd grown aware of a dark fog swirling in my brain. Presuming myself to be tired from Grayson's meeting, I forged onward, scanning ahead for familiar landmarks and CR 49½. Strangely, everything looked foreign and new, as if I'd never driven the route a day in my life. I looked to the street signs for affirmation, but the letters jumbled and then blurred. With every passing U-turn, I grew more and more disoriented, and no matter how hard I tried, I could not find our road.

The brute fact of the matter was, I was lost—one-half-mile away from the house we once called home.

Sensing my distress, Carol called off our outing and directed me home, where she literally tucked me into bed. I was not awake long enough to hear the front door latch shut; nor do I remember how long I slept.

The nightmares started that night, filling in for Grayson's absence with their unwelcome presence. As I lay sleeping, I could have sworn my eyes flew open to behold Grayson standing above me on a ladder, a devilish look in his eyes. A huge anvil hung over my chest, supported by a rope that looped over a pulley and wrapped around Grayson's slowly loosening grip. I watched, paralyzed, as Grayson opened his hand and then awoke to the sound of my screams filling our empty room. I reached for Arin before remembering he was working.

The next morning, my chest felt deflated. Drawing a full breath felt impossible as if an anvil truly had crushed my chest. Sitting up and stretching, I scratched off the white salt lines that had trickled into my hairline, drying as I slept. My dream, however, was not so easy to erase.

That night, I preventatively tried to ward off another nightmare with a sleeping pill. But as I slept, three new images flashed slowly through my head. First was Grayson and Rylee on the outside of the railing—just standing. Their faces were emotionless. No fear. No smiles. Next, they leaned out, holding on with one hand. In the last scene, they were dangling from the ledge by four fingers. They had black holes for eyes and their bodies were limp as rag dolls.

Once again, I woke up screaming and gasping for air. This time, Arin was home, and he jolted upright in a panic and talked me back to reality before wrapping me in his arms.

"It's just a dream," he consoled, already drifting back to sleep. But I could not stop my tears from flowing. I slipped from his arms into the hallway; I needed to see the railing for myself, to prove to my brain that it was just a dream. *See! There's no one hanging from the edge. Grayson is safe in California. Rylee is in her bed. Go back to sleep.*

Still, I sobbed and shook.

Friday, the following night, I awoke to large hands shaking my shoulders and Arin's voice yelling my name. As I came to my senses, I discovered my hands buried wrist-deep in the bottom of my sock drawer, frantically rummaging for the pair of metal sewing scissors I had *just seen* in Grayson's hands. They had been poised at the back of my throat—somehow inside my mouth—open wide around the thickest part of my tongue. His hands each possessed a silver handle, and he had been pressing down with all his might, fiercely determined to cut my tongue from my mouth. My nightmare had been so realistic that a metallic taste lingered near the back of my throat—whether from blood or scissors, I do not know.

It took me a long time to calm down that night.

Finally, Saturday arrived. Arin's boss had gifted us with a night in a luxury suite in celebration of my thirty-second birthday. The suite had a set of French doors that opened up to a Juliet balcony overlooking the Denver skyscrapers, and I couldn't imagine what neanderthal approved operable doors on the hotel's top floor. There was no metal cage, no glass barrier, or even a posted warning sign. Anyone could potentially open those doors, climb up and over that flimsy steel railing, pace along its outside, and dangle one-handedly from its edge.

As fate would have it, Arin immediately dropped our bags, flung the doors wide open, and leaned out as far as humanly possible. My head nearly burst into flames, and my legs turned to jelly. Scrunching my eyes tight, I held my breath until the doors clicked shut. With a gulp, I once again forced down my fears and then met Arin's unsuspecting eyes with a broad, masking smile.

It was late by the time we returned to the hotel after dinner, and a strong wind howled through the gap of our French doors, lulling Arin straight to sleep. But rather than feeling comforted by his deep, rhythmic breaths, I suddenly felt abandoned, alone, and afraid.

I closed my eyes, willing myself to sleep, but whenever I drifted off, I saw Arin standing on our hotel balcony—just standing. But in my dreams, the railing was gone, and he stood on a shallow platform, body flattened against the building. I awoke each time in a cold sweat, increasingly incapable of breathing. Over and over, this vision flashed before my eyes the moment they fluttered asleep. Eventually, as the images worsened, Arin moved closer to the edge and then leaned out as far as humanly possible. Last, I saw Rylee and Grayson—yet again hanging from the platform by four fingers.

When I came to, my pillow was soaked with tears.

But whether asleep or awake, I grew acutely aware of two sounds. First was the gusting wind whistling through rattling doors. The second was a long strain of repeating words: *Let not these Holy Gifts be to my condemnation because of my unworthiness, but for the cleansing and sanctification of soul and body. It is good for me to cling to God and place in Him the hope of my salvation.*

I recognized these words from our pre-Communion prayers. We recited them every Sunday without fail.

Growing progressively fearful of falling asleep, I slipped from our bed to the bathroom, unwilling to rouse Arin with yet another crazy dream. I splashed my face with cold water and lightly slapped myself on the cheeks. Then I sat down on the fancy heated toilet that had a touch-screen bidet. Forcing myself to breathe, I fiddled with the buttons and scanned the marble shower walls for human or animal faces, in hopes of distracting myself.

But blood pulsed through my ears as loud as a kettle drum, and my panicking heart relentlessly hurled itself against my rib cage, desperate to break free from my chaos.

Boom, boom, boom beat my heart, while the words in my head marched alongside: *Let not these Holy Gifts be to my condemnation. It is good for me to cling to God.* I began mouthing the words—urgently and continuously—as if their very incantation could somehow save the life I seemed to be losing.

Slowly, very slowly, my heart decelerated to a dull thud, and the drumming ceased hammering in my ears. In the wee hours of morning, I crawled into bed next to Arin and slept a restless slumber.

For the first time since his birth, Grayson's absence proved to be a greater challenge than his presence. His bodily presence had served as a cork in the proverbial dam. As long as the cork was in place, the dam remained fortified. But Grayson's departure permitted a trickling letdown—and the slightest release in pressure was enough to capsize the dam.

Therefore, what I intended as a peaceful week of leisure instead turned into a bulimic soul purge. All my suppressed fears and anxieties spewed forth in the form of nightmares and uncontrollable sobs. And all I could do was keep breathing.

By Sunday night, Grayson was home, and I slept soundly through the night—nightmare-free.

The proverbial cork was back in the dam.

Still, the words from the hotel repeated themselves like a looped recording, another silent mantra of sorts. I'd occasionally notice them running through my head as I vacuumed or did laundry, but unlike before when the words sprung forth from inside me, these words were not part of me. Yet.

One day, completely out of the blue, their meaning erupted with crystal clarity. In a single moment, I somehow understood beyond the shadow of a doubt. The fear, the nightmares, the panic—*these were the holy gifts.* On one hand, they could condemn, sentencing me to anger, cynicism, and hopelessness. But on the other, they could sanitize my oozing, festering soul. Every trial contained an equal opportunity for either growth or destruction, and I suddenly realized that I possessed not only the freedom but the *ability to choose.*

Could I tolerate the debridement of my wounds, allow all my decaying, stuffed fears to be lanced, scraped, flushed, and exposed in hopes of a scarless healing? Or did I prefer to tamp them down the back of my throat with two fingers until I was so chock-full of fear and pain that I involuntarily purged the second I relaxed?

I wasn't entirely sure what such a purifying procedure might look like, but I felt fairly certain it had something to do with the last line, which reverberated louder and slower than the others: *It is good for me to cling to God.*

I always carried a sense of emptiness within me, perhaps better described as empty-handedness. Feeling depleted day in and day out, I believed I had nothing to offer the world. Life with Grayson had already begun stripping me of my false identities and pseudo-confidence. All I once wore as badges—obedient children, an enviable marriage, a put-together life—had dissolved like a desert mirage.

I recalled the parable of the widow's mite—the poor woman who offered her last coin back to God—and He deemed her meager gift more precious than all, for she'd given no less than everything.

I took inventory; my soul-pockets were completely empty, and everything in me hurt. Was it possible to offer my pain and emptiness back to God as a widow's mite of sorts?

I began adding my own words to the lines that were slowly becoming my life mantra: *It is good for me to cling to God. All that I am and all that I'm not, I offer it back to You. My brokenness, my pain, my emptiness—I offer them all.*

Little by little, and completely without realizing it, I was gradually learning to pray from my heart—from the deepest, darkest, most jagged crevices.

From then on, I approached the Communion chalice quite differently.

My external situation varied from week to week. Some Sundays, I drew near with Grayson in a headlock, my hand clamped tightly over his mouth to silence his steady stream of cuss words. Other weeks, I arrived late, tousled and out-of-breath, adorned in bite marks rather than jewelry. Often, I never even made it to church.

Those were the mornings Grayson barricaded his naked body beneath mounds of pillows behind a locked bathroom door. Even then, I lamely offered God my unproductive exasperation, though perhaps through gritted teeth and clenched fists, "It is . . . good for me . . . to cling . . . *dammit, Grayson, open the door!*"

On the days I was physically present in church, I approached the Holy Gifts meekly, oftentimes embarrassed, as if I'd arrived at a party empty-handed and underdressed. My insides were chaotic, and my outsides felt disheveled—had I even remembered my pants?—and claw marks streaked the length of my arm. My son had just dropped an F-bomb in the Communion line, and I sensed curious eyes burning holes in the back of my head.

It was in those moments that I took a deep breath, straightened my back, and gently reminded myself: *These—yes, even these—are the holy gifts given for the cleansing and sanctification of soul and body.*

I envisioned my shame and rage as exposed soul-wounds, invisible but real as the claw marks on my arms. Then, I clutched the napkin beneath the cup and opened my mouth to receive.

It is good for me to cling to God . . .

13

Laughing

The body heals with play, the mind heals
with laughter, and the spirit heals with joy.

—AUTHOR UNKNOWN

I sat across the table from Grayson, swiping away any unwelcome, escaping tears. A paper Krispy Kreme hat was pressed low on his brow, scrunching his forehead like a wrinkly Shar-Pei. His cheeks and ears burned with red, scaly eczema patches that had erupted in protest over his as of yet unchanged and exacerbating diet. A round, glistening pastry, minus one colossal bite, was being crushed in his chubby hand, and if I close my eyes, I can still hear his excited squeals over that last, stupid, heart-wrenching doughnut.

D-day had finally arrived—the eve of Grayson's new diet. I had prepared like the type-A person I'd never been, staying awake until 2:00 a.m. every morning for a week, cursing, crying, and laboring to plan a regular menu for the kids and a special one for Grayson. Drafting his menu felt like completing a crossword puzzle. I'd figure out one line, only to discover I'd messed up another.

On this gut-healing diet, Grayson was allowed one grain per day, such as rice or tortilla chips, and one serving of low-glycemic fruit, such as berries. The only permissible sweeteners were stevia, honey, or agave, which meant my mom and I spent an entire day home-cooking all the quintessential kid condiments—jelly, barbecue sauce, and of course, ketchup.

Ultimately, my mission was to wean a child off of Eggo waffles and Goldfish crackers and successfully transition him to a regimented diet of mostly veggies and meat.

Wandering the aisles of health-food stores and big-box grocers, I cross-referenced all processed foods against my eight-page list of forbidden ingredients while talking to myself like a crazy lady. I mumbled the names of ingredients I'd never heard of, much less knew how to pronounce: *Triticum vulgare, seitan, durum, hydrolyzed wheat proteins*—all indicative of gluten. Words like *acidophilus* and *caseinate* signaled the presence of dairy, not to even mention the endless synonyms for soy, yeast, and sugar. A single shopping trip initially consumed a three-hour chunk of time, and a decent portion of gluten-free food ended up in the trash. Even our dog wouldn't touch it.

By the day of our final Krispy Kreme outing, I had overhauled my kitchen. The fridge was chock-full of fresh meat and produce. Egg-free, yeast-free, and gluten-free loaves that tasted like disintegrating cardboard replaced cloudlike loaves of Wonder Bread. I had boxed up cookies, chips, and any other flavorful snacks and stored them high atop pantry shelves.

Everything was ready but me.

There I sat at the doughnut shop, staving off tears and watching Grayson's last bites of normalcy disappear one huge gulp at a time. With every swallow, my heart twisted into a tighter knot. All I could think of was everything my sweet five-year-old boy was unknowingly relinquishing—all he'd be missing in the days still to come.

Can it even be considered a proper childhood if you haven't chased an ice-cream truck down the street on a midsummer's eve? And what's a movie good for, if not boxes of candy and buttered popcorn? And birthday parties—what would he ever eat at his friends' birthday parties?

In hindsight, I needn't have worried about those. Parties become somewhat irrelevant in the absence of friends. No, those would not be an issue. But doughnuts—I would have moved Heaven and Earth to keep doughnuts.

Even as a high schooler, he still dreamily whispers as I tuck him into bed, "I can't wait to die and go to Heaven. Then I can eat all the doughnuts in the world."

Miraculously, the first morning of Grayson's diet, the child who rarely obeyed a single command, woke up in a good mood, ate what I placed before him, and never once questioned his missing food. He didn't fuss when I told him no, never tried to sneak any outlawed treats, and only once did he ever put anything in his mouth without my permission.

Like a drill sergeant, I'd ordered my sister to keep a vigilant watch while I quickly ran upstairs to use the restroom. But somehow, a lone Goldfish cracker snuck past her watchful eye. No worries—I'd address her negligence later. I barreled down the stairs two at a time and tackled Grayson with a highly disproportionate fervor. Wrestling him beneath the kitchen table, I pried his clenched jaw loose, cleared that venomous cracker with the proficient finger-sweep of a veteran parent, and then flung it mercilessly against the nearest wall, where it met its untimely death. Breathless and proud, I stood tall to accept my medal. Crisis averted, thanks to me.

Looking back, I find the whole situation rather humorous. What did I think would happen if Grayson consumed a single cracker? Did I believe his head would spin in circles and then spontaneously combust?

Yet in hindsight, I also understand that for the first time ever, I had a clearly defined, tangible way of helping Grayson. For once, I could potentially *do* something to improve his quality of life, so I funneled every last ounce of energy into that stinking diet. I needed a way to release the pressure and longed to hurl myself on the altar of motherly guilt. The gods of such altar had been hounding me incessantly since Grayson's birth, and perhaps I subconsciously believed that my impassioned sacrifice might somehow assuage their vengeful wrath.

Besides doling out his routine medications, Grayson's new diet flaunted the allure of control like a sparkling oasis in the Sahara, and I'd be damned if I wasn't going to give 250 percent. If there was even a chance my actions might improve Grayson's behavior or make him more "normal," then I would find a way to do it better, longer, and more perfectly than anyone else ever. Failure was not an option. Behind the fact that Grayson never snuck anything past me was the fact that *I never allowed it.*

If I was on duty, I would be absolutely certain that zero errors occurred on my watch. I enrolled myself in mommy boot camp and then demanded nothing less than my all: *Buck up! Quit yer belly achin'! Do you not know that other people are facin' much harder situations than you and doin' it far better than you? Yes, Drill Sergeant! And do you not know that there are smarter, stronger, and significantly prettier women who manage both a thrivin' career and their households? Yes, Drill Sergeant! And is yer husband not workin' himself into the ground while you lollygag around the house in your pajamas, eatin' leftover chicken nuggets off your children's plates and whinin' over a few ole' dietary changes? Drop and give me twenty, you pathetic maggot!*

Drill-sergeant me was right. My house was a mess because I was undisciplined and lazy. Self-compassion was for those who earned it, and I had a long way to go. I was unworthy and unlovable. Somehow, I'd even managed to scare off my newfound sense of peace from the monastery.

Push, demand, chastise, repeat—I slipped naturally into this vicious cycle. But after a while, despite my unrelenting self-applied pressure, a small opening emerged in my life.

In July 2011, in honor of our twelfth wedding anniversary, Arin and I renewed our wedding vows in the Orthodox Church and then uncharacteristically left our kids with my parents *for an entire weekend.*

Once again, working in the hospitality industry had its perks, and Arin reserved a hotel room in Vail, Colorado, for just twenty-five dollars per night. I raided my sister's closet for a strappy date-night dress and a few non-mom outfits, and we were off—kid-free for the first time in neither-of-us-could-remember-how-long.

We walked hand in hand through town the first night like lightly starched shirts—crisp and presentable to the eye but stiff and slightly scratchy to the touch. Our first dinner was served over candlelight in a quaint alpine restaurant, and while my mind was finally free to disregard words like *triticum vulgare* or *acidophilus*, it was still firmly entrenched in the worries of home. No one was careful as I. What if Grayson ate a forbidden food? Would my self-indulgent getaway end in his intestinal pain?

Thus, our starched-shirt evening continued and ended—nice and formal but too proper to be fun.

A good night's sleep helped clear my head, and a brisk morning hike put more miles between me and my worries of home. Arin and I talked and reminisced as we hiked, and when the conversation lulled and then ceased, the rhythmic crunching of gravel filled a comfortable silence. As we settled into a challenging pace, I sucked the thinning oxygen deep into my lungs while taking the opportunity to study my husband.

Not much had changed. He still had the same impenetrable optimism of youth, and the immutable bounce to his step had simply grown nimbler to keep up with our busy life. Despite his exhausting work situation, life had yet to crease the corners of his eyes with worry; nor had it revealed any twists of fate too unusual or cruel for him to withstand. In so many ways, he was the same boy I'd met thirteen long years ago—quick to laugh, slow to complain—and he would still rope the moon if it meant my happiness. After all the years and challenges, his love for me had not even begun to cool. Something inside me began to relax.

It felt good to be together as husband and wife (without five trailing attachments), to remember our initial stirrings of love, and most importantly, the depth of our friendship. And perhaps it was the altitude, but as we reached the peak of our hike, giggling and posing like children on lingering snow crusts, I felt a bit lighter and less formally "starched."

After a well-earned nap, we went for another dinner—this time over martinis. I intentionally wadded up my old Presbyterian guilt and stuffed it deep in my purse alongside the kids' chewed-up gum in crinkled receipts. With each sip, the heaviness of life fell further away. Halfway into the glass, I was no longer worried about my parents or our kids, and by the time my glass was empty, I had forgotten we even had kids. Slowly, we had transformed from mom and dad to husband and wife and back to plain old Arin and Corey, once again blissfully happy and carefree.

Color seeped back into my ordinarily gray world, and my eyes opened as if reawakening from a long sleep. Outside, a man was pushing a golden retriever on a bellhop's cart. Had we ever seen anything so ridiculous? No, never, we avowed. And when Arin mentioned his steak was undercooked, our waiter told him it was the lighting, though the cow slab before us was still practically mooing. We tried to suppress our snorts as the waiter turned hotly on his heels, and then we erupted into peals of laughter like he was the funniest comedian we'd ever heard. We laughed until tears rolled down our cheeks. Then we laughed some more.

We laughed over absolutely nothing and every little thing. We laughed to make up for lost time and because we couldn't see a reason not to. Mostly, we laughed because it just felt so damn good.

After dinner, we followed the sound of music to a bar with a live band. The hostess led us to a front table, where we were close enough to see the weathered crow's feet etched into the lead singer's tanned and leathery skin. His overprocessed, bleached-blond feathered hair suggested it might be '80s night in the bar—or more likely, the rock star had never parted ways with the decade. Over a break, he asked where we were from and the reason for our visit. When Arin informed him it was our anniversary and that we had five children back home, the singer promptly made a congratulatory announcement and ordered a round of drinks on the house.

Irish Car Bombs were delivered—one for him and two for us—and the surrounding tables began bouncing beneath a multitude of pounding fists. The raucous bar of middle-aged locals demanded that we *chug, chug, chug,* as if we were at a frat party. We exchanged unrestrained smiles, shrugged our shoulders, and obliged them.

Newly initiated into the Irish Car Bomb Club, we sheepishly wiped the foam from our lips and locked eyes, and that single glance conveyed more than a thousand words: *All is forgiven. I've missed you. I need you and love you more than the very breath I breathe.*

That night, buried love was unearthed in a bar, and a tanned, weathered man with fried and feathery hair served as the conductor. Perhaps it's true that God uses the simple things of the world to shame the wise, though I've never felt particularly wise.

Was it possible that God was larger than the minuscule box I'd locked Him in years prior?

Eventually, we called it a night and shuttled back to our hotel. As everyone else unloaded, I uncharacteristically made a demand, "Don't get off, Arin. I'm not ready for bed—I'm having *too much fun!*" He cocked his head and raised a quizzical eyebrow; then he laughed and acquiesced. We rode back to town and split a late-night pizza.

Leading up to our anniversary weekend, I had been relentlessly pushing against a door intended to open the opposite way. I'd been ruthlessly striving for perfection and control and in doing so, had blocked out light, laughter, and happiness. The moment I stopped laboring, the door floated effortlessly open, and I realized that not all worthwhile things are necessarily hard-won. *Sometimes, they are simply gifted with love.*

Our twelfth anniversary weekend, Vail, Colorado

For so many years, I had viewed God as a tyrannical despot—demanding, unrelenting, evasive—just waiting to catch me red-handed in sin. The only way I knew to gain His approval was by following the rules—don't drink, don't cuss, read your Bible, and pray. Probably even in that order. But that night, despite having violated my old prohibition code—and quite possibly *because* of it—I learned that life was meant to be *lived*, not avoided. Even within the biblical Garden of Eden, only one tree was off-limits. The rest were a wonderful series of "yeses." I had spent years trying to avoid the few forbidden fruits without ever once lifting my eyes to behold the surrounding paradise.

That weekend, a choice unfolded before me. I had been intently focused on the negatives—surrendering, dying, and clinging. But I realized I could also choose positively. I could choose happiness, joy, and laughter. *The choice was all mine.*

Ultimately, I could *survive* my life, or I could *live* it.

I chose to attempt the latter.

Three months later, my decision would be severely tested.

14

———

Dissolving

In my relationships with people suffering with cancer, AIDS, and other life-threatening illness, I am always struck by the mixture of sadness and relief they experience when illness interrupts their overly busy lives. While each shares their particular fears and sorrow, almost every one confesses some secret gratefulness. "Finally," they say, "at last. I can rest."

—Wayne Muller, *Sabbath*

The body sensations started slowly. Sporadically. Minor flukes here and there—all rather undeserving of mentioning. I'd be blow-drying my hair, and a few fingers would tingle and turn numb. No big deal; I'd just wiggle my arm, and they'd return to normal. Additionally, I randomly started dropping things; one minute, my phone would be firmly gripped in my hand, and the next, clattering to the floor like my brain had no say. Weird, but whatever. Other times, I'd be aiming for the center of a door-way, but a slight spatial misjudgment would cause me to clip my shoulder against the frame and send my body reeling. I didn't usually crash into walls, but stranger things have certainly happened. Right?

But then, my muscles began burning when scrubbing down countertops, and I had to pause and rest, letting my arms dangle limply like wet noodles. I assumed it to be my penalty for not working out and quickly resumed, scrubbing harder than ever.

It felt like—little by little—my body was resigning one part at a time, and for the life of me, I could not understand why my normally reliable thirty-two-year-old body had suddenly decided to up and quit working.

But I wasn't asking the right questions; I didn't yet know which questions to ask. I didn't understand the interconnectedness of body, brain, and soul. I never knew that repressed emotions could stifle an entire system, pilfer my strength, energy, and motivation. And I certainly never considered how a traumatic blood draw could undulate into the very fibers of my being.

Several days before the onset of my symptoms, I had taken Grayson for a routine blood draw. The date was October 27, 2011, his sixth birthday. Things shouldn't have happened the way they did. He had been poked multiple times before—vaccinations, IVs, prior blood draws—but that particular morning, I grew careless.

Typically, Grayson got his blood drawn at the Wholeness Center, where a gentle nurse consistently instructed me to hold him close to my body, comfortingly, chest to chest. Standing behind him, she so proficiently distracted him that he never even noticed the sharp needle penetrating his soft layers of flesh. But Arin had recently accepted a job in the oil field, and our new insurance company didn't cover the Wholeness Center's lab fees.

Consequently, Grayson and I found ourselves seated on hard plastic chairs at a large corporate laboratory, surrounded by fake greenery and wooden racks of outdated magazines, awaiting what I believed would be an ordinary blood draw. He had been on his new diet for approximately six months, and Dr. Mary wanted to recheck his food sensitivities.

He was calm and agreeable that morning—it *was* his birthday after all—and I was feeling pleasantly relaxed myself. However, I now know bad things happen when I let down; so begins the hypervigilance of a special needs parent: sleep with one eye open, sift through every new sound, keep your phone at arm's length, and never, ever lower your guard. You just never know what might happen.

Regardless, in my laid-back state, I failed to notice the nurse's gruff and hurried mannerisms, the way she brusquely positioned his back to my chest—where he'd inevitably witness the oncoming needle and her pinched face drawing near. I never even considered that Grayson might respond poorly. He had been successfully pricked so many times prior the thought never entered my mind.

But suddenly, he was flailing, headbutting, foaming at the mouth, clawing, and biting. Splattering blood was flying through the air, and the nurse was screaming for help. We all struggled—but none more than Grayson—and bumbled through the chaos until the debacle ended as abruptly as it had started, and the weight of my suddenly sleeping child made my arms concurrently burn and feel weak as limp noodles—a connection I'd not make for years.

I awoke the following morning feeling like I'd been hit by a truck. When my floundering arm landed on the cold, empty bedsheets beside me, I was dolefully reminded that I was alone. What little morale I had left evaporated instantly as my groggy brain staved off the reality of Arin's absence. He had left for Wyoming a few days prior to train for his new position. He would be gone for ten days total, an eternity as far as I was concerned.

The thought of facing another day of screaming and tantrums felt unbearable, so I stared at the ceiling and imagined my way to the desolate plains of Rock Springs, Wyoming. I pictured sneaking soundlessly to my car, still in pajamas, and then driving four-and-a-half hours in total silence to a rundown motel with a janky bed, where I would be soothed by my husband's warm body. There, in that barren oasis, I could stay in bed all day, indulging in Taco Bell and watching back-to-back reruns of *The Price Is Right*. There, no one would know where to find me.

But then, Grayson barged into my room, famished as always, and reminded me with a slap on the face and a yank of my hair that I would *not* be luxuriating in bed all day munching on cheap burritos and watching Bob Barker.

Begrudgingly, I forced myself upright as a thought I'd never before allowed to pass my lips burbled to the tip of my tongue: *I hate my life. It's a living hell.* I swallowed it back down to the pit from where it came and stormed down the stairs to make breakfast for the mini-tyrant who refused to wait a single minute more.

I got sick shortly after Grayson's blood draw. But it was merely a head cold, so I pressed on, unwilling to be the weak link in the chain. If Arin was working, then I should be too—at least, that's what I told myself.

One morning after the kids left for school, I carried a load of laundry down to Caleb's room and allowed myself the rare indulgence of sitting down, if just for a moment, on the edge of his bed. My muscles were searing like I'd just run a marathon, and lately, I'd started feeling like electric bugs were skittering about beneath my scalp. The charged sensation felt so real I frequently touched my head to ensure no robotic arachnids were tunneling through my hair—an act that instantly made me feel crazy. Furthermore, my buzzing head and limp arms had grown so heavy that my burning muscles felt incapable of supporting their weight. Like a bobblehead doll, my bowling ball-sized melon seemed to wobble about precariously on my flimsy neck, and this perceived weakness made me nauseous.

After resting momentarily, none of my sensations had waned. In fact, I felt even more fatigued than before. Succumbing to my exhaustion, I flopped back onto Caleb's bed and closed my eyes. My bowling ball head sunk blissfully deep into his mattress, and I fantasized about sleeping till I could sleep no more.

But there was still more laundry and no shortage of housework. I tried to peel myself from the bed, but just the thought of trekking back up the long staircase made my heart sink, so I picked up the phone and called Arin instead.

"It's okay. We'll talk later," I promised when Arin whispered that he was busy. Then I proceeded to reassure him regarding the hollowness in my voice. "Yes, I'm fine. A little tired, but it's just a cold. See you soon. Love you too."

Summoning my strength, I rolled over and elbowed my way off the bed, embarrassed for lounging while Arin was working. I shuffled to the stairs, where, leaning against the wall for support, I scaled them one slow step at a time. Upon cresting my personal Everest, I collapsed on the nearest couch—wearied and breathless—to fold a heaping basket of mismatched socks.

However, as I stared at the pile, a funny thing happened. No matter how hard I tried, I could not make a match. I eyeballed a short white Nike sock, easily distinguished from the crowd. But by the time I started digging around, I'd already forgotten the aim of my quest. I tried again—a lacy pink one this time. But the socks swirled before my eyes, jumbled into a solid mass. Disgusted, I swept the heap to the floor without finding a single pair.

The following morning was Saturday. I was so weak I slid down the stairs on my rump then stumbled straight to the couch, where I dozed in and out of sleep the whole morning. I don't remember much other than the kids climbing on the counter to toast waffles for breakfast and eight-year-old Rylee making sandwiches for lunch. For once, I was oblivious to Grayson. As long he left me alone, I don't think I would have cared had he burned down the house. The worst part would have been forcing myself from the couch.

It must have been the next day that I loaded myself and my kids into the van and drove to my parents' home. At least there, I reasoned, a capable adult could care for my children.

I had spoken nothing of my symptoms to my parents. I didn't see the point. Nothing good could come from them knowing.

True to form, my mom had sandwich fixings spread across the kitchen island by the time we arrived, and the kids immediately began shouting their orders. Their voices bounced off the walls of my head like a cavern, and I grew so disoriented I couldn't even think to quiet their noise.

Once again, objects began muddling before me. The mayonnaise jar melded into the mustard bottle, creating a strange new hybrid, and the cheese welded seamlessly to the ham.

Suddenly, the room grew deathly silent save the rhythmic pounding of the oversized clock. Every echoing tick and tock loudly announced that yet another second had passed with me failing to assemble a sandwich.

Abruptly, I turned and strode out of the kitchen, repulsed by my incompetence, and uncharacteristically barked at my mom to figure out lunch for herself. Fully aware of her questioning stare, I face-planted on the couch and disappeared into its softness.

In hindsight, I wonder why I didn't ask for help, confide in my parents, or confess to Arin how terrible I felt. And then, I remember.

Earlier that year, Grayson had been screaming all day, and I was fit to be tied. I called my mom, and like the cavalry, she valiantly came riding in to rescue me. She loaded him up in her car, his tears already subsiding. As I watched her pull away, Grayson's little hand waved happily out the window. I broke down right then and there in the middle of the street and cried ugly tears without even considering which neighbor might be watching. I couldn't even handle my own child without requiring assistance.

Resolving never to feel so helpless again, *I determined to stop needing help.*

Historically, I'd been "the strong one" in my family. My sisters looked to me for guidance and support. I wasn't emotional. I didn't cry. I was tough. And as the oldest daughter, I felt a fervent responsibility to protect everyone else.

But with the onset of Grayson's issues, I had witnessed my parents agonize over my struggles and their inability to ease my pain. I had watched, bleary-eyed, as my middle sister drew back and covered her mouth in shock the first time I crumbled before her and wept. And I had observed the fire in Arin's eyes as he wrestled against his own deeply primitive instincts to protect his cherished wife.

I didn't want to be the source of anyone's anguish. Why should everyone suffer if I could stomach the pain on my own?

And so I said nothing.

Yet there I was, face down on my parents' couch, my brokenness on full display, unable to match socks or even make a sandwich. I lay there, worthless as a bump on a log, while my mom prepared lunch for my children.

After a while, I heard the far-off tinkling sounds of laughter and happiness, but even that couldn't rouse me. At that moment, I didn't care whether I lived or died. Besides, eternal slumber sounded sublime.

A few days later, Arin returned home from Wyoming around 3:00 p.m.

As far as he knew, I had a head cold, so he immediately offered to watch the kids while I napped. I slept through dinner and all through that night. Arin woke early the following day, but I didn't stir. He fed the kids breakfast and got them off to school, astonished I'd slept through the morning melee, and then came to check on me around 8:00 a.m. Still, I remained deeply slumbering. He peeked in again around 2:00 p.m. after running his errands, certain he'd find me awake. But it quickly became apparent I had not moved. Slightly distressed, he gently shook me and later reported that my eyes opened and flickered, and I incoherently mumbled a few words. Then my eyes rolled back in my head, and I was dead asleep once more. Regarding these things, I have no recollection.

Arin's mind leaped wildly to the worst possible scenarios. At once, he pictured me ill unto death, himself as a single father and our children motherless babes. Then he promptly did what I should have done much earlier: He asked for help. Almost immediately, my parents and sisters arrived with groceries. They cooked meals and tended to me and our children for the next few days. Still, I remember nothing.

I slept through day two and then day three. Finally, on day four, Arin made an executive decision and—loading me into the car like a sack of potatoes—drove me to see Dr. Farley, his respected friend and a family physician. I snored the entire way.

Five weeks had passed since Grayson's infamous blood draw.

Ironically, my first memory is of the doctor's office—specifically the sound and crunch of the crinkled paper covering the examination table. Dr. Farley was a handsome older man with a kindly chiseled face and even kinder eyes. They were blue but not overly so, rather more transparent and watery. Had his eyes been excessively blue, their intensity would have certainly drained what little energy I possessed. Regardless, they were comforting, and their softness drew forth my stifled words like a poultice.

My voice was flat and thin when I spoke. I felt certain the doctor would chuckle at my bizarre symptoms and then send me home with a prescription for a little R&R and some ibuprofen. Instead, he pulled out his clipboard to take notes. Dr. Farley listened, truly listened, and the more he furrowed his eyebrows and clucked his concern, the faster and easier my words spewed forth. I spilled out my fears, my frustrations, my difficulties with Grayson, and all the while, he furiously took notes. Somehow, the notes felt significant; they implied my struggles were real, severe enough to require transcription.

When I finished speaking, my voice already stronger, Dr. Farley pulled out his phone and wrote down a list of people to call. Teri knew all about local resources for autistic children; Betty could help with long-term financial planning; Envision was a nonprofit organization for the developmentally challenged. And, last but not least, he scribbled his personal cell number—noting and underlining that I should "Call Anytime!"

Finally, laying a sympathetic hand on my shoulder, he looked down at me through compassionate eyes and declared, "Sweetheart, you are not crazy. You're exhausted . . . and you're clinically depressed."

His conclusion caught Arin and me completely off-guard. I didn't feel sad, and I rarely cried. I only felt numb, empty, and internally dead.

Of course, I didn't know then that I manifested every classic depression symptom: a lack of motivation, anxiety, excessive tiredness, trouble focusing, hopelessness, irritability, slowed thinking or speaking, and feelings of guilt or worthlessness. I also didn't realize how many emotions I'd ignored and suppressed for years upon years.

The truth was, I knew if I indulged in a single tear, I'd most likely never stop crying.

For me, the only permissible emotion was anger. It was strong. It was fuel. It ignited me and kept me moving. And although I was cautious to keep it contained, still it burned white-hot within. People constantly commended my calm disposition. But I knew better. Inside I was churning, the threat of eruption always bubbling just below the surface.

What I didn't know was that grief often disguises itself as rage.

Unlike some grief that starts with a wound and heals with time, mine was like the sore of a chronic scab picker that never stood a chance of coagulating and healing. Each day brought about new losses, some larger than others. Many were known only to me. I buried the sadness, concealed the rage. But now, everything I had suppressed deep in my body revolted and began demanding the attention I had so long denied them. As much as

I tried to buck up and power through, my body—and my emotions—were letting me know they were no longer interested in being ignored.

As we drove to the pharmacy to pick up my antidepressant, Arin verbalized his unspoken fears. For days, he'd been racking his brain, trying to figure out how to work while caring for the kids and his "Sleeping Beauty," whom he worried would never wake. Then he expressed his relief over Dr. Farley's prognosis—that I should feel better in just a few days with medication. Gingerly, Arin let me know a few days were all he had left before officially starting his new job.

Likewise, my family felt relieved that my symptoms could be alleviated with a pill. They wished me a speedy recovery on their way out the door and assured me I'd get better soon. I appreciated their well-wishes and hoped the same for myself. But rather quickly, everyone's words of encouragement began to feel like pressure. A *speedy* recovery, getting better *soon*, and *a few days* until Arin's new job suddenly started to feel like blaring, red-ink to-do items on a list already overwhelming and full.

I returned to my closet to petition a recovery expedient enough for everyone's deadlines. But alone in front of my icon, the thought of praying felt burdensome—another despised box on an unwanted checklist. The only thing that sounded good was lying flat on my back in the dark.

From my supine position, I called a friend for advice, a priest named Father Tom who lived in Seattle. Although the lights were off, I shut my eyes. It was easier to hear with closed eyes.

With great tenderness, Father Tom speculated, "Perhaps you feel the need to get better quickly because you haven't had anyone *just sit* with you and love you through your yucky places. Maybe you could try lighting a candle and sitting in front of your icon for, say, two minutes a day—just sitting, no thinking, no praying with words."

It sounded doable but overly simplistic. Then I paused.

Was not the very root of my current predicament actively entangled in *doing*? Over the last few months, perhaps even years, I had never stopped, never rested, and only felt valuable when I was *doing*. When I lost my ability to *do*, my self-worth disintegrated. *What good was I if I couldn't fold socks, make a sandwich, or clean the house?*

I decided to follow Father Tom's advice, and soon two candlelit minutes turned into five and then ten. From the floor in my closet, I watched the flame's shadows flit spastically over rows of clothing, as the icon of Christ glowed steadily, patiently, without expectation.

I passed many hours that way, lying awake in the dark while my family slept. At that hour, I could have found privacy anywhere, yet I preferred the four womblike walls of my closet. Ironically, it was the only room in the house without a vent, where even the airwaves stood stock-still, respecting my severe need for peace.

Perhaps what I craved was control.

Regardless, a cluttered closet morphed into a makeshift soul-incubator and a little oval pill co-labored with the Creator of the Universe to gradually restore my strength. Secular became sacred and mundane matter made holy, as *doing* slowly dissolved into *being*.

15

Awakening

A kind of light spread out from her. And everything changed color.
And the world opened out. And a day was good to awaken to.
And there were no limits to anything.

—JOHN STEINBECK, *East of Eden*

Having felt like one who walked among the dead, my recovery from depression was a resurrection of sorts.

Within days of starting my antidepressant, my energy improved, and within weeks, the strange physical symptoms all but disappeared. In time, the icy deadness entombing my heart began to thaw, and my stiff, dormant soul-limbs awakened as if from hibernation, curling and stretching toward a sun long obscured. Its gentle rays melted my frozen tears, which trickled down my cheeks like spring runoff.

The world around me started blossoming, and a zest for life I hadn't realized was missing slowly returned. Food that recently crumbled in my mouth like dry clods of dirt now erupted with flavor, and I reveled in the forgotten delight of satiated cravings. Books felt weighty and substantial in my previously tingling hands, and their jet-black words—once dead on the page—now leaped forth from their bindings, freshly robed in rich meaning.

Additionally, my children had a new feeling of permanence. Pre-depression, they were ghostlike—vaporous and intangible; present yet somehow not. But as I recovered, everything about them grew excessively and painfully *real*—their sweet smell after bath time, the silky, slippery fineness of their hair, the rustic aura of soil and sky that clung to them after playing outdoors—and they existed to me then in a way they never had.

For the first time in years, Arin's new job allowed for two weeks of work, followed by one spent at home. Therefore, ordinary events became grounds for celebration, and mundane moments grew so round and full I feared they might pop. In response, I dusted off my camera to preserve our memories in the making, and after years of neglect, our cobwebbed albums once again brimmed with happy photos.

There we are in December, picking Christmas trees with our neighbors and making snow angels on a bright winter morn. Then it's Valentine's Day, and I'm baking gluten-free doughnuts—Grayson's first in over a year. There's Arin and me in mid-April. Rosy-cheeked in winter coats, we're walking hand-in hand on the riverbank as our kids skip rocks across the partially frozen water.

The photos confirm—our time was well spent.

In June, Arin and I hiked and biked through Vail with our three oldest kids, and then we vacationed as a family at a horse ranch in July. We became "regulars" at a local Mexican restaurant, where we shared many a fishbowl margarita and devoured endless baskets of chips. We spent every weekend at the neighborhood pool, where Arin catapulted shrieking children into the deep end to retrieve his wedding band he'd just hurled. Afterward, we barbecued in our swimsuits and then drove to the skate park, where our oldest boys "dropped in" on their boards and Arin catastrophically tried to follow. The other children slid arm in arm down concrete ramps until their pants grew threadbare while I laughed behind the lens, capturing every golden minute.

For the first time since Grayson's birth, I was the mother I'd always hoped to become.

Arin trying to "drop in" at the skatepark

I let Reagan "cook" her own recipe in her underwear on the counter, which required water, food coloring, and flour. Caleb and I ran a 5K race in Boulder. The kids painted the back of Grayson's decimated bedroom door with rainbows and handprints. We frequented the library, and I read *James and the Giant Peach* aloud on the porch with one child sprawled across the back of my chair and the others piled at my feet. And when Arin was working, I took the kids to the lake where Caleb, our avid fisherman, hooked worm after worm for his siblings. Grayson had the time of his life riding a nearby, swaying branch, which he magically transformed into a mind-blowing roller coaster.

For eight short months, a peaceful lull followed that period of darkness, and my soul grew refreshed and replete. Grayson's tantrums decreased, and my children's happiness waxed while my loneliness waned. For one tiny window, our lives felt *normal.* Our kids felt normal, Grayson felt *more* normal, and above all, *I* felt normal. And for the girl who'd grown up feeling only halfway normal, all the way normal was the best feeling in the world.

Undoubtedly, I should have considered the source of such change, but who questions life when it's good? We interrogate the storm, doubt its timing and violence, and shake our fists at the gathering clouds. Yet the instant breakthrough rays beam down like a spotlight from Heaven, our cynicism dissipates, and—tempest forgotten—we pull up a lawn chair, pour a cold drink, and bask in the warmth of the sun.

Besides, as the saying goes, only in hindsight do we see twenty-twenty.

Looking back, it's clear. For the first time in as long as our kids could remember, dinners were a family affair. Their parents slept in the same bed all night long, they had someone to wrestle with while their mother was cooking, and should Grayson's temper flare, their father extinguished his flames.

Every evening after supper, Arin relieved me so I could visit the gym. He juggled bath time and story time, nightly prayers, and endless requests for water while I weight-lifted and stair-stepped my way to physical, mental, and emotional health.

I worked out for ninety minutes, five nights a week, until every last muscle quivered from physical exhaustion. Then I dissolved any lingering traces of stress in the stringent vapors of the women's eucalyptus steam room or sent them swirling down the shower drain as I shaved my legs—alone and in peace—or spiraling into space as I absent-mindedly blow-dried my hair. Finally, when I was good and ready, I packed up my bag, drove home in the dark, and sidled up to Arin's sleeping body, smelling fresh as a spa and feeling just as serene.

For quite possibly the first time in my life, I was routinely practicing my own bit of self-care, though I was unfamiliar with such words. Our previous religious circles would have labeled my behavior self-indulgent, and blessed guilt was always lurking, ready to pounce should I let down my guard. Even the very act of ignoring the shameful, nagging voices in my head felt hedonistic. Still, my husband's never-critical, unconditional generosity allowed me to cherish my gym time in the spirit he intended—as a no-strings-attached gift of love—and one I felt oh-so-grateful to receive.

With Arin consistently home and rested, we both had a surplus of energy for the first time in years, which we redeposited back into our family. Had we comprehended the full impact of his presence, we would never have made our next move.

❖

Toward the end of June, just as I was weaning myself off antidepressants, Arin accepted a new drilling position in the oil field. Although his previous pay was adequate, his new salary surpassed our wildest dreams, and after years of financial struggles, the decision seemed a no-brainer.

Despite the fact he'd be working twelve-hour shifts every night, he could still sleep at home during the day; and if I started cooking a few hours earlier, we could still eat dinner as a family. Not much would be different; we'd just have to make a few changes.

However, what neither of us knew was that the drilling side of the oil field functions much like the U.S. Postal Service *but on steroids*. While the postal service avows that "neither snow nor rain nor heat nor gloom of night" will prevent the delivery of mail, the oil field swears on its employees' lives to procure "liquid gold" twenty-four hours per day, seven days per week, 365 days per year. It stops for nothing and no one—not Thanksgiving or Christmas, not for weddings or funerals, not even for blizzards, tornadoes, or electric bolts from the sky. (Honest to goodness, lightning once struck a rig hand atop the derrick. His coworkers carried him off stiff as a board, but he returned the next day, declaring his slight heart arrhythmia as "no excuse to miss work!")

Regardless, entirely naive to the inner workings of his new position, Arin eagerly committed himself. With one wildly scribbled signature, he unknowingly signed away his life and our peaceful days of summer.

Initially, everything transpired as planned—Arin sleeping, me shushing the children and shooing them outside, afternoon cooking, early family dinners, and evening giggles as Arin tucked the kids into bed before leaving for work. My nights at the gym were no longer an option, but I planned on resuming them once Arin adjusted to his new position.

But rather quickly, the oil field sunk its grimy claws deep into my husband's time, laying claim to his every waking moment and eventually even his hours of rest. It ingested him imperceptibly at first, like quicksand. Yet before long, it wholly consumed him before my very eyes, and I perceived his absence as a great, gaping hole.

Reality dawned slowly through a multitude of questions: "What time will you be home? What do you mean you're not coming home? You're sleeping at the rig every day? Well, when is your next day off? What do you mean you don't have days off? Check the schedule. What do you mean there's no schedule? There has to be a schedule. So you just work every day unless the rig moves or breaks down? That can't be right. Talk to your supervisor. Doesn't he know you have a family? How can we ever plan anything? Check again. This can't be right . . ."

No part of my brain could process my husband's words. Surely there were laws against such conditions! I railed against the backward, rednecked injustice of the oil field, but as usual, Arin never complained.

While it's true the oil field is and always has been a demanding task-master, what I didn't know until years later was that Arin had *willingly* laid down his life; he'd *freely* sacrificed his time. In the same way Grayson's diet had hooked me with its whispered promises of change and control, so the oil field ensnared my husband.

Finally, the boy who grew up without running water or electricity would be free from financial concerns. Driven by an unexamined past and a personal oath to never clean another urinal or sweep another street, Arin silently swore to become the best directional driller in the basin—no mat-ter the cost. At last, he could afford the muscle cars and lifted trucks that would forever sever his adolescent self-image from the dilapidated, rusting Nissan his mother could barely afford. After years of wearing white Hanes His Way T-shirts, Arin could line his closet with enough flannel shirts and steel-toed boots to sufficiently validate his masculinity. Finally, he could leave generous tips at restaurants once beyond his means. He could take his family on vacations he'd never experienced and ultimately provide his children with the lifestyle he'd never known.

Additionally, I believe Arin secretly hoped, on some deep subcon-scious and childlike level, that news of his unrelenting work ethic might somehow reach his deceased father's heavenly domain. Whereupon, Jay Hatfield, burning with paternal pride, would claw his way through death's fragile veil to quell his own fire and his son's doubting heart. At last, Arin might uncover enough confidence to claim his rightful title as a "man"—if he'd only surrender his life.

Eventually, experience confirmed what my brain could not initially compute. Arin's presence in our home would be the exception, not the rule.

But for one glorious summer, everything in the world had been right. The clouds had parted and the sun had shone, casting a golden hue over our life.

And then, Arin disappeared.

Almost immediately, dark clouds reconvened, and lightning bolts started flashing across the sky.

We should have made the correlation, but we didn't.

Who questions life when it's good?

16

Seeing

The only thing worse than being blind
is having sight but no vision.

—Attributed to Helen Keller

I always heard him long before I could see him. That day, I could tell Grayson was somewhere near the back of the school, although his screams sounded strangely muffled. As usual, the aide met me at the door. Her cheeks were flushed, her breath rapid and shallow, her tone elevated and choppy.

We walked briskly down the hall as she began filling me in. "He got really mad and jumped up on his desk—I have no idea what set him off! I tried to get him down, but he grabbed me by the hair." Then, pulling down her cotton neckline, she revealed eight red scratch marks that started at her collarbone and disappeared into her bra. "He also tried to grab me by the breasts," she quietly confided, her hot shame rivaling mine. "Afterward, he flipped his desk, ran out of the room, and hid in the janitor's closet. We've kept him there while waiting for your arrival."

I didn't know whether she intended that last piece of information to comfort me, but the thought of my six-year-old son trapped in a dark closet full of chemicals and foreign objects did nothing to soothe my aching heart.

Grayson tumbled into my arms the moment I opened the door. Splotchy-faced and wild-eyed, he clung to me, trembling and weeping.

Out of the corner of my eye, I grew aware of several indistinguishable figures nervously milling about—teachers and administrators I still cannot visualize to this day. I perceived their blurry heads bowing close, discussing my child's fate in low voices. Momentarily, the faceless bodies straightened and turned toward me, and one of them spoke, letting me know that home would probably be the best place for Grayson that afternoon. Surely, *he* needed to rest.

I scoffed internally as I scanned the demolished classroom and then nodded compliantly and retreated down the hall.

The faceless bodies held the exit doors wide open, eager for our departure, and as I passed through the double metal doors—Grayson still clinging tightly—even the school walls seemed to heave a sigh of relief.

It's not that I hadn't tried setting him up for a successful year. Although he had done exceptionally well in half-day kindergarten, I knew the long days of first grade would prove overwhelming, so I preemptively met with his new teacher to express my concerns and desires. Establishing my intentions from the start, I asked whether it might be possible to bring Grayson in before school officially started. I suggested he help decorate bulletin boards or arrange furniture, hoping to encourage his gentle acclimation. Then I began describing Grayson's behaviors and my concerns.

But I was quickly interrupted.

With a tight-lipped, condescending smile, Ms. Frasier informed me that she had been teaching for *twenty* years, thank you very much, and preferred getting to know her students without being swayed by their parents' preconceived opinions. She was certain Grayson would do just fine starting the same day as everyone else.

Feeling as small as a first grader myself, I cast my eyes downward—half expecting to see my childhood patent-leather Mary-Janes—then timidly acquiesced. After all, Ms. Frasier had been teaching for *twenty* years, and I was *just* a mom. What could I possibly teach her about my son that she couldn't learn for herself?

But perhaps she regretted her decision on the first day of school when Grayson bolted from her classroom and tore through the parking lot. Or maybe her remorse was delayed until the second or third day when he ran away again and again. Possibly, she didn't doubt her decision until months later, on the day Grayson was ranting atop his desk, arms upraised like Moses parting the Red Sea, half the class cowering in one corner and the other half flattened against the opposing wall.

Regardless of *when* she rued her decision, after just a few weeks of school, she so often requested my assistance that I began restricting my daily activities to a five-mile radius of the school.

Eventually, I started observing his classroom to better understand his explosions and potentially contrive a solution. But what I witnessed boiled my blood, and I had to bite my lip in restraint.

The students' desks were arranged in clusters to facilitate group work, and Ms. Frasier's golden rule was that no one could ask for help without first consulting their peers. Rotating from one station to another, their tasks for the morning included copying sentences from the board, listening to stories through headphones and answering questions, and writing paragraphs using complete sentences.

Grayson could barely write his name, much less read.

At Ms. Frasier's command, all the students, except Grayson, burst into action. His hand nervously fluttered about his mouth, and his eyes darted from side to side as he desperately tried to track his seatmates, who were dispersing every which way. They swarmed about him like he was invisible, and he began turning in circles, trying to decide who to follow. He was so small and lost, and watching him cracked my heart into a thousand pieces.

Grayson didn't have a friend in the world—never had—and hadn't a clue how to make one.

But then, something shifted, and Grayson spun on his heels and marched determinedly to his teacher's desk. Still, I watched—my broken heart now swelling with pride—as he patiently waited his turn and then politely asked for her help.

I faintly heard her reply above the din, "Don't ask for my help until you've asked all your friends."

My hopeful heart deflated with his slumping shoulders. He trudged back to his desk and buried his head in his arms. Both his presence and absence had gone equally unnoticed. So much for his so-called friends.

Everything in me yearned to gather him in my arms and whisk him home, never again to return. But a deeper, more sensible part of me somehow knew that the most merciful thing to do was allow him to struggle in the world where he'd one day have to live.

Sitting on my hands with brimming tears, I waited until class ended. After the last student had filed out of the room, I summoned *my* courage and marched to Ms. Frasier's desk. I calmly told her Grayson's work was far too advanced and—alongside the constant chaos—was contributing to his frustration and, ultimately, his angry outbursts.

Completely disregarding my opinion, she looked down at me over the top of her tortoise-rimmed glasses. In her primmest, twenty-year-veteran teacher voice, she let me in on a little secret my uneducated pea-brain had apparently failed to observe.

"Oh, he can do the work all right," she contended. "We just need to figure out *why* he's refusing."

Now, I'm not a fighting woman by any stretch of the imagination, but that day, I pictured myself slapping her smugness clean into the second grade or, at the very least, giving her a tongue-lashing she'd never forget.

Instead, I said nothing and stared at my hands cordially folded in my lap. When I lifted my head, politely smiling to mask my rage, Ms. Frasier had already resumed grading her papers. Clearly dismissed, I thanked her for her time and backed out of the room.

Rather than confronting Grayson's problematic teacher, I started volunteering three mornings per week in his classroom. I sat next to him in a little plastic chair and read the words on the board one letter at a time so that by the end of the exercise, he'd at least have one sentence to his classmates' paragraphs.

Back home, mornings were torturous. The more Grayson came to hate school, the more vigorously he resisted attending. Suddenly, the collar on his uniform shirt grew unbearable and his khaki back pockets intolerable. He only wanted to wear his fuzzy Lightning McQueen pajamas, and when I refused, all hell broke loose. Packing a sack lunch in light of his food sensitivities felt absolutely overwhelming, and getting his socks "just right" in his shoes could have tried the patience of a saint. Brushing his teeth was a battle I largely avoided; I had gotten headbutted and finger-chomped far too many times to persist. I lamely reasoned that his baby teeth would fall out one day, regardless.

To neglect such basic hygiene seemed unthinkable, and I felt confident that a scarlet letter—"D" for Dirty—had been branded on my forehead. Besides considering myself a "neither-nor," I additionally began labeling myself a "less-than."

Our kids' school required parents to volunteer twenty hours per year. Although I should have already been a paid staff member (as much as I was physically present), I still tried to meet my annual quota, though I never quite succeeded. I signed up for the solitary jobs whenever I could, like grading or laminating papers. But occasionally, I got stuck supervising science experiments or reading groups and was forced to interact with other parents.

I kept my head low, hoping they wouldn't notice my scarlet letter, but I needn't have worried; something about me was as repelling as a magnet, and no parent ever addressed me. I ran my tongue across my teeth, reminding myself that *Grayson's* teeth were unbrushed, not mine. *I* had showered, put on makeup, and even curled my hair.

But a cloud of chaos swirled about me, reinforcing my belief that I should have stayed home—where I belonged.

I slipped away as soon as my volunteer hours ended to return to the safety of my house. Finally alone, I sat at my kitchen table, gathering my thoughts and assessing the damage from the morning rush. Dishes with dried parcels of food inevitably littered the countertops, and laundry from the previous day lay strewn across the railing. The milk had been left out (again), and toys remained randomly scattered wherever my children had dropped them. Without even looking, I knew the evidence of my boys' poor aim would be splattered all over the toilet seats, and all the bathroom trash cans would be overflowing.

My "D" for Dirty morphed into a "D" for Disgusting.

What was wrong with me, I wondered, that I couldn't keep up with my life?

Out of necessity, our four other children grew fiercely independent, even little five-year-old Reagan. They prepared their own breakfast, got themselves dressed and ready, and then slipped from the house to meet their carpool without even a kiss goodbye.

Those days were the worst.

On one such morning, I was rushing about looking for a pair of socks that Grayson would actually keep on his feet and chastising myself for being so disorganized. Grayson was losing his mind, but for whatever reason, I paused long enough to peer over the railing and check on my other kids.

All four children were seated at the kitchen table, sharply dressed in school uniforms. The boys had tucked in their polo shirts, and the girls' hair was surprisingly combed and neatly adorned in matching ribbons. (Had I done that? I couldn't recall.) They all slurped their cereal with rounded backs, except for tiny Reagan, who still had to sit tall to reach the lip of her bowl. Each child had placed a cereal box before them, and the row of boxes formed a tight line. Instantly, an image of wartime barricades flashed before my eyes. Something about my children crouching behind the tall boxes made it appear like they were hiding, and I briefly wondered if their makeshift line of defense wasn't their subconscious way of blocking out Grayson's noise.

Then, just as I started to turn away, I suddenly noticed *how* they were eating.

Each child was sitting *the exact same way*—elbows propped on the table and index fingers plugging their ears like miniature corks. They removed their fingers only to shovel in new mouthfuls of cereal and then quickly replaced them in their ears. Their movements were casual yet mechanic, and I wondered how many mornings they'd eaten that way. Beyond that, I wondered how long I'd taken to notice.

I silently complimented my children's resiliency, indulging in a moment of motherly pride. Then, noting their expressionless faces with a twinge of jealousy, I thought there was nothing, it seemed, that could faze them.

I savored the moment a split second more and then quickly averted my gaze.

For somewhere deep in my body, I knew that something about that scene had the potential to destroy me. Already, I could taste the acrid failure bubbling up the back of my throat like hot bile, but I forced it back down, turning away from the four to the one.

Outwardly, I resembled the four. My face was expressionless, my movements as casual and mechanical as theirs. But internally, I raged like the one who couldn't make peace with a pair of socks. Inwardly, *I* was autistic—rocking backing and forth, pulling my hair and slapping my face, desperately trying to self-soothe.

My poor children—they had the undying love of two dedicated parents yet still had been unintentionally orphaned. There was never enough of me to go around, and how does a mother ever choose between her own children?

And yet I did.

Even as I write, a white-hot pain ignites in my chest and saliva begins flowing from the old lump rising in my throat. All the sadness I never allowed myself to feel gushes down my face in torrential sheets, drenching my cheeks and filling the concave spot at the base of my neck.

That year, I painted my kitchen and living room four times.

The largest wall spanned the entire length of the house, and the vaulted ceiling was maybe fifteen feet high. I had to stand on tiptoes on the ladder's top rung and use an extension rod to reach the peak, but for some reason, I was determined—come hell or high water—to find the perfect color.

It started as creamy Lambskin (builder's choice), but I painted it a happy Tuscan yellow on a whim. But I didn't feel happy inside, and the wall quickly exposed my hypocrisy. So I tried blue because it's supposed to be tranquil. But it looked babyish instead, and my whole house felt like a nursery, so I feverishly redressed it in two coats of brown in one day. The brown was better, but it didn't feel warm and cozy as promised. On good days, it looked like earthy clay; on bad ones, my wall looked like someone had smeared it with feces.

Most days, it looked like it had been smeared with feces.

Eight coats of paint later, I settled for poop-brown. I'd grown tired of climbing up and down my ladder. Finally, I conceded: My painting experiment had been an abject failure—a complete waste of time, money, and precious energy.

I see now what I couldn't see then. I wasn't searching for the perfect color; I was searching for something, anything, to counterbalance my internal unrest.

But no matter the number of coats or size of the canvas, I still remained entirely uncomfortable.

During Grayson's first-grade year, we all started unraveling.

By midyear, Caleb's sixth-grade teachers had started calling home. He had grown quite disruptive and argumentative. Could we please come in for a conference? I was shocked. Caleb had always been exceptionally bright, a good student, and well-liked by his teachers. Since when had he started mouthing off in class?

Arin made it home for that meeting—no son of *his* would be rude. Caleb was sullen, his eyes dark as we conferenced with his teachers. We apologized, assured them it wouldn't happen again, scolded Caleb, and chalked the rest up to puberty.

The one thing we failed to do was listen.

Shortly after, I took Caleb to see Father Evan, hoping he could break through to our son. After making small talk, Father Evan asked Caleb if he missed Arin since he was gone more than usual. Caleb was slouched so low in his chair that his head was nearly even with the table. He had wrapped his arms protectively around his body, a moody scowl clouding his face. He mumbled, "No, I don't care. I get that he has to work."

But a lone tear leaking from his eye said otherwise. It escaped halfway down his cheek before he swiped it away in preteen embarrassment.

I missed what that tear was trying to say; it spoke all the words that Caleb could not.

Back home, his anger kept growing in hostility and volatility.

Unfortunately, Grayson screamed louder.

One afternoon, Rylee stormed into the house with tears streaming down her face to tattle on her brothers. They told her they had a surprise—a fuzzy baby bunny just beyond the front yard. But they failed to mention the bunny had been flattened beneath moving car wheels. The boys thought it hilarious; Rylee was distraught.

I scolded the boys and sent them to their rooms, but I never followed up with my brokenhearted daughter. I'm sure something more pressing occurred. Something like Grayson.

Another time, she came home from school with a certificate in hand for good grades. She stared inquisitively into my eyes and softly asked, "Mama, why didn't you come to the assembly today? You told me you'd be there. I made the fourth-grade honor roll."

"I was there, sweet girl," I told her, blinking away stinging tears, "but I was in the hallway looking through the glass. Grayson was having a hard day, and I had to keep him with me. You couldn't see me, but I was there."

Such came to be my children's life narrative: *You couldn't see me, but I was there.*

Jacob's third-grade teacher also called home that same year. There was a boy in his class with a disability. He couldn't carry his backpack, so Jacob had taken it upon himself to transport the boy's bag between classes, often arriving late to his own. Did I know what a good boy he was?

I most certainly did. Jacob was our easiest child. He always did what we asked without a complaint. However, lately, he had developed severe and random stomach aches, inexplicable to even our doctor.

Eventually they went away.

I couldn't see the invisible stressors that were tying his stomach in knots. Jacob has carried others' burdens his whole life—even when they left him writhing on the floor.

Early in the school year, Reagan and I spent many quiet afternoons bonding and making up for lost time. We baked cookies, painted pumpkins, and went to the salon for mommy-and-me haircuts.

But then something changed, which I can't remember to save my life, and I enrolled Reagan in full-day kindergarten. She was our only child who ever attended a full day of kindergarten, and I'm sure it had something to do with Grayson.

Like Jacob, she never complained. She seemed oblivious to the surrounding chaos and always happy to entertain herself. But to this day, she's reticent to speak of her troubles. Instead, I've learned to read her silent cues, like a row of missing eyelashes or the scabbed-over cuts on her thigh.

Father Evan once said that children with a special needs sibling either create significant issues to gain their parents' attention or conclude their problems don't matter.

In time, Caleb and Rylee sought recognition by creating issues too large to ignore, whereas Jacob and Reagan went silent, having deemed their troubles inconsequential.

It's not that I was ignoring Father Evan's wisdom; I deeply took it to heart. I just didn't know what to look for.

But it was all there in plain sight for everyone to see but me: Caleb's angry outbursts, Rylee's lonely neglect, Jacob's burning need to help and heal, and Reagan trailing behind—silent and alone.

All my children were symptomatic. They were all reacting to life with a special needs sibling, and isolated events were coalescing to paint a coherent picture.

Unfortunately, I didn't notice. I was too busy painting a wall of my own.

17

Diagnosing

For after all, the best thing one can do
when it is raining is let it rain.

—Henry Wadsworth Longfellow, *Tales of a Wayside Inn*

I've only recently grown accustomed to "feeling my feelings." So it's merely in hindsight that I can flip through my Rolodex of memories and deposit the appropriate emotions like a postdated check. From my armchair vantage point ten years down the road, I can now correctly label the shame I experienced over not brushing Grayson's teeth and the missing emotions I sought in colorful gallons of paint.

But years ago, when anyone asked how I was *really* doing, I simply smiled, shrugged, and evenly offered my standard line of deflection: "It is what it is. We're doing just fine."

What else could I say? There was nothing. And besides, I mostly believed it.

Recently, I had the unique opportunity to observe how I must have appeared back when I was void of emotions. A visiting friend was drowning beneath the rage, violence, and hopelessness of not one but *two* special needs children. Her face looked relaxed as she spoke, sublimely beautiful and free from contortion. Anticipating the crack in her voice or a free-falling tear, I watched closely and prepared to gather her in my arms while she wept.

But her voice never faltered, and her eyes remained dry and clear as a hot summer day.

As she spoke, I marveled at her unnatural calm. Her resolve was stoic, her strength supernatural. I admired her resiliency and ability to hold life together under such dire straits.

But in a flash, I remembered and then understood. Allowing myself to slip back in time, I put myself in her shoes and realized I'd been applying the wrong adjectives as others had so often done to me.

My friend wasn't calm or stoic; she was dead. She felt neither strength nor resilience, only perpetual numbness. Her heartbeat had flatlined, and her lifeblood had run dry. In her zombified stupor, all she could manage was one step, then another, and the robotic imitation of those more fully alive. Sure, she could mimic laughter, and she could smile. But beneath her mechanical outer shell, I knew she felt hollow.

I wondered if she was plagued by the same question that once throbbed endlessly through my brain: *How will I ever survive my own life?*

Finally, I understood how I must have appeared—when I was a Walking Dead.

In the 1960s, a University of Pennsylvania graduate student named Martin Seligman conducted an experiment. Pairs of dogs were harnessed together, and Seligman and his colleagues administered multiple series of light shocks. One dog could press a lever with its nose, thereby ending the electric current, while the other had no choice but to endure. Later, the same dogs were placed in a kennel divided by a low-lying fence. Again, light shocks were administered. The dogs who could previously eliminate their suffering with the push of a lever jumped over the fence to safety; the other dogs laid down on the electrocuted floor in resignation.

Seligman termed this behavior *learned helplessness*, stating, "Learned helplessness is the giving-up reaction, the quitting response that follows from the belief that whatever you do doesn't matter."[1]

I felt crushed when I read his conclusion. The dogs who had endured and made peace with their sufferings understood life to be uncontrollable and had adapted accordingly. Yet they would forever go down in history as quitters—the dogs who gave up.

The funny thing is, before learning of Seligman's deduction, I thought he'd surely label his dogs as *resilient*.

The implications of his experiment felt personally staggering. Was I resilient or just a paralyzed, defeated quitter? Was I summoning a primal level of adaptability when surrendering to life's unpredictability? Or did I merely lack the internal fortitude to hop over a low-lying fence?

In hindsight, perhaps the dogs were simply a mirror image of my friend and former self—perpetually numb, internally hollow.

The day Grayson was diagnosed as autistic, Arin and I attended his appointment and then stopped to visit Carol, who was recovering from surgery. Walking into her hospital room, I witnessed my bandaged and broken friend reclining on her bed but felt nothing.

As Arin shared the news of Grayson's diagnosis, his voice rose several octaves. He was distraught, incredulous, overwhelmed, and his rising intonations irritated me to no end. *What was the big deal?* We already knew something was wrong with Grayson, and *autism* was just six tiny letters strung together to make up some nonsensical word.

No matter what the label, Grayson would still be Grayson. The fits would remain the same, his rage no different. Autism was incurable. There were no magic pills, no light at the end of the tunnel. His diagnosis was simply an inconsequential hyphen connecting an endless chain of chaos.

The diagnosis passed through my body like electric shockwaves, but I'd grown as immune as Seligman's dogs. But unlike his dogs, I had no time to lie down in resignation. I had errands to run, kids to pick up, and a family to feed. By that evening, I had cooked dinner, picked up groceries, library books, dry-cleaning, and an autism diagnosis—and nothing on that list felt more significant than the other.

The morning had started with the faintest buzz of a sensation that bordered on excitement. I had a good feeling about Dr. Ramirez, a psychologist referred by the Wholeness Center. I felt expectant, as if the information she bestowed would somehow enlighten us like a magic crystal ball.

But when the word *autism* landed in my ears with a thud, it felt as dull and anticlimactic as unwrapping a jar of pickles on a birthday. *This? This is what I've been waiting for all year?*

Arin and I questioned the doctor's prognosis, and then Arin pressed her even further: How could she be sure? Was the testing process truly accurate? Did Grayson even comply?

But I had watched; I'd seen her in action. I liked her—no, I *loved* her the minute she walked through the exam room door. She grasped my hand warmly in two of hers, and her twinkling, rich brown eyes flashed me an encrypted message, letting me know that Grayson and I were safe and literally in good hands. I could have melted with relief. Her wave of goodness nearly bowled me over, and everything inside me settled.

Without a word, Dr. Ramirez plopped to the floor, as far away from Grayson as the room would allow. Appearing uninterested, she began playing with toys, and Grayson, who was hiding behind my legs, investigated with only one eye. Her gaze affixed to the floor, she spoke as if to herself, "Hey, Grayson. I'm Dr. Ramirez. I'm going to be playing with you today."

She picked up one toy and then another, each time watching from the corner of her eye to see which would pique his interest.

Her testing had already begun.

The cars didn't budge him, and the flashing firetruck elicited a two-eyed stare. But it was ultimately the coveted marble ramp that lured him from behind my legs. Inch by inch, he lowered himself to the ground, still gripping my ankle as if I were his prisoner on house arrest. Slowly, he crawled toward her on hands and knees until he landed directly in front of her—calmly seated and in his right mind.

Still, the doctor ignored him and kept her eyes glued to the ground.

She waited for him to initiate conversation, and once he did, they played together the whole session as if they'd been lifelong friends.

I watched in awe as she charmed the one so normally quick to strike. Never in my life had I witnessed Grayson interact with a stranger in such positive ways.

I recalled our first psychologist, Dr. Keller—how she grabbed hold of his foot when he tried to kick her and her sharp, commanding words: "No! We do not act like that in here!"

Hers was one method, and before me, another. One felt harsh and controlling, the other loving and calm. In a single moment, I realized that I could force, corner, and physically manhandle my son, or I could learn to sit silently, eyes lowered in peace, thus settling his apprehensions with my calming presence. I didn't specifically know *how*, but for the first time, I realized it *could* be done.

Two very different paths had been illumined before me. One led straight back to my legalistic past, while the other pointed promisingly forward. Little by little, I was being shown that gentleness and mercy cause life to flourish, whereas compassionless justice shrivels a soul.

I should have made a bumper sticker: All I Really Need to Know I Learned from Autism.

At any rate, when Dr. Ramirez declared Grayson to be autistic, I questioned her, but I didn't doubt. I knew *she* knew all *I* needed to know.

Of all the questions we asked that day, only one stands out in my mind: "How could my son be autistic?" He made eye contact and gestured appropriately; he didn't flap his hands or make strange, guttural sounds

But truth be told, there was a larger, burning question hiding behind my question, peeking out with one timid eye like my son: *How could I, his mother, have not known?* Although I'd danced around the idea of autism numerous times, Grayson never seemed to match the stereotype in my head.

Immediately, my internal critic was off to the races, thrilled to possess yet another piece of incriminating evidence that proved my maternal ineptitude.

As if reading my mind, Dr. Ramirez leaned forward, her eyes brimming with tenderness. "The thing is," she explained, "if you've seen one autistic kid, you've seen . . . one autistic kid. *They are all that different.*"

My internal critic started stammering uncomfortably as the doctor continued, "Even *I* have a hard time identifying kids on the spectrum, and I've done *hundreds*, maybe even *thousands* of diagnostic tests."

With these last comforting words, my critical inner voice vaporized into thin air.

It took me a long time to fully accept Grayson's diagnosis. Autism existed "out there" and belonged to anyone other than us. It reminded me of a thrift-store T-shirt worn by countless others that smelled like a conglomeration of drugstore detergents. Someone else's friction had worn the fabric thin, and others' experiences had raised balled cotton pilling. No matter how often I washed it in *our* detergent or made Grayson try it on for size, it never seemed right. I tried to make the word leap from my tongue, but it refused. I couldn't make it *mine*. I couldn't make it *ours*.

So I stashed it in the back corner of a dark closet. Instead of referring to it by name, I spoke of Grayson's "behavioral issues" or his "special needs." Eventually, I transitioned to mentioning that his doctor thought he *might* have autism and then graduated to admitting that he actually did. It took me much longer to assert that he *was* autistic, and many years passed before I uttered the word aloud in his presence. Instead, I whispered it behind a concealing hand, mouthed it like it were a foul four-letter word, and cringed should anyone blurt it too loudly.

Again, it's not that I disagreed; I just never wanted Grayson to feel different or less-than—like me. It seemed unfair to bundle such a beautiful, complex soul into a single, reductionistic term. To me, he was infinitely more.

I initially refrained from using the word, hoping that if I left it untouched in the back of the closet, perhaps one day I could return his diagnosis for a full refund, or at least partial store credit. I think I secretly believed that if I ignored it long enough, we'd one day pull it out to try it on for size and—much to our delight—realize it no longer fit. Part of me felt confident that, with time, Grayson would outgrow his "little phase."

I asked Dr. Ramirez one final question before leaving her office that day: "Why does it even matter? There's no cure, no treatment, so what good is a diagnosis?"

I eventually would learn that diagnoses, while potentially labeling and limiting, can also be highly efficient. I could communicate what would typically take pages to convey with a single word. I could succinctly explain Grayson's behavior, thereby silencing even the rudest of strangers, like the time Grayson shoved Reagan in Costco and sent her sprawling in front of an old woman's cart. She waggled a crooked finger in his face and chastised him for being a "bad boy." I expressed that he had "difficulties," and her scolding finger then pointed my way. "Well then, next time, leave him at home," she croaked, wobbling away. I deliberated momentarily and then chased her down. "I'll have you know my son is *autistic*," I all but yelled before turning on my heels and leaving her sputtering in the aisle.

Of course, I hadn't changed her heart with my impulsive declaration, but for the first time, I had taken possession of the word. Made it mine. Made it ours.

Years later, as Grayson neared adolescence, he would begin studying his face in the mirror. Lamenting its perceived ugliness, he would tearfully demand a face transplant or that I burn his face off with acid. He would question why no one ever invited him to their birthday party, wonder why his siblings had multiple friends, and he had not even one. After exploding like the Hulk, Grayson—upon coming to his senses—would behold the wake of his destruction. Buckling to the ground in remorse, he would punish his ugly face over and over with two fists while dissolving into a heap of howling, lamenting sobs: *Why am I such a bad boy?*

Dr. Ramirez said I would know when the timing was right. She told me Grayson would find a way to let me know when he was ready to learn of his diagnosis—and she was right. One night, while sitting on the edge of his bed post-tantrum, he would launch into a stream of unrelenting questions: "But *why* am I different? *Why* do I struggle with everything? *Why* do I feel so angry?" His questions would break my heart, for I constantly wondered the same about myself.

At that moment, resolve would settle over me like Grayson's weighted blanket, and I would *know* the timing was right. It would become crystal clear that the most painful, loving, and merciful thing to do was speak the word—his word—out loud. I would say it firmly, sympathetically, and with pride, "Autism. Autism. Autism."

In time, I would educate him about its implications, and he would receive the information as calmly and matter-of-factly as I presented it. The word that had long felt foreign in my ears would ring intrinsically true in his.

From that night forward, I would no longer treat his diagnosis like a crumpled thrift-store T-shirt. I had dug it out of a dark closet corner, and lo and behold, it fit Grayson like a glove. After that night on the side of his bed, the word would slip easily off my tongue.

If my son could own it, then so would I.

Grayson has taught me that there are situations in life that refuse to be controlled, painful sensations that can't be avoided. They roll around you and through you like electrical currents, and sometimes the best choice is to lie down in quiet acceptance.

I've since concluded that Martin Seligman got everything wrong.

His dogs weren't quitters.

They were heroic. They were stalwarts. And above all, *they were resilient.*

18

Beautifying

You must have chaos within you to give birth to a dancing star.
—Friedrich Nietzsche, *Thus Spoke Zarathustra*

I hated the house the first time I saw it. It was as if someone had built a brand new home and then projectile-vomited the color yellow everywhere—on the carpet, the walls, and the hardwood floors. I had been disappointed by yellow once and recalled it to be incapable of producing any sort of chipper happiness as promised.

Based on its listed features, I should have loved the house: four bedrooms plus an unfinished basement, a designated office, four-and-a-half bathrooms, a stunning chef's kitchen, and a golf course community with swimming lakes for the kids.

But the house was yellow. Disgustingly so.

I dismissed it the second I walked through the door—as quickly as Arin surmised it was perfect. The house was in a much better school district for Grayson and closer to our church.

"Besides," Arin reasoned, "you know we can change anything you don't like, right?"

Shocked, I silently admitted to myself that, no, I didn't realize that at all. The thought had never crossed my mind.

That night in bed, I spent several long, sleepless hours staring at the ceiling, marveling at the simplicity of Arin's suggestion.

After years of dealing with Grayson's uncontrollable chaos, I, like Seligman's dogs, had accepted the narrative that nothing would ever change. Subconsciously, I had lain down and resigned myself to the fact that life was simply immutable.

Yellow would remain yellow forever.

But as the night progressed, my incredulity over having missed such an easy solution morphed into open-ended imaginings, and I loosened the reins on my normally rigid brain and allowed it to graze freely among fields of *potential*.

Surprisingly, picturing what the house could become came easily, and I discovered that I could mentally walk through each room and envision it complete. I drifted off to sleep in the early morning hours, feeling empowered. *I can change the house,* I silently murmured. *I can change anything I don't like.*

We made an offer on the house the next day.

I fell in love with Fiona the first time I saw her. Her catalog description eloquently read: "Graceful tufting, elongated back, and gently flared arms combine to create our stunning Fiona Cushioned Sofa. Its feminine silhouette is accentuated by chic and luminous fabric—a vintage-inspired velvet in soft tones that evoke a sense of decadent Parisian luxury. A row of nailhead detailing surrounds its base in a subtle antique brass, adding a perfect final touch to this classically styled masterpiece."

Although we had yet to close on our new house, I drove straight to the furniture store and ordered her on the spot. It didn't matter that she was made of white velvet or that we had five young children; Fiona was *beautiful.* I uncharacteristically plunked down my credit card without a second thought and gladly paid extra for the fabric protection plan.

With the purchase of our new house, I began studying paint decks as if they were sacred texts. Arin would come home to find endless gray swatches spread from one end of the dining table to the other and his entertaining wife deep in thought.

Holding one up to the window, I marveled at the way some grays turned quickly brown and then purplish once more beneath artificial lighting. The sun-loving grays grew prickly in the cold light from the north, but once again inviting and warm when facing south. Almost always, rippling beneath the surface, ran the undercurrent of another tone. There were brown-grays, purple-grays, blue-grays, and green-grays, but very rarely did I ever come across a gray content to simply be itself.

Unbeknownst to me, from choosing Fiona to finding the right paint color, something inside had started shifting. Having been a rule follower since I was old enough to walk, my life choices had been dictated by black-and-white terms like "right and wrong," "should and shouldn't." There was no sliding scale, no gradient middle ground.

But then, Fiona came along and illumined a new way, where *Beauty* was revered as the regal queen Fyodor Dostoevsky claimed would save the world, rather than relegated to the sideline role of ditzy cheerleader.

I once heard it said that the longest distance in the world is the eighteen inches from one's head to one's heart, but I'd never understood what it meant. Even so, I was slowly being loosed from the binding cord of obligation to grope my way—hand over hand—through dark, uncharted territory where the only thing I had to follow was the thin, wispy strand of desire.

Words from my legalistic past accosted me from the shadows: *Hedonist! Materialist! Shallow, petty female!*

Regardless, I immersed myself in Beauty like she was the therapist I never had.

When Grayson had a rough day, I found myself awake past midnight, vigorously painting until I was dripping with sweat. Alone at last, I could release the angry energy I'd deemed unbefitting of a woman, daub cuss words into the drywall with bristles mashed every which way, and reveal my pain to a color that was gradually disclosing its true self to me.

In the end, Benjamin Moore agreed to keep my rage concealed beneath two, thick coats, and I felt content to let him have it.

Initially, very few endeavors transpired so smoothly as painting.

One afternoon, I loaded my car full of throw pillows from Home Goods, only to end up hurling them against the wall when they didn't coordinate as I intended. Another time, I googled how to build and hang window cornices and then sat fuming through an entire football game, loathing their very sight, my shoddy workmanship, and my abominable taste.

Even so, Beauty smiled knowingly, maternally understanding that beneath my outraged frustration was an untapped passion.

In time, I would hone my skills. I would spend hours perusing photographs on Pinterest and Houzz, evaluating what worked and what didn't, and borrow every interior design book our library offered.

When a contractor bid exorbitantly high, I would build out our mudroom myself, thanks to YouTube and the helpful folks at Home Depot. (Only my closest friends and family know that, unwilling to make one more stinking trip to the hardware store, I used a carrot peeler to plane the last one-eighth inch off a sheet of plywood I'd erroneously measured.)

From there, I would learn to read blueprints and then teach myself how to use SketchUp to design our kitchen and backyard remodel. While working with contractors, I lingered while they built and drilled them with boatloads of questions.

Ultimately, I would start my own interior design business, where I would have the immense joy of renovating multiple homes, a century-old schoolhouse, a multigenerational farmhouse, a man-cave storage unit, and even our church.

And all the while, Beauty was my ever-present guide. She taught in patient whispers, never once using words like *should* or *shouldn't* yet definitively confirming when something was absolutely and perfectly right. Her approval came in the form of a subtle release, a soft exhalation, a deep-rooted satisfaction. And when life turned tumultuous mid-project, as it often did, she would absorb my internal chaos as gently as if catching a thin-shelled egg and then simply use it to fuel my creative process. Somewhere along the way, my inner discord inevitably dissolved into a rhythmic flow, where all that remained was *Beauty*.

I spent the first forty-two days in our new house as a single parent. The neighbors assumed I was a lonely divorcée; they certainly got the first part right. Arin had been working on a rig in North Dakota, so on day forty-three, when he crossed the threshold of our home for the first time, he entered as a guest. He had to ask for a towel, a glass, his socks—and I never even bothered to show him where they were. I just handed him whatever he needed. He'd be gone in two days, regardless.

On his first night home, he fell asleep in my arms with the lights still on, and I didn't dare wake him by moving. To have a warm body in my bed felt almost more than I could bear, so I watched him sleep, savoring the dwindling moments. Silver strands peeped through hair that permanently wreaked of oil, and I inhaled the fragrance, savoring it in the same way I'd come to cherish the throaty rumble of his diesel truck.

Both the smell and the sound meant his presence.

Two days later, he was hastily packing his bag, and I was unpacking it, teasing and half-jokingly begging him to stay.

"You know I want to," he apologetically replied, retrieving his shirt from my hand, "but they need me up there. I have to hurry and *get back home*."

The words slipped effortlessly from his mouth, but judging by the way his eyes shot wide open, I knew he immediately wished to recant them. With a heavy sigh, he laid his shirt on the bed and turned toward me. His flecked hazel eyes had lost their luster, and dark rings clung to their corners, drooping beneath the weight of the world.

No longer rushed, he rested a calloused hand on my shoulder and pulled me close, "I'm sorry. That's not what I meant to say."

But the words had been spoken, and they were not wrong. Our home had become a trading stop, a place to replenish supplies before moving on.

I buried my head in his chest to hide my pooling tears and deeply breathed in the pungent oil I had simultaneously come to love and despise.

After the last vibrations of his diesel truck faded away toward North Dakota, I leaned my weary body against our bedroom window, pressing my forehead into the pane.

Outside, a father passed a football to his son before tackling him to the ground. Their dog ran tight, yapping circles around the boy as the rest of the family barbecued and laughed. Next door, an older couple was pulling weeds side by side. Their heads leaned crookedly toward one another as if gravity somehow affected them differently than the rest of the world. They waved affably as a young family pedaled past on bikes with matching flags. The shiny family was smiling so broadly I could have counted every one of their sparkling teeth from my second-story window. I imagined them filming a Colgate commercial, and their sunny cheerfulness enraged me to no end.

Donning my director's cap, I crafted the next scene—the one where they crash into each other—*hard*—smashing their bikes together into a tangled heap of metal. I sardonically wondered if they'd still be smiling.

Weeks later, Arin texted a photograph. The blurry image settled in my stomach like a pile of rocks, and confirmed he was indeed far enough away from home to witness the Northern Lights. It also solidified the fact that my two-hour gym sessions were officially a thing of the past. If I were to continue caring for my body, I'd have to figure out how on my own. We had no capable babysitters to watch Grayson, and so anything I did would have to include him.

One morning, I surprised Grayson (and myself) by suggesting a run. Typically, I hated running, and he only enjoyed sprinting when it was away from me. Therefore, I turned it into a game. We raced from one fire hydrant to the next and then walked to the third. So we continued—running and walking, running and walking—for two miles down the length of the golf course and back.

As we crossed the "finish line" (i.e., a crack in the driveway), an unrecognizable expression flashed across Grayson's seven-year-old face. He stood tall, eyes gleaming and chest heaving, until finally it dawned on me—it was the first time I'd ever witnessed *pride* in his eyes.

Back inside, I juiced fresh carrots and apples in celebration, and we shared a cold drink from two straws. I didn't think much of it, but an instant connection was forged in Grayson's mind: *run-juice.* The words rolled together in a single, inseparable unit, and from then on, every summer break ceremoniously commenced with a fire hydrant run and fresh-pressed apple-carrot juice.

I learned that Grayson needed a schedule in the same way I craved solitude. Consequently, we fell into our first easy rhythm. A daily run-juice bought me a brief period of much-needed respite. I quickly learned that I would not be filled unless he was first satiated, and is this not the essence of motherhood?

Nine years later, we have neither broken nor deviated from this tradition.

Despite Arin's extended absence, the kids and I passed our first summer in the new house rather pleasantly. They swam in the various lakes and chummed for massive carp using canned corn and chopped-up hotdogs. Upon befriending the neighborhood children, they discovered a fifteen-foot plastic tube abandoned on a dirt lot and then dragged it to the park, where they climbed in one after another—head-to-foot to head-to-foot—and rolled down the grassy embankment, tumbling like wet clothes in the dryer.

Grayson's outraged screams occasionally drifted through my screened window, which I deliberately left open for such moments. Then, I would rush to the park, where I would find children fleeing in all directions from his poised-and-ready fist filled with rocks.

Even then, the summer was largely peaceful.

But I only ever felt like half of myself.

As the days of summer started descending into fall, Arin returned to working in Colorado, and I began girding my loins for a new school year. I knew four of my kids would be fine in their new setting, but it was the *one* who caused me concern.

In preparation, I called Grayson's new school and left a message requesting a meeting with the principal. Two weeks before school started, Ms. Pritchard returned my call. She told me she didn't think it necessary to connect us with Grayson's second-grade teacher in advance; nor did she deem it essential for him to visit the school. He would be fine, she assured me; they were a wonderful school with a highly trained staff. It was *not* their first rodeo, she confirmed with a chuckle, perhaps intending to sound kind.

But like an eye-rolling horror movie, the plot was overly redundant, and the outcome lamely predictable.

The first call of the year came within two hours of dropping him off the first day.

The secretary was just calling to let me know that Grayson was fine, not to worry, but he had, as a matter of fact, run away. But not to worry, everything was under control. Although he was running loose through the neighborhood, they had eyes on him while chasing him down the street. "Don't worry, though," she tittered nervously, "someone wisely thought to block traffic." No, no one had caught him quite yet, but the police had been called and were on their way, not to worry. Oh, and just as a side note, she did need to inform me that the school was *legally* obligated to inform the officers that Grayson was violent because he *had*, after all, hurt a teacher.

She finished her spiel with one final piece of advice: "Don't worry!"

New to police involvement, I sat on my hands at home as instructed and was eventually given the play-by-play rundown from my new inside informant, the secretary.

Eventually, the staff caught up with Grayson in the park, where several police officers had pinned him to the ground. He was escorted back to school in the caged back seat of a police car, but—not to worry—all was now fine.

I didn't permit my brain to envision the scene. The mere thought made me sick. *Why did they have to call the police?* I lamented, a thick lump forming in my throat. *He's only in second grade.*

After three days of nonstop struggles, Ms. Pritchard tapped out. She should have listened, she conceded through tears. Perhaps it wasn't the right school for him, but did we know there was another school nearby with a special program called SOAR for kids with extreme behaviors? There, the teachers were trained in restraint, and should Grayson get upset, his classroom contained a door that could be held shut from the outside until he grew calm. Of course, the district would never *force* him to attend, but she had already submitted the paperwork to make things easier, *just in case*. All we had to do was attend a quick orientation. There was an immediate opening, but it was our choice. Still, she really didn't feel her school was equipped to handle our son.

I guess Grayson had introduced her "highly trained staff" to their first *real* rodeo.

Speaking of which, I had personally started feeling like a cow being prodded through a narrow, one-way chute toward an end point I assumed would be catastrophic. Although my line of sight was limited, it seemed the highly trained staff were the ones doing the prodding.

What I didn't know was that I was being gently guided toward greener pastures by One who carries a shepherd's rod—not a bully stick—and that He had plans to prosper and not harm Grayson, to give our family a future and a hope.

But I was still hesitant to believe in a *Good* Shepherd—the opposite had been too long engrained. For years, I'd experienced His staff as the choking, obligatory rope around my neck; but the noose, it turns out, was man-made.

Yet I couldn't fully trust God to be "everywhere present and filling all things," as the Orthodox Church affirms; I assumed my chaos sufficiently deterred Him, alongside my unbecoming, unfeminine rage.

I hadn't yet learned to perceive Him in the light reflecting off my sun-strewn swatches or the therapeutic paint absorbing my pain. I didn't understand that His guidance could feel practically imperceptible—a subtle release, a soft exhalation, a deep-rooted satisfaction, or the thin, wispy strand of desire followed hand over hand in near darkness.

I didn't yet know His name could be *Beauty*.

19

Soaring

There will be a bird today. It will be white with streaks
of gold like a crown atop its head. It will fly.

—TAHEREH MAFI, *Shatter Me*

M rs. Pielin looked nothing like the matronly warden I'd expected to
find at Grayson's second new school of the year. In fact, she scarcely
looked old enough to be a teacher. Dressed in leggings, an oversized top,
and silver bangle bracelets, she jingled merrily as she walked down the hall.

Already accustomed to disappointment when it came to teachers, I
imagined her horns were hiding somewhere beneath her cute, bouncy bob.
It wouldn't be long till they poked through, I presumed. Grayson was an
expert in provocation.

As Mrs. Pielin cracked the classroom door, I sucked in my breath and
prepared to witness the cold cement floors, metal bars, and padded room
that could be locked from the outside. I was split seconds from meeting the
worst-of-the-worst, the wayward misfits that all other schools had rejected.

Instead, I encountered radiant faces and peals of laughter. Straightaway, a short, round boy with spiky hair came up to me and roughly began patting my stomach before wrapping his arms around my waist in a tight embrace.

"Patrick," Mrs. Pielin softly chided, an amused half-smile forming, "you know better. What's the correct way to greet our guests?"

Drawing himself to his full height (which wasn't much), Patrick turned toward me and methodically stuck out his hand, looking me straight in the eyes.

"Hi, I'm Patrick," he enunciated in a loud, monotone voice. "It's very nice to meet you."

I could tell he had rehearsed his salutation *ad nauseam*, and Mrs. Pielin beamed her approval before ushering him back to his seat.

As she did, I glanced around the room. A total of six students sat divided between two low tables, with an additional teacher at each. Several kids bounced on round medicine balls in lieu of chairs, while those who preferred chairs sat calmly pedaling on what appeared to be miniature half-bikes under the table.

On the right side of the room, an oversized beanbag was snugly stuffed behind a half-wall, and I pictured Grayson launching himself into its center when his energy bubbled over or wriggling beneath when the world grew too large.

Presently, the kids left for lunch, and Mrs. Pielin motioned for us to sit. Nodding toward the door, she let us know her students ate lunch alone in the cafeteria, arrived at school ten minutes early, and had separate passing periods to ensure the noisy, crowded hallways wouldn't overwhelm them.

As much as I was prepared to dislike the school, Mrs. Pielin was making it difficult.

She walked us through a typical day in her SOAR classroom, which followed the Boys Town Education Model. Both focused on "managing behavior, building relationships, and teaching social skills" by utilizing "preventive and proactive practices."

Every day followed the same schedule, starting with direct eye contact and a firm handshake in the hall. From that moment on, teachers immediately rewarded positive behavior with points that students could redeem for prizes and patiently redirected any negative behaviors.

Each of the three teachers had been meticulously trained to use the same vernacular, and over the years, I, too, would adopt their jargon.

"Grayson," I would eventually learn to say, "I've noticed you're choosing to ignore me and not pick up your toys. A better choice would be to finish your work so we can move on to something new."

In response, Grayson would automatically intone, "I'm sorry for not listening. A better choice would be to pick up my toys right away. Do you accept my apology?"

But those days were still quite a ways down the road.

Regardless, by the end of our one-hour orientation session, Arin and I had changed our tune about the SOAR program and were eagerly anticipating Grayson's *second* first day of school.

He had to be restrained several times that first day, but this time by the school's *actually* highly trained staff. Grayson also spent a significant amount of time talking with his teacher in what I had initially called a padded room. (The school had wisely and more appropriately dubbed it "The Opportunity Room.") Remarkably, Mrs. Pielin had requested a substitute for the entire day so she could devote all her attention to Grayson.

She debriefed me at my car window that afternoon, shaking her head and laughing at Grayson's "feistiness." He had a strong kick, to be sure, and she had swiftly learned to be wary of his bite. But even so, she was standing before me, smiling. Shockingly, there were no heavy lines of frustration etched into her forehead. No exasperated sighs heaved between phrases.

Her time would come, I reminded myself realistically. But it never did.

Grayson had to be restrained slightly fewer times his second day, and by the third, he sat in his chair like a civilized child and made it through an entire day of school without a single crisis.

Never in our four years at the school did I ever witness a single teacher express anger or even irritation with my son. They treated him like a precious, struggling child rather than a troublesome problem to be eradicated. Day in and day out, they gently coaxed him from his protective shell and provided the necessary routine for him to learn and grow with confidence.

Slowly, he began interacting with other classmates and conversing with his teachers. Before long, he was sharing stories from home and regaling them with countless random facts about water slides, roller coasters, and his newest infatuation—marble ramps.

Anyone who possessed the eyes to see would have noticed how frequently his right hand slipped down every sloped surface and launched into the air like a marble set free from gravity's pull. His eyes followed the trajectory of the imagined marble so intently that I almost expected to see one. Grayson saw ramps where I beheld only stiff-armed church pews and racing, curving water slides rather than bendable twelve-inch rulers. He was the king of envisioning. For him, possibility and reality were conjoined twins, with no veil of separation between them. His mind conceived the ideas, and his heart birthed them into existence.

When I grew still enough for the eyes of my soul to focus, it became readily apparent that he lived in a dazzling universe of faith and potential—one such as I had never known. Grayson was my introduction to many things in this world, but his ability to dream surpassed them all. If he could believe it, he would achieve it.

In the right environment, Grayson rapidly and surprisingly evolved into a model student. I bought him his first watch, a white Cassio, of which we have since purchased at least twenty—never knowing the security it would provide. Before long, he was the official timekeeper and never failed to remind his teacher when to switch classes.

No longer was I attached to my phone or the five-mile leash that once kept me tethered to his school. For the first time since becoming a parent twelve years ago, I had five days a week and seven hours a day entirely to myself, not to mention the gift of peace that came from knowing my son was as safe and happy as could be. For the first time since Grayson's birth, I felt really and truly free.

I don't imagine the need to explain my sheer giddiness. No combination of words would suffice. But I did experience a strange sense of solidarity with Grayson's marbles when they were launched off a ramp and set loose into a galaxy of endless possibilities. I could fully relate to the way those marbles must have felt at the peak of their ascent—the sublime stillness, the momentary sensation of weightlessness, and the joy of belonging to no one and nothing but yourself.

From second through sixth grade, Mrs. Pielen, and then Mrs. Auton, Mrs. Jacoby, Mr. Roth, and countless other specialists and aides would love Grayson—dare I say, almost perfectly—and would vicariously love me by caring for him. I spent countless hours observing their every move; I mimicked their tone, emulated their body language, and echoed their well-rehearsed lingo. And I cannot even begin to recall the number of mornings I watched through my rearview mirror—tears leaking from my eyes—as my son disappeared into school hand in hand with one of his trusted teachers.

In my newfound stretches of uninterrupted silence, I suddenly realized it was physically possible to think linear, coherent thoughts (who knew?). Therefore, three months into the school year, I found myself seated on a leather barstool at my kitchen counter. Sunlight was streaming through our back door, her soft rays welcoming my pent-up words and emotions.

For the first time in fifteen months, I cracked open my journal and—with hovering pen and poised fingers—scanned the room, soaking in all my hands had audaciously dared to create.

From the kitchen, I could see through the dining room's widely arched doorway straight to the front of the house. The smoky gray walls had turned out perfectly—neither too cold nor too warm but just right. Rich navy-blue satin curtains framed an elongated picture window, and gauzy panels hung airily between. The left adjacent wall had two narrow windows—each bordered with a paisley panel and covered with another breezy sheer. And situated perfectly between them sat Fiona.

My eyes misted over as I lowered my pen, recording one pensive thought at a time.

I had spent the last year racing about frantically—packing, unpacking, and decorating—and being still that morning allowed my soul to finally catch up. In the midst of a new and beautiful life—Grayson's amazing school, a gorgeous home, and Arin's well-paying job—I became acutely aware that my same heart-holes were still present and patiently waiting to be acknowledged. Amid our uncharacteristically calm, ideal life, I was the one who stood out like a sore thumb—a swollen, unmanicured, and glaring sore thumb.

As I laid down my pen, the words of an old children's song came to mind: "One of these things is not like the others; one of these things just doesn't belong."

The answer to the riddle was *me*, I concluded through streaming tears. In our gorgeous new home and incredible life, it was *I* who didn't belong.

Suddenly, the rays that had just been softly slanting through our back door turned garish and—like sunbeams through a woman's skirt—now shamefully exposed my insecure parts. The parts I preferred to keep covered. The parts I'd neglected to tend.

Now, alone on my barstool, enveloped by a surplus of time, space, beauty, and light, I could admit that I felt as naked as an emperor in imaginary garments—ashamedly homely and plain.

Yet for once, Beauty stepped in to challenge my vulnerability rather than soothe it.

You could not have imparted that which you did not already possess, she whispered, reminding me that our home had not been created *ex nihilo* (out of nothing) but from a vision born of myself.

I reluctantly conceded her point.

It was true. There I sat, encircled by the visible end product of my creativity. But despite the tangible evidence, I was blackballing my own goodness. While I didn't hate myself as I once did, I hadn't yet grown accustomed to embracing my internal beauty. And just as the kindness of strangers could buckle my knees, so—oddly enough—could encountering my own strengths strip me bare.

I couldn't yet comprehend that the beauty I had created was simply an outpouring of the beauty I already possessed.

Still, despite feeling so woefully unworthy of my new surroundings, it was wonderfully freeing to acknowledge my nakedness. Rather than frantically trying to cover my insecurities as usual, it felt blissful to brazenly bathe them in the sun.

After exposing myself to me, the light now graciously wrapped herself around me like a cloak. Covering my stripped-down, forlorn state, she *honored* my vulnerability rather than rebuking it, leaving me clothed in a radiant, transparent garment of herself.

For only when we are naked can we be clothed.

Like Grayson, I, too, would need years in the right environment before settling into my natural skin and stepping into the fullness of the woman I was created to be. Similarly, I would need to be reminded over and over that I was not a problem to be eradicated but a child to be loved. Also, like my son, I would need to learn and trust that failure led—not to solitary confinement in a padded room—but to *new opportunities*.

With a little time, space, freedom, and love, I, too, would one day learn to SOAR.

20

Restraining

The need for control always comes from someone that has lost it.

—Attributed to Shannon L. Alder

The list was two pages long and contained maybe forty names and phone numbers. I had been staring at it for weeks, trying to conjure the energy to call as many facilities and providers as potentially necessary. As excellent as Grayson was doing in school, nothing had changed at home, and summer was looming large on the horizon.

A friend with a physically disabled daughter told me she received multiple hours of respite per month through a government-funded program. I was ecstatic, confident I had found the key to maintaining my sanity over summer break. But the representative informed me Grayson was ineligible as he was not physically disabled. Had he needed a feeding tube or a nightly diaper change, I could have received *eighty hours of respite per month* and thousands of dollars for home modifications and other services like house cleaning. But since he was *just* autistic, only behavior-modifying therapies would be covered. Strike one.

Another woman in our church worked for a nonprofit charity. They kept kids overnight *for up to a week* to give parents and siblings a break. I attended the tour and was chomping at the bit to sign on the dotted line until the counselor mentioned the center had a zero-tolerance policy for violence. Any singular act of physical aggression would result in the child being immediately sent home. Strike two.

The counselor was, however, kind enough to send me home with a list of private agencies that might be willing to provide respite or additional behavioral therapies. That was the two-page list.

Line by line, I crossed off one name after another. Some didn't accept our insurance, while others only worked with children who resided in their county. One location mistakenly ended up on the list; it was a live-in rehabilitation center for adults with brain injuries. Moving on, I marked the facility "non-applicable."

Finally, I found *one* company willing to support violent children that also accepted our insurance. They could send two therapists to our house (a violent child automatically mandated a two-person team) for a copay of $60 per therapist. For only $120, I, too, could have one idyllic hour alone amid the chaos of summer. Tempting, but no. Strike three.

With every crossed-off name, my list was shrinking alongside my hope. I sat, massaging the stress from my temples, and tried another number. It rang for a while before a tired voice answered the phone.

"Hello?" the woman on the other end said flatly. She sounded suspicious, as if I were a telemarketer.

I told her my story, how I had an autistic son—yes, he was violent—and that I was hoping to find someone to help with respite over the summer.

There was a long silence and then a cold, demanding question: "How did you get my number?"

Confused, I explained how I got the list and waited through another long pause.

"I shouldn't be on there," she snarled. "No one should be giving out my number. I'm not a provider; I'm a parent. My adult daughter was in a car accident and has a brain injury. I was looking for respite but haven't been able to find any live-in facilities accepting adults with brain injuries. There's no way those people should be giving out my number."

Suddenly, a light bulb flipped on in my head. The facility I had just spoken to—they were a live-in clinic accepting adults with brain injuries!

"Ma'am, I don't know why you're on their list, but I just spoke with someone I think can help you," I excitedly explained.

I shared all the details—the name, phone number, and location—and the other end went once again silent. After several long seconds, she spoke, though not to me. No longer gruff, her voice was thin and shaking.

"Honey," she said with a controlled effort, presumably to her husband, "there's some lady on the phone telling me about a place for Katie. I've never heard of it before, and I think maybe they can help us."

Then, all control went out the window, and her voice rose and fell and cracked like a prepubescent boy. She was sobbing.

"Thank you. Thank you so much. Thank you," the woman squeaked before hanging up.

And that was all; I never heard from her again. I always wondered whether she was able to find help for her daughter. Somehow, I felt certain she did.

No longer stressed, I sat at my desk, my own eyes filling with tears. I could only imagine what that poor family had gone through to evoke such a heart-wrenching response. As challenging as Grayson was, other families were suffering just as greatly or more, and all it took was one short, random phone call to remind me I was not alone.

As I was working through the list, someone had referenced an agency that provided applied behavior analysis (ABA) therapy, a highly recommended treatment for autistic children that focused on behavior modification. I had scribbled the agency's name in the margins; the school year was quickly winding down, and my desperation was rapidly amping up.

Surprisingly, the agency accepted our insurance *and* made house calls. After amassing a great deal of information about Grayson, the scheduler opted to send her lead therapist. Truthfully, I didn't care if she sent Ronald

McDonald and he turned cartwheels the entire time—I just wanted another adult in the house, if only for commiseration.

The morning of our first appointment, I opened the door to an underwhelming lead therapist named Elliott. Small and unimpressive in stature, he reminded me of a redheaded weasel with thin, slanting eyes and a slightly hunched back. He was wringing his hands and shifting his slight weight from one foot to the other. Nothing about his demeanor inspired confidence. He seemed sweet, kind, and soft-spoken, and I knew instantly that Grayson *would eat him alive.*

As soon as Elliott entered our home, Grayson appeared from nowhere, swiped the sunglasses from the crook of Elliott's button-up polo, and skipped gleefully straight out the door. Then Elliott, the lead therapist, turned toward me and sought my advice.

After several challenging visits, Elliott arrived with a new "behavioral aide." Robert was tall and willowy with pale skin, black over-dyed hair, and sallow, pockmarked cheeks. He reeked of cigarette smoke and seemed like the type to accept a job simply because he had nothing better to do.

Elliott and Robert spent their morning chasing Grayson around, trying to get him to play games that would teach him to take turns or complete activities to soothe his sensory-seeking ways. But Grayson was a fast learner and soon realized that compliant behavior earned him a brightly colored Skittle. His behavior was, in fact, quickly modified, and he soon began refusing to do even the most minor task without *first* receiving his reward. Soon, he was ordering and dictating the therapists' actions.

It became readily apparent that behavior modification could go either way.

Eventually, the supervising manager was called in. No progress was being made, and I was growing weary of advising the therapists who were supposed to be advising me.

Liam was sharp and professional-looking. His erect posture and towering presence conveyed authority, and his voice demanded respect. When he spoke, Grayson listened. He was a man with a plan and immediately asked me to empty an unused office on the main floor of our house so we could escort Grayson to a safe place when he refused to obey. The door would lock from the outside, and I was delighted to hear that a professional's plan matched my earlier neophyte idea, back when Grayson stood only thigh-high.

Everything was spelled out in writing. We would issue a simple command: "Grayson, please pick up that toy." If he refused, we'd escort him to the office and leave him alone behind a locked door. It was assumed that a temper tantrum would ensue, which we would ignore until he elected to self-soothe. Once calm, I would ask Grayson to sit facing forward against the back wall. Opening the door, I would repeat the request for compliance. If he agreed to pick up the toy and stayed calm, we would enter the room to talk through the situation, but if his rage reignited, we would back out, lock the door behind us, and restart the process. Liam's number one rule was that Grayson *could not* come out until he was *completely* docile.

It took all four of us to simply get him to the room the first time he refused to cooperate, and it became quickly apparent that Liam had grossly underestimated Grayson's strength and sheer wiggliness. Then, once we arrived at the door, no one could figure out how to get Grayson *into* the locked room while simultaneously getting four grown adults *out*.

Finally, I asked the men to step back and, in one swift motion, flung Grayson into the empty room, ran back out, and locked the door. Mission accomplished. In this one insignificant skill, I was a pro.

Back on track, we reminded Grayson that we would not open the door until he was calm. But when his screams turned into sounds of ripping drywall and crashing metal, we reneged and opened the door to inspect. Grayson had wrenched the metal clothes bar from the closet and was going to town on my office walls. That home improvement budget from the government would have certainly come in handy.

From start to finish, the "intense therapy session" led by a supervising manager lasted well over three hours.

I could only imagine how much fun I would have implementing Liam's process alone.

After seeing the severity of Grayson's behavior, Liam arranged for me to attend a staff training where I would be coached in restraint. With my mom babysitting our children, I geared up for a full day away from home.

Right off, I was paired with one, then two, staff members, and we spent the day learning various holds. The instructor showed us what to do if a child dropped and refused to walk; then we practiced moving an unwilling participant to a safe destination. I learned how to safely transport an agitated child with the assistance of several staff members and a chair. But in every scenario, the staff member who was supposed to be emulating the child was sane and cooperative, or at worst, resistant, dead weight. No one ever tried to claw my eyes out or choke me or spit on me, but regardless, every restraint I learned required two people.

As the day drew to a close, I asked the instructor, "So far, everything you've modeled requires a partner. Are you going to teach any single person restraints?"

No, she explained, looking at me like I was crazy. They worked in pairs. All holds and transports were always to be done by two adults. It wasn't safe to restrain a raging child alone.

That much, I knew.

I returned home as empty-handed as I came.

Three months of therapy and thousands of dollars later, little to no change had occurred. I was an excellent parent, Elliott confirmed, and was doing everything right. He wasn't exactly sure what was going on. Grayson wasn't responding well to their proven techniques. Perhaps it was time to try something new.

His words felt like a breakup: It's not you; it's me. But can we still be friends?

Strike 573. Throw in the bat. Call it a game.

Although Elliott had warned me to Grayson-proof my house—to lock up the knives, screwdrivers, or any loose-lying machetes and hand grenades—he must have forgotten to mention the candlesticks, brooms, lamps, picture frames, forks, chairs, curtain rods, and rollerblades. Not to mention the shovels, rakes, and thousands of rocks in our yard.

What good did it do to lock up the "weapons," I wondered, when everything else served the same purpose?

I tried to incorporate the restraints I'd learned to see whether they could be adapted for single-person usage. But a solid headbutt to the face informed me that no, they could not, so I returned to my surefire method: survival of the fittest.

For that, I could have written the manual.

Grayson's record-breaking restraint lasted for three solid hours. It started downstairs on the main level, which might not have been so bad if I could have escorted him to my empty office. But the door had been smashed to smithereens by a curtain rod (thank God I locked up the "weapons"), and its solid wood replacement had yet to arrive.

My only recourse was to get him up to his room—and *up* was a daunting seventeen stairs away.

Had I been a lead therapist coaching myself, my lesson that day would have sounded something like this: No, don't pick him up from behind—he'll headbutt you or kick off a higher stair to knock you backward. Grab his hands like this and drag him upstairs. I know it sounds mean, but you have to keep as much distance from his body as possible. Keep all of his fingers within your grasp so he can't scratch your hands. Stay away from the spindles so he can't hook his foot! Dang. You lost one of his hands, and he grabbed a spindle. Now his foot is wedged in, too. Pry his fingers loose but watch for the hair grab once they're free. Keep your head back—he'll push off the stairs for another headbutt. Now, yank his foot free. Yes, I know the spindle might snap. Just add it to your growing list of repairs. Okay, you're almost there. Go fast over the top stair. Whoops, too slow. Now he's hooked his toes on the top step. Good grief! His toes are freakishly strong! Okay, give him a good pull. You're up the stairs now. Use the momentum to drag him to his room. I know; you're out of breath. You'll get to rest in a minute. Ha! Who am I kidding? No, you won't.

Now, go fast through the door so he can't hook his heel on the frame, and in one swift motion—pull-him-forward-spin-drop-on-top-of-him-and-pin-him-down. Yeah, I see. He's got your hair. Watch out! He'll bite your face. Okay, grab the wide part of his hand and squeeze to release his grip. Good, now pin his arms to the ground above his head. Brace yourself with your arms. He'll hip thrust and throw you over his head into the wall. Ugh, too late. Better luck next time. You lost his arms, and now he's flipped on his belly. Okay, recapture his arms and pin them to his sides with your legs. Cover your back. He's going to kick! Oops, too slow. Sorry, bet that one hurt.

On and on it went. I couldn't create enough separation to make my escape. Grayson was a raging fire that refused to be quelled.

Of course, as luck would have it, Rylee had a birthday party to attend, but it was still two hours away. Certainly, I could resolve our little situation by then.

But when one hour turned into two, and Grayson was still blowing his top, I reluctantly asked Rylee to grab my phone. Via speakerphone, I hesitantly asked Carol to take Rylee to the party; there was no way I could let go of Grayson.

Soon enough, Carol's head peaked timidly around the corner. At the sight of her concerned expression, the corners of my eyes began leaking drops of saltwater. I wasn't crying, for crying implies emotion. It was more like my exhausted body was shutting down and squeezing out the last remaining drops of liquid. After my cheeks dried, there would be only white, crusty salt and a hollow, brittle version of me.

With Carol's arrival, I grew instantly aware of how I must have appeared to a lucid adult. Like a wild cavewoman crouched brutishly above her writhing prey, there I was, straddling my eight-year-old son. He was thrashing wildly beneath me on the carpeted floor as if I was going to eat him alive. My eyes were surely bloodshot and crazed, and my knotted, ratty hair presumably looked like it hadn't been combed for weeks. Grayson's face was mottled and swollen from the struggle, we were both scraped and welted, and there was a good chance one of us was bleeding.

Carol's eyes opened wide enough to absorb everything and then filled with the emotional tears I was incapable of crying for myself. Her tender silence respectfully acknowledged there was nothing to be said. She gathered Rylee into her arms—kissing the top of the head and loving her in a way I could not—then drove her to the birthday party.

That pain I felt.

I had five children, but four of them were motherless.

❧

That summer, Grayson decided to take his show on the road and go public with his fits.

Because of the impossibility of finding a respite provider, the school principal hesitantly allowed Mr. Roth, one of Grayson's SOAR teachers, to serve double duty. A young, single man—who before becoming a teacher had traversed the world on a Navy submarine—Mr. Roth was unflappable, and his sunny disposition was impossible to darken, even for Grayson. In all the years I've known him, the only time I have ever seen him enraged has been over the mistreatment of puppies, particularly pugs.

Mr. Roth was the perfect solution. He spoke the SOAR lingo, was familiar with all of Grayson's peccadilloes, and—out of love for our family—was willing to work for a measly fifteen dollars an hour (although we always paid him more).

Therefore, we thought nothing of it the first time we left them alone. Jacob even volunteered to stay behind to help soothe any potential nerves on either end. Arin had the evening off, and we planned to attend a Wednesday night church service in peace (i.e., sans Grayson).

The ride home from church was relaxed and jovial, and the three children were ecstatic to have our full attention, particularly Arin's. Halfway home, my phone lit up with Mr. Roth's number, and I answered it, a smile still lingering on my lips. But it instantly faded the second I heard Jacob's rapid-fire, staccato speech on the other end.

"Mom, it's Grayson. He ran away—well, Mr. Roth has him now, but he can't talk 'cause he's talkin' to the police. We chased him, and I helped hold on to him. But someone thought we were chokin' him and called the police. But we weren't actually. We were just tryin' to bring him back home."

Arin instantly kicked into hyperdrive—accelerating fast and braking hard, and we made it home in record time. Our whole block was lit up with alternating flashes of blue and red. At least three police cars and one ambulance lined the street leading to our house. Straggling neighbors gathered in small huddles on street corners, and I could only imagine the number of inquiring eyes peeping through parted blinds—all because of our son.

Arin jammed the car into park and was speaking with the officers before I even opened my door. Meanwhile, my breathing and heart rate decelerated, and my eyes slowly scanned the scene, absorbing every minute detail. Mr. Roth was surrounded by a ring of officers that Arin had since broken through. Grayson sat on the curb, tracing shapes in the dirt, looking bored and perfectly calm. Jacob was running toward me, but I bypassed him, ordering him to wait in the car.

Jacob had given us a decent rundown of the night, but Mr. Roth filled in the missing pieces. Just as they were getting ready to do a science experiment involving Mentos breath mints, Grayson turned and, without a word, slipped through the front door. He made it down our street and the next before they caught up with him, and when they did, Mr. Roth restrained him in the most professional way possible. And, as I already knew from experience, the most professional way possible meant doing anything necessary to keep him from running further. That night, it involved a collar grab, some street-corner wrestling, and a headlock. Passing neighbors reported a grown man strangling and possibly trying to kidnap a small child.

Arin was distraught and repeatedly murmured, "I can't believe this is happening." But I was calm—unnaturally calm—almost as if something inside me was preemptively warning: *Brace yourself. This is only the beginning.*

21

Despairing

Trauma is not what happens to us, but what we hold
inside in the absence of an empathetic witness.

—Peter A. Levine, *In an Unspoken Voice*

June 29, 2014. I was back in the massively domed Greek cathedral, where I had experienced my first Orthodox liturgy six years prior, this time for a wedding. But that particular day, I couldn't have cared less about my surroundings.

Grayson was a hot mess, a whirling dervish, and couldn't seem to decide whether he felt more comfortable inside or out. When he could not refrain from stomping on the marble floors to hear the echo bounce around the dome, we would step outside, and when he started stealing furtive glances at the roped-off construction zone, we went back in. Then, when he bolted from one fire alarm to the next, tempted to see my reaction should he pull the lever, we went outside, and when he sprinted back in the same doors he *just ran out of* to look for his gramma, I, of course, followed him back in.

Although I'd made it a personal rule not to attend large gatherings with Grayson in tow, I'd known the bride, Cosette, since she was fifteen and refused to miss her special day. Besides, I was growing weary of sitting on the sidelines, watching everyone else have all the fun.

In hindsight, I should have super-glued myself to the bench.

Apparently, all five of my children were present that day, but for the life of me, I can only remember the *one*. I have no recollection of the ceremony, Cosette's dress, or a single person in attendance.

I only remember Grayson's every move.

At the reception, I noticed some of his mannerisms growing agitated. He had been eyeballing the cake and was irritated it wasn't gluten-free. The other guests milled about, completely unaware of the catastrophe that could occur at any moment.

But not me; I was ready.

In a single instant, Grayson's agitation mutated into a spark of inspiration. His eyes lit up like the skies on the fourth of July, and I knew— something bad was going to happen.

In the blink of an eye, Grayson turned and raced full-speed through the reception hall doors, and without a second to think, I spun on my high heels to chase him—leaving my phone behind on the table.

As always, I knew what kind of streets surrounded our location and how quickly the traffic flowed. I was always prepared for him to run, always knew where the exits were, and always anticipated which direction he might go.

As my eyes adjusted to the outside brightness, I caught sight of Grayson ascending a paved incline. He was speed-walking up a sidewalk that ran parallel to four lanes of traffic, all traveling fifty-five miles per hour in the same direction.

Intent on keeping his distance, he set his speed according to my pace. Like a game of tag, if I ran fast, he ran faster. All the while, the massive cathedral dome was growing smaller and smaller behind me. As I neared the peak of the hill, heels now in hand, a dark-colored sedan pulled off on the shoulder of the road and slowed to match my pace. A window rolled down to gradually reveal a slightly older, sharply dressed man.

"Hey there," he drawled, looking me up and down over the top of his sunglasses, "How *you* doin'?"

My mind could not comprehend his actions. The man felt as pesky as a housefly on a hot, humid day, and all I wanted was to swat him away. Snapping a short "Fine!" without glancing his direction, I refocused my attention on Grayson. Still, the man in the black car rolled alongside me, undeterred.

Suddenly, Grayson picked up his pace and broke into a jog. Distracted by my unwelcome companion, I unthinkingly (and regrettably) followed suit.

Game on.

Grayson lived for the thrill of the chase, and finally, his boring old mom had joined in the fun. He broke into a sprint and veered sharply left—*straight into oncoming traffic.*

Cars slammed on their brakes and screeched sideways, while others laid on their horns and swerved to avoid a collision. Within seconds, cars were facing every which way, and I had lost sight of Grayson. My innards liquified as I pictured his body lying bloodied and broken on a shattered windshield. Suddenly, he reappeared, unfazed and zigzagging in and out of sharply angled cars. He returned to the sidewalk, and traffic straightened itself and resumed as if nothing had ever happened. Not a single person stopped to help.

Still, the man in the car had not resumed his travels. He remained at my side, unbelievably oblivious—even for a man. He was annoyingly unshakeable. Couldn't he see I was busy? I started wondering whether his intentions were malicious, but the thought never had time to unfold. With my eyes now firmly fixed before me, the man finally caught on and followed my gaze to the object of my pursuit.

As if on cue, Grayson cut left into a fresh stream of traffic, and the horror repeated itself once more.

Immediately, the man accelerated down the shoulder of the road straight toward Grayson. I was at a complete loss. I yelled, knowing full well Grayson would never hear me—much less *listen* to me—and pleaded with him to stay away from the black car. I watched helplessly as cars continued to zoom haphazardly around his fragile body.

As the man approached Grayson, he yanked his steering wheel sharply to the left and used his vehicle to carve a strong angle into traffic, which only resulted in more angry honking. His car was then evenly aligned with Grayson, and I felt confident my son would be snatched up and swallowed whole by a black sedan.

Instead, Grayson returned to the sidewalk, and the black car mirrored his actions. Whichever way Grayson turned, so did the man, thereby keeping Grayson's body to the right of his car.

Finally, it dawned on me. The man was using his car as a shield to protect Grayson from oncoming traffic. At that moment, regardless of anything I thought prior, the man in the black car became Grayson's guardian angel.

A wave of weakness washed over me, and I became aware that my muscles were twitching spasmodically. Even my body was not mine to control. People's indifference—their unwillingness to help, even their disdain—only fueled my fire and made me stronger. But a kind human being buckled my knees.

Yet, try as I might, I could not persuade Grayson to stop running or return. I frantically flipped through my mental parenting manual. The section I needed was conveniently missing, so I summoned my last bit of strength and resolved to do the hardest, most counterintuitive thing a mother could do.

With a deep breath and something unspoken that bordered on either cussing or a prayer (and perhaps they were one and the same), *I turned my back on my child*, who was cutting in and out of fifty-five-miles-per-hour traffic, and started walking back toward the church. Alone.

I hoped to God that no one was watching, that no one would misinterpret my actions as neglect. I looked over my shoulder. Grayson hadn't yet noticed. The distance between us was widening, and I was doubting my decision beyond all belief. I even forgot about breathing until I found myself instinctively gasping for air as if resurfacing from a long dive.

Finally, when I was on the verge of despair, he turned and noticed I was no longer following him.

"Mommy?" he cried out.

Biting down on my lip for added reinforcement, I kept my mouth shut and ignored him. And if that all didn't feel crazy enough, I started running. The game had been flipped; it was his turn to chase me. The faster I ran, the harder he tried to catch me, so I ran until my lungs were flames of fire.

I allowed him to catch me only when we reached the church parking lot. Snatching him by the shirt and wrapping it around my fist, I gathered him into my arms—torn between my desire to choke and embrace him—and clung to him as if my life depended on it.

Traffic had resumed its normal flow. The man in the black car was nowhere to be found. Anything that justified the panic I felt inside had simply up and disappeared. All I wanted was to collapse into someone's arms. Anyone's arms.

Yet, when we reentered the reception hall, it was as if we had never even left. My family stood in the same back corner; people were dancing, laughing, and celebrating. But I had been to hell and back. The disconnect was more than I could bear.

With a trembling hand, I signaled to my parents. They followed me to my car, where I filled them in on the bare-boned details and roughly strapped Grayson into his front passenger booster seat, where he would remain within an arm's length. By then, he was raging again for no apparent reason, and so was I. My parents held the door shut until I got to my side of the car. Wrapping his shirt around my fist once again, I began backing out of my parking spot. My mom and dad begged me to reconsider. They didn't think it wise to drive with Grayson, flared up as he was. But I knew with 100 percent certainty that I had enough adrenaline coursing through my veins to keep him in place. All I could think of was *home*.

I left my parents standing in the parking lot. I suppose I assumed they would bring my other children home. Apparently, I forgot they were even present. I drove for ten minutes, impervious to Grayson's screams. He clawed equally at the door handle and my arm, leaving a nice bite mark and future scars on my hand. But I felt nothing. I lacked the energy even to hurt.

Eventually, he fell asleep, and I drove on. There was nothing left to think, nothing left to feel. I watched the yellow line on the pavement alternate between straight and dotted, straight and dotted, and drove the rest of the way home in a white-hot silence.

22

Drifting

Here I am, in borrowed bones, in makeshift skin,
looking out of eyes that are a construct, breathing with lungs
that are only a step—a basic rearrangement—away from leaves.
How funny, to have a body when I am not a body? How funny,
to be inside when I am outside.

—HELENA FOX, *How It Feels to Float*

The summer of 2014, no matter how far I stretched my groping fingers into the darkness, I could not connect with either Arin or God. One was physically absent; the other achingly silent. The chains of my life felt too heavy to bear alone, yet what choice remained? Summers simply became long strands of conjoined drownings, and I could barely come up for air before being shoved back down into oblivion.

Grayson seemed intent on showing the world exactly how miserable he felt, and as his episodes grew increasingly larger and more public, my world seemed to close in around me until at last I felt trapped like a prisoner in my home.

Church services with Grayson had grown torturous. He bluntly declared that if I made him attend church, he would scream the second he walked through the door—and he wasn't lying. My other kids knew the drill. They proceeded inside while I remained outside with Grayson, reasoning with him and blocking the church's entrance so he wouldn't go tearing in like a holy terror.

Each passerby handled the situation differently. Many offered sympathetic half-smiles and kind pats on the shoulder, while some brushed politely past as if the mother-son wrestling match taking place on the wheelchair ramp was simply a mirage. Still others stopped to speak as if nothing were wrong—chatting pleasantly as if I didn't have my son's head in a vice-grip and as if cuss words weren't streaming through the finger-cracks of the hand I'd clamped tightly over his mouth.

Grayson was always fried by the end of church, and I was just proud of myself for not becoming an alcoholic over the hour-and-a-half-long liturgy.

Why even bother attending? I questioned week after week.

Even so, my stubborn streak would not allow me to surrender. I adamantly *refused* to let Grayson win the war, to permit his behaviors to dictate my life. I needed something stable, something normal for myself. And that ground that I dug my heels into just happened to be church.

I never imagined my stubbornness could lead to another's pain.

One Sunday, my mom, who also attended our parish, offered to watch Grayson over the coffee hour so I could visit with other adults like a civilized human being. I rounded the church corner just in time to nearly collide with a speeding Grayson and to witness a horde of people hovering above my mom, who—half-reclining—lay propped on her elbow in a pile of rocks. Making a quick decision, I spun around in hot pursuit of Grayson.

I caught up with him and restrained him. Straddling him on the corner of a stranger's lawn, I pinned down my dress with one hand and Grayson's arm with the other.

Eventually, some men from our church arrived. When asked, they informed me that Grayson had pushed my mom, and she had tripped, fallen backward, and hit her head on the rocks. Standing around me in an awkward semicircle, unsure of how to proceed in such uncharted territory, the men respectfully asked how to help. Cheeks burning, I instructed each to grab one of Grayson's limbs while I attempted to modestly swivel my leg off his body.

My humiliation quadrupled that day. Not only did I have to publicly restrain Grayson on a street corner, but I also had to rope three good men into partaking in my shame. I watched each one struggle to control Grayson's singular, thrashing limb—a job I normally did alone—and they became like three mirrors.

In their eyes, I witnessed pangs of consternation and helplessness. Those same feelings resided somewhere deep within me. But I'd so deeply buried them that to observe them in others caused an uncomfortable stirring. I longed to erase the men's faces like a chalkboard—to make them blank like mine. The mere sight of their flickering emotions incited a weakness I could not afford.

When Grayson finally calmed down, the men rose and—with a pitying hug—returned to their families. Smoothing my dress, I brushed away any feelings the men's emotions might have surfaced and gathered my children for the drive home.

Many hours passed before I finally realized I hadn't even checked on my mom. More heaping guilt, more piling shame. Dig a deeper hole. Bury it all; then turn and walk away.

I always scheduled the kids' dentist appointments for the summertime so I wouldn't miss a single school day of independence. The summer of 2014, I decided to get Grayson's visit out of the way first. But immediately after the appointment, he demanded that I leave the others behind to go get lunch. I took him to the car to wait for the other children and the inevitable blowup that was well underway.

By the time everyone else finished, Grayson was irate, and I only made it out of the parking lot before realizing safe travel was impossible. Every time I attempted to drive, Grayson jerked the steering wheel sharply to the right, so I pulled off on the shoulder, gave Caleb my credit card, and told him to walk across the street with the other kids and buy breakfast at Sonic.

I was stuck. I couldn't go anywhere, but I also couldn't stay. I couldn't physically constrain Grayson in the car much longer, and I was unwilling to chase him through traffic yet again.

Fortunately, there was a police station next door to the dentist. After much deliberation, I inched my van toward the parking lot. It was the last thing I wanted to do, but the only thing I could think of. I dragged Grayson into the station, kicking and howling, and explained the situation to the receptionist over his incessant screaming.

When two officers stepped out to greet us, Grayson flew from my grip, rushed at the first, and dove straight for his gun. Everything immediately turned into a mad scramble of arms and legs.

I remember cajoling Grayson through blinding tears, attempting to calm him down. But a recent conversation was blaring in my head like a siren.

Constantly worried about future police interactions, I often attempted to prepare Grayson for their occurrence. "Always be polite and do what they say," I instructed. "If they ask you to sit down, do it! *Do not ever, ever run away!*"

Grayson had asked what would happen if a bad guy tried to steal a police officer's gun. Used to his wandering mind, I envisioned a masked bandit and told him not to worry; the police officers would shoot the bad guy before he could steal their gun.

I had been trying to reassure him; I had no idea he was asking for himself.

As soon as Grayson lunged for the gun, I instantly realized he had been plotting his move from the moment we first entered the station. He had asked me to shoot him numerous times prior and grown desperate when I obviously refused. He'd even preemptively warned, "If I find a policeman, I'm going to grab his gun so he'll kill me."

I had just dragged Grayson headlong into his ideal scenario.

On some level of consciousness, I heard my soon-to-be third grader begging the police officers, "Just shoot me! Please kill me! *I want to be dead!*"

His wailing entreaties froze my veins, and I catatonically turned from the scuffle to shuffle stiffly toward the chairs. It broke my body to sit, but I did so regardless. There was nothing more I could do. I was only getting in the way. My soul detached from my body and hovered above the unfolding scene. I watched them struggle—the policemen and my son—for three minutes or thirty years.

By the time control was regained, I was an old woman inside.

Sitting in the station's conference room, Grayson—having already forgotten what made him mad in the first place—had transitioned to speaking of lunch. Paperwork was completed, and reports were filed.

The police officers were exceptional human beings, and I sensed their kindhearted concern and the same despairing helplessness as the men from our church. They gave me business cards of consolation and welcomed me to stop by any time.

I called my children and told them to start walking back. All was fine.

My face was red and splotchy when I walked out to meet them, and I was squinting and shielding my eyes from the sun. Luckily, none of them seemed to notice. Grayson was happy as a clam; reminiscent of the wedding, the only trace of chaos remained trapped within me. Nothing in the outside world was even slightly ajar, and the kids jumped back in exactly where they had left off:

"Mommy, can I have a friend over when we get home?"

"Can you drop me off at the lake?"

"Mom, guess what Caleb did while we were at Sonic?"

I wavered for a moment while examining their lively, expectant eyes. None of this was their fault, I reminded myself, and my children deserved more than my bloodshot eyes and weary exhaustion. So, with a single decision and a big gulp, I tipped my face to the sky and swallowed the morning whole.

Forcing a broad smile in my children's direction, I replied, "Sure, your friend can come over," "Of course, I'll drop you off at the lake," and "I can only imagine what Caleb did at Sonic. Do tell."

※

It was still summer 2014. Having lived at our new house for slightly over a year, more and more kids began finding their way to our backyard.

Grayson, halfway interested in making friends, often resorted to unusual tactics when attempting to impress the neighborhood children— much to his siblings' dismay.

Once, while locked in his room two stories above, Grayson watched the playing children from his east window, which I had permanently locked the day he decided to climb out of it and shimmy down our wooden pergola. His north window, however, was *not* locked. Since it overlooked a two-story drop onto hard concrete, I'd dismissed it as a viable escape route.

But where there's a will, there's a way.

That particular afternoon, Grayson opened his north window, climbed up and over the ledge, and hung by eight strong fingertips. Little by little, he inched his finger along the sill and walked his toes around the corner of the house until he felt the rough wood of the pergola. Wrapping his arm around one corner of the house, he pulled himself to standing and then once again shimmied down the posts.

Attempting to impress the neighborhood kids in our yard, who were already gaping, Grayson tied a jump rope around his neck and—threatening to hang himself—tightened the rope until his face turned purple.

The kids all scattered like dust in the wind while my kids stormed into the house to report Grayson's misdeeds.

I had to make several explanatory phone calls to parents who barely even knew my name—reason number *five billion* why I've never struggled with the deadly sin of pride.

There were few places I could go where my reputation as Grayson's mother did not precede me. I had difficulty knowing who "I" was when his presence constantly foreshadowed mine.

First, church had ceased to be my refuge, then my community at large, and finally, my neighborhood. Only when I was within the privacy of my own four walls did I feel free from pity, judgment, or disgust—save my own—and even those four walls were closing in tighter every day.

I moved Grayson to the basement bedroom after that second death-defying escape. Although I could no longer lock his actual window, I could lock the egress cover we'd recently installed. I weighed out the risks—trapping my son in a fire or allowing him to escape and run free. One seemed far riskier than the other, so I locked the cover.

Immediately, Grayson forced his way through an impossibly small gap—scraping his back on the plexiglass until it bled—and ran straight back into the house, laughing like a madman. I placed the lawnmower on top to weigh down the cover. But again he slipped through. Next time, I waited outside with the garden hose and sprayed his head the second it popped through the crack. But that only enraged him and made me feel horrible.

Finally, I resorted to sitting in the hallway outside his locked door and opening it only when I heard the sliding sound of his window. I always had a bribe or threat prepared to hold over his head: "If you open your window one time, we won't go swimming tomorrow. Frogs or spiders or mice will get in if you open your window." I even briefly considered using his window well as a terrarium to house a harmless bull snake and the hairless baby mice he so despised but then quickly changed my mind after envisioning them loose in the house.

I already knew from every book I'd ever read that it was wrong to use bribes and threats to control Grayson's behavior. But I had yet to uncover any other techniques that actually worked. At least my ways—unprecedented though they may be—kept my son confined to his room instead of tearing naked through the streets.

After all, survival belongs to the fittest, not the most studious one who religiously adheres to the textbook.

Therefore, large portions of my summer were spent sitting in a dark hallway outside Grayson's door. Light bulbs had long burned out alongside my give-a-shit levels, and I possessed zero energy to replenish either one. I rarely knew where my other kids were or who they were with, as I often ended up downstairs without a phone, unable to leave my post lest Grayson break free.

Already, Grayson had pulled two doors off their hinges and had decimated many, many more. He lost the privilege of having a doorknob after ripping one off and using it to smash holes in his walls. After that, he asked his friend Siri "how to escape from a locked room." Preemptively hiding a library card in his closet, he walked so willingly to his room that I knew he'd been plotting. Sliding the card down the jamb, he unlatched his door and ran upstairs, giggling delightedly. He was so proud of his ingenuity that I *almost* felt tempted to celebrate with him. After confiscating his library card, my credit cards constantly turned up missing, and when I started locking my purse in the car, he improvised with folded pages torn from a book.

Out of options, I hired a handyman to install a deadbolt on Grayson's bedroom door, and I can only imagine the explanations he mentally contrived while he worked. The only downside to a deadbolt was that the entire door frame had started wobbling from being battered by Grayson's ramming body, and fresh cracks were squiggling up the wall toward the ceiling. I seriously wondered if, at some point, he might not hurl his body against the door only to tear down the wall and then collapse our whole house.

Sitting in the darkness, I waited for eight little fingers to curl their way beneath the door and then whacked them with any object lying within my reach, unwilling to lose yet another door. I felt squalid—like part-Japanese, part–White trash. My beautiful new house seemed to be collapsing around me, and all I could do was sit sentry outside a beat-up basement door.

For hours on end, I sat outside Grayson's room and listened to his highly detailed descriptions of what a terrible mother I was, how much he hated me, how much I surely hated him, what a bitch I was, and how he was planning to kill, stab, maim, and burn me. He ranted on and on, screaming until his voice grew hoarse, and while on one level, I knew not to let it faze me, on another, it broke my heart into a million tiny pieces.

Our basement became my prison, and like an inmate, I felt outcast and cast down. Grayson's constant screaming and banging were driving me mad, and I recalled the woman who "accidentally" smothered her autistic son beneath a beanbag. The public was outraged, demanding to know how any loving mother could suffocate her beloved child. But I shed tears for that woman; I ached for that poor mother. I had tasted the depths of her despondency in my own vile blackness. I knew what it felt like to be driven to the brink.

After spending what felt like days in solitary confinement, the dankness of my subterranean dungeon began coiling and seeping its way inside me, snuffing out anything with breath. It washed over me like an unholy baptism, cleansing me of all hope and joy. I felt abandoned first by God and then by my husband, and I wasn't sure which felt worse. I knew in my heart that neither was *actually* true, but I was so sick of trying to rein in my thoughts, feel the right feelings, and suffer like the righteous woman I wasn't.

So instead, I let my loneliness commingle with my liberated despair. Crashing head-on, they swirled together to create a powerful undertow, and—closing my eyes and leaning back against my cell wall—I surrendered to its pull.

Nothingness rolled over me in waves, and I allowed myself to be enveloped in obscurity. Any thoughts and emotions that kept me harbored in reality, I cut loose, and they sank like a metal anchor into the abyss. If I could control nothing else, at least I could refuse to think, refuse to feel.

Relief appeared to me then in a welcomed cloud of white numbness and enshrouded me in a silent mist as I floated weightlessly out to sea, drifting wherever the waves pulled me. Grayson's screaming faded and then disappeared completely.

From then on, numbness became my preferred drug of choice, and I learned how to get my fix with relative ease. Unlike summertime, numbness was controllable. I could snap my fingers and rapturously disappear into an opaque, silent mist.

Eventually, the tide would turn with the start of the school year, and I would once again find myself washed ashore on solid ground.

But until then, it took everything in me just to stay afloat.

23

Light-Bearing

How then does light return to the world after the eclipse
of the sun? Miraculously. Fraily. In thin stripes.

—Virginia Woolf, *The Waves*

The storm has passed. I open Grayson's battered door and crawl to
him on hands and knees. I have been to the precipice, but his tears of
humanity call me back, melting both his rage and mine. Through his tears, I
catch a glimpse into his tormented soul and am crushed beneath my woeful
lack of love. My smallness of heart grieves me to no end, and my inability to
contain both his light and his pain is the true origin of my darkness.

I have been deemed worthy of caring for an angel, yet I continuously
proclaim, "I cannot."

I collapse before him in an unworthy heap of remorse and offer him a
glimpse into my tormented soul. Forgetting his pain, he weeps for mine,
and as he tenderly strokes my hair, his tears wash me with divine forgiveness. He loves me in a way I don't deserve to be loved.

Mary, the mother of Jesus, is called the Light Bearer. She knit flaming cells of light within her womb, but like the burning bush, she was not consumed. She carried light and became light. Yet when I try to do the same, I groan and stagger beneath its weight. My soul-womb is not yet spacious enough to bear my son's light.

But he has been expanding me since the day of his conception. His limbs of light extend into my dark places time and again. They ground me in hope and joy and laughter, and in his eyes, the veil is thin, and I can almost see straight into Heaven.

Just as black is not the absence of color but the union of all, so is Grayson not an absence but a brimming fullness. The complete embodiment of all things—all joy and sorrow, all blessings and pain. The universe is contained within him, and I am being widened to contain them both.

A friend once asked, "How can you love him when he causes so much pain?" I answered truthfully, "While Grayson has been at the center of so many challenges, I've never once viewed him as the source of my pain. I am who I am because of him."

I've written much on the pain and sorrow and would be gravely remiss to overlook the blessings and joy.

Whatever Grayson gives, he does so wholeheartedly, without expecting anything in return—like the morning he woke me up early, bursting at the seams to celebrate *his* birthday. A cup of coffee, a spoon, and some creamer lay on the table next to my reading chair, alongside my journal and pen and a heartfelt note he'd dictated on his iPad: *I love you mommy I think about you in my heart so does god and Jesus if I could I would give you a piece of my heart god and me thank you for being my mom sorry you didn't sleep well god prays for you every night and day.*

His theology is better than most.

I delight in his notes. I savor and study them, especially the handwritten ones. All his eclectic parts collide in a hot, jumbled mess and are captured and preserved on a whole sheet of paper. I notice the nuances no one else would and laugh to myself. That hole is where he drooled. I picture him growing irritated and feverishly scrubbing the wet spot until the paper dissolved beneath his finger. The scribble blacker than night is where he wrongly formed a letter and buried it alive beneath a pile of ink—pen clutched in his seething fist. The ballpoint dots that nearly pierced the paper's skin suggest a serial stabbing and are one of the primary reasons my wood tables are covered in glass. I imagine the heap of crumpled paper snowballs thrown carelessly over his shoulder—prior mistakes cast angrily to the ground. Where others may see only 8.5 × 11 lined sheets of disaster, I see tremendous sacrifices of love.

Such notes epitomize his life. They condense the vastness of his struggles on a singular sheet. No matter his age, on paper he appears perpetually four. Large, misshapen letters clutter the page, and he can only fit several words before running out of space. Every line slopes sharply downward as if by each end, his arm had wearied of writing, and words trail off the paper's edge, resuming wherever they left off on the next line.

His drawings are even more rudimentary. When I once let him borrow my journal, he returned it with an entry of his own. A bodiless head that could have been drawn by my three-year-old niece had two dots for eyes and one for a nose. An upside-down U formed a mouth, and beneath were the words *sad monster*, as spelled out letter by letter by me. The next page contained the same head but jagged black eyebrows and a straight-lined mouth. That one was captioned *angry monster*.

Grayson's sad and angry monsters

On one level, his simplistic drawings are endearing. On another, their insights shatter my soul.

His notes are compilations of recycled phrases; Grayson collects sayings like others collect stamps or coins. "You rock" was one of Mr. Roth's favorite phrases and, therefore, a frequent greeting in Grayson's letters. Another expression originated with Grayson. It popped out of his mouth when he could barely speak, and he's said it every night since: "I think about you in my heart, Mom. I think about you in my peace."

I'm not exactly sure what he means by this, but I like the idea of being thought about in someone's peace.

I find many of his letters humorous, especially when angrily written. One such note was written on a paper towel and conspicuously left on the counter after dinner: *I love you mom love Grayson your food was grose I just ate it to make you happy.* Another, found when he was eight years old, had been written on a piece of cardboard after packing his suitcase: *Imaparprsen Ineedsmunee Iwintlivewmuhfamlee,* which translated to *I'm a poor person. I need money. I won't live with my family.* His name is signed at the top because he ran out of room at the bottom. Apparently, he had big plans to run away from home and panhandle for a living.

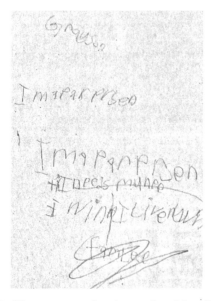

Grayson's note: "I'm a poor person. I need money. I won't live with my family."

While his letters provided helpful insight into his brain, Grayson's crazy stunts were more amusing than anything. He became obsessed with feeling weightless, and all his quirky infatuations—like water slides, roller coasters, and marble ramps—partially satiated this sensation. But right around the summer of 2014, Grayson added a few new activities that could lend to the feeling of buoyancy, like levitation, sky diving, and scuba diving—and he dubbed me his lucky assistant.

Every day, a fresh idea led to unique props and relatively appropriate costumes. One morning, he came downstairs dressed in a life vest with a garbage bag tied to the front and declared it "Skydiving Day." He traipsed to the park, leaped from the jungle gym, and grew enraged when his parachute failed to slow his landing.

On "Scuba Diving Day," he came down wearing Jacob's tight-fitting long underwear as a wetsuit, with two grocery bags taped around his feet to keep them dry. Why dry feet were so important I'll never know. I trailed behind him to the neighborhood lake and then dealt with his fit when he discovered his wetsuit and "boots" were insufficiently waterproof. But his

Grayson's "skydiving" outfit

tantrum came to a screeching halt in a brilliant flash of inspiration. To be a *real* scuba diver, he needed to breathe underwater. Could I just run back home and grab him a straw?

His fascination with levitation lasted the longest. He watched one YouTube video after another, studying the exact placement of a plank between two chairs. Grayson squealed with excitement when the magician removed the board, and the volunteer's body remained hovering in midair. Our living room became his stage, with a thin sheet of plywood connecting two chairs. He repeatedly ordered any compliant person to yank the board from beneath him to test whether he could float. His siblings were exceedingly happy to oblige him and watched him tumble to the ground again and again—laughing each time harder than the last. Grayson would jump up, muttering and shaking his head in disgust, and then dust himself off as he set out to find a new-and-improved method.

When, at last, we helped him understand there was a trick behind every levitation, he reluctantly settled for the mere illusion.

One summer morning, Grayson dragged me outside when there was barely enough light to see. A YouTube video had provided the key to his success. He instructed me to bury the head of a shovel and pack the surrounding dirt *tight*! Then, planting his feet on the shovel head, he leaned back on the wooden handle concealed by his shirt, and let his head fall forward, closing his eyes as if under a spell. I snapped many photographs to prove the authenticity of his illusion. The shovel stayed buried all summer, and I often caught him talking to his imaginary audience while "levitating" on its wooden handle.

His most serious weightless attempt came in the form of a red balloon. While cleaning, I lost track of Grayson. Suddenly, I heard the garage door creak, followed by Jacob's hesitant voice. I could tell he was trying to suppress a laugh, and nothing about the situation sounded promising.

"Um, Mom," he called. "You'd better come see what Grayson did."

More muffled giggles.

Knowing that whatever awaited me in the garage could not be good, I dropped my dish towel and responded promptly. Before I even rounded the corner, I saw the red glow. A giant, rubbery red balloon was filling

Grayson "levitating" on a shovel

my garage—its string wrapped around the handlebars of Grayson's bike. Flabbergasted, I paused while piecing together the story in my mind. Knowing it would take something massive to lift his body into the air, Grayson snuck away when I wasn't looking—a pair of scissors tucked in his pocket—and rode his bike to the neighborhood model homes, where he snipped the string of the largest balloon he'd ever beheld in his life. It occurred to me then that he had ridden through our entire neighborhood dragging a bobbing model-home balloon behind him. Although my jaw was on the floor, I had the presence of mind to snap a picture, and the second I did, the balloon drifted toward the top of the garage, hit something sharp, and popped. All hell broke loose, followed by a massive fit and concurrent apologies to the model-home salespeople.

They hadn't even realized their balloon was missing.

More than half of our adventures ended in Category 5 meltdowns. Still, I found myself doing my son's crazy bidding: I tracked down magnifying plexiglass, rescued plastic pipes from dumpsters, and searched the internet for the coveted infomercial "Ostrich Pillow"—all while wondering: *What in tarnation am I doing?*

Honest to goodness, I have stood outside in the heat of summer before God and all our neighbors, attaching branches to my son with a belt as he pressed himself against a tree trunk to test whether he could successfully disappear. I have rolled and bound him with plastic wrap and packing tape just to see if he could roll faster down hills, and I have stuffed sweatpants full of T-shirts and arranged them with shoes on a chair so Grayson could lie on the floor, his legs hiding behind the couch—thereby creating the illusion of being sawn in two.

His wacky ideas drive me half mad. My other half is thoroughly entertained.

But most hilarious of all is Grayson's YouTube history, which I've often reviewed with tears streaming down my cheeks. His sought-out topics have included *how to make a shocking spy device, how to walk through a closed*

Grayson trying to disappear via camouflage

door, how to do freaky body tricks, how to charge your iPod with a sock, how to make string go through your head, how to shock yourself, how to break your arm in three seconds, and my personal but totally random favorite, *Kevin Hart women anger issues.*

Grayson's zest for life is like a blinding ray of sunlight—intense and impossible to ignore. If he is elated, rest assured, the world will know. But the joy he bestows is subtle, like floating particles of dust drifting on slanting shafts of light. Some will be repulsed, beholding only sloughed-off flakes of dead skin. But others with the eyes to see will be enchanted by the sparkling glitter dancing in the sun.

Much of life with Grayson has been loud and turbulent. The lows have been extremely low, and the peaks more like barely perceptible hills. Our victories have been measured in slivers—an intentional smile, sitting still in the dentist's chair, not leaping from a moving vehicle—events that most parents take for granted. Such gifts occur in the cracks of time, the in-between moments, and when I forget to pay attention, they slip by—uncelebrated and unnoticed.

The joy that comes from being Grayson's mother trickles in through holy streams of effervescent laughter. It hovers in silent, marveling wonder and sneaks in unannounced when I come to my senses and find myself knee-deep in his outlandish schemes. Being his mother has peeled my fingers from any semblance of perceived control. He has made me belly-laugh and blubber like a baby; he has humbled me and made me so proud I could burst. Above all, he reminds me daily, in the words attributed to Mother Teresa, that "I can do no great things—only small things with great love."

I once read that the difference between a fly and a bee is that a fly will be drawn to the single pile of dung amid a field of wildflowers, whereas a bee will seek the lone flower in a landfill. Day by day, I am striving to be like the bee, though I fail more often than not. I am fighting to cling to the good and let the rest slide. I am attempting to grow still and widen my eyes to the in-between moments, the cracks, and the fragile slivers of time.

In the rare moments when my insides stop churning, I lie fallow and watch sparkles of dust dance across sunbeams. I bathe in their light, and the rays reach deep into my darkness and ground me in a calm, quiet joy.

24

Cutting

It is not easy to find happiness in ourselves,
and it is not possible to find it elsewhere.

—AGNES REPPLIER, *The Treasure Chest*

Arin and I sat quietly, parked beneath a streetlight at the Guadalajara Mexican Restaurant. We had gone to grab a late-night dinner but were apparently too late-night—the doors were already locked. My bare feet were propped on Arin's dashboard, and he was scrolling through the texts he'd received while driving and responding to the ones that couldn't wait—which was all of them.

I shifted nervously in my seat, gathering the courage to speak the words I'd been thinking for weeks.

In fact, I'd been asking some form of the same question on and off for the last few years.

"Arin, I have a question," I always began. "Do you ever worry that one day we'll wake up and realize we aren't as happy as we think? That maybe we only *think* we're in love, but we're actually deceiving ourselves, and that one day we'll wake up and realize none of this is real?"

Arin immediately stopped whatever he was doing and turned to stare at me—one eyebrow shooting for the sky in terror and the other dipping in total confusion.

"No! I never think that!" he always exclaimed; then came the inevitable pause and his recurring question, "Do *you?*"

I replied honestly that, no, I didn't believe that either.

But I *had* wondered.

Over the last three years, our lives had become so compartmentalized. There was the "fun us" that came out to play between Arin's hitches. That version of us filled our days with lunch martinis on restaurant patios, weekend football games, missed birthday celebrations at the Hibachi grill, Zac Brown concerts, and midweek getaways. We rarely fought, and our time together was smooth and easy. Ecstatic to be in each other's presence, our happiness so filled each and every waking second that there was little room for anything else.

Then there was the completely inverted "oil field us"—all work and no play. We infrequently talked on the phone about surface events—kids' sports, Grayson's fits, work problems—and if the rig's reception was good enough, we occasionally FaceTimed each other. Overall, I didn't know much about his workdays, and he didn't know much about mine.

When we were together, every moment was authentically full of joy. Yet when we were apart, the abrupt deficiency was equally and excruciatingly hollow. With such drastically varied versions of "us," I sometimes wondered which was *more* real.

Behind my recurring question was the nagging sense that something was *off.*

But lately, my nagging sense had bubbled over into a full-blown concern and was just waiting for the perfect opportunity to burst free.

"Arin," I began, back in the Guadalajara parking lot, "you're working really hard; I know the thought of retirement keeps you afloat, and I know you pass hours daydreaming about how we'll spend it. But if we don't start nurturing our relationship now, I'm worried there'll be nothing left by the time you retire."

I stopped talking and waited for my words to penetrate Arin's exhausted brain, knowing full well that any additional statements wouldn't be heard. Arin was so burned out he seemed incapable of processing any information except that which his job required. In response, I'd gradually started prescreening my words, selecting only the most essential, and then condensing even those to their most reduced form. I knew I had only a small window of time with my husband's attention.

Arin's eyes glazed over and flickered distractedly between his constantly dinging phone and some faraway point beyond his windshield.

"Yeah," he replied dully. "I understand what you're saying. I'll try to do better."

I sighed as Arin fired up the ignition, thus signaling the end of our conversation. Somehow, my concerns had been relegated to another chore on his endless to-do list, and I couldn't help feeling like the conversation might have gone better over a few Guadalajara margaritas.

Lately, alcohol seemed to be the one thing capable of elevating Arin and me above his heavy workload, and the majority of our happy times revolved around its consumption. It helped him sleep through the empty moments, escape the ones that felt too full, and supercharge the good ones—always too few and far between. It had become the liquid bridge that consistently reconnected our disconnected lives, a trustworthy fortress that shielded us from reality, and the neon-lit road stop that never failed to provide a good time.

To us, it was anything but a problem.

But somewhere between the clearly defined "fun us" and "oil field us" existed a hazy, nondescript void. I could detect traces of it in the normative, wordless lulls that lingered between Arin and the kids when they ran errands together, or in the long list of their friend's names he didn't know, or the questions he couldn't think to ask.

Whereas alcohol conveniently bridged the gap between him and me, it was an unsuitable conduit between him and the children. So Arin supplanted any missing intimacy with fun outings, bouts of after-dinner wrestling, and movie parties on the couch that found him inevitably snoring halfway through.

But the truth was, the kids were growing accustomed to Arin's absence, and he was forgetting what it meant to feel present.

Occasionally I tried to resurrect our old ways. I'd casually mention a book I'd been reading or some meandering thought I'd been pondering. But Arin's reserves were so depleted that even my seemingly innocuous words descended on him like a heavy yoke, draining what little energy he had left.

Feeling like a massive burden, I doubled down on my attempts to make Arin's home life as pleasant as possible. Whenever he returned home, the fridge was stocked full of his favorite beer. A home-cooked meal was simmering on the stove. The sheets were freshly laundered, and the house was sparkling clean. I, too, was freshly showered, dressed to impress, and I made every effort to present myself as happy, emotionally level, and ever-available to work, play, or let him sleep.

But my actions never seemed to elicit the desired response. Arin's affect remained flat, and his disposition dead-dog-tired.

All this I perceived as rejection.

My overactive brain kicked into hyperdrive. It began throwing out desperate accusations—regardless of whether they were logical.

Does Arin even love me? Maybe he's not attracted to me. Surely, it's because of the weight I've gained after having five children. What if he's cheating? Gasp! Perhaps he's hiding a second family!

Arin had always been forthcoming about the rig prostitutes, the insane money his coworkers dropped at strip clubs, and the online dating profiles created by "happily" married men. Although any of Arin's colleagues could have attested to his integrity and fidelity, the dormant insecurities I'd been too preoccupied to consider began rearing their ugly heads and demanding my full attention.

For weeks, I stewed and wrestled with my thoughts. I pestered Arin to reassure myself of his faithfulness and drove him crazy with questions regarding my self-alleged declining looks. For the first time in our marriage, I imagine he was excited to return to his rig.

Finally, for whatever reason, on September 8, 2014, something inside me snapped, and I could no longer tolerate myself. I lay awake that night feeling angry, resentful, ashamed, and adamantly determined to not sleep until I'd settled whatever was churning inside.

After a long while, I opened my journal and finally allowed the words to fall freely and truthfully onto the page:

> *I have stopped feeling like I "belong" with Arin. I feel unworthy of our relationship and his love. I'm always striving to be what I think he wants me to be—the woman I think he deserves—so that he doesn't feel shortchanged. With all the pressures of the oil field, I feel constantly pressed to be "on," happy, pretty, available, on top of everything—and sometimes I act as though I exist solely for him.*
>
> *Although we are no longer Reformed, I still don't understand what it means to live in freedom. I'm married but feel alone. Alone, but still dependent on another for my happiness. I feel like a sailboat, blown about whichever way the wind decrees. Despite the fact that I'm a grown woman, I have yet to take control of my own life. I did first as my father told me, and then my religion, and while Arin would never order me to do anything, I am still living my life to please him—even in his absence.*
>
> *At what point will I start making decisions for myself?*

My thoughts continued, snowballing faster and faster with the weight of additional insight.

> *Perhaps it's not that I'm not good enough for Arin but that I'm not good enough for me! If I can't love and respect myself, how will I ever be capable of receiving love and respect from others—including my husband, double including God? I am not presenting myself as I am, but as I think I should be. Ironically, maybe I am withholding the very thing that both*

*Arin and God so longingly desire—the gift of my authentic
and unified self.*

*Am I being honest with Arin and bringing my true self
to the table, or simply the version I think he desires? Does he
appreciate me for who I am, independent of him? Do I? Who
am I without Arin?*

I rolled over to check the time: 4:00 a.m., and nothing but more
questions.

Now desirous but incapable of sleeping, I began growing more agitated; Grayson would be awake in a few short hours.

In a flash, the clarity I'd been seeking appeared, though certainly not in
the form I'd imagined. It emerged from my rambling thoughts like a rugged iceberg, and no matter how hard I tried to avoid it, its magnetic pull
kept drawing me back.

Finally, I conceded. First thing in the morning, I would call several
gyms to find a personal trainer. My body had been beaten on, and I was
tired of feeling hurt and weak. As Grayson grew strong, I would need
to grow stronger. I would check in with Arin, as we always did if our
actions could cause each other discomfort. I would *not*, however, ask his
permission.

Additionally, I would make an appointment to chop my hair, which
nearly grazed my waist. Arin had always vehemently professed his love for
my long hair, and while I wouldn't cut it *to spite* him, I would do it *despite*
him. It wasn't a choice *against him* but *for me.*

I lay in bed thinking a while longer. Why the gym? A new haircut?
Drastic outward manifestations of my subtle inward changes? A final purging of Reformed ideas about long-haired femininity? An angry middle
finger because I was sick of worrying about everyone else's opinions? A
determined effort to do something for me instead of constantly considering Arin?

And in all of this, where *was* Arin? Why was I not confiding in him?

Anger started bubbling to the surface. I *had* tried to talk to him, but he
was always too tired to listen. Should I try again? Fight for the friendship I

was so desperately missing? Or should I take a step back and figure things out myself, seek a healthy level of independence, and move on with my life, even—and *especially*—in his absence? Could I do that without feeling bitter?

Yet when the majority of our days did not include each other, how could we expect to remain an intimate part of each other's lives?

What are we sacrificing for the oil field? I wondered rhetorically before finally falling asleep.

Ironically, I couldn't cut my hair when it came right down to it. It ended up being a much bigger part of my identity than I'd realized, and the decision was much harder than I'd imagined. My insides hadn't yet changed *enough* to go through with the act, and come to find out, I—not Arin or the Reformed church—had wrongly embedded my femininity in my hair.

Like the biblical strongman Samson, I considered it my only redeeming quality, my sole good feature. Cut my hair, and I'm no longer me. I was once told as much by a boy in high school—that my name and long, flowing locks were synonymous. No hair, no Corey. For whatever reason, I swallowed his statement hook, line, and sinker. Accepted it as God's honest truth.

As shallow as it may seem, cutting my hair meant severing my ties to *myself*. But before I could do that, I had to figure out who my new self was—or more accurately, my *true* self.

Unlike cutting my hair, returning to the gym *was* a return to myself. It forced me back into my body—a place I'd not inhabited for years. I showed up to my first session highly nervous, wearing a long, baggy T-shirt and sweats and looking every bit the part of a frumpy old housewife. My scoliosis-riddled back made me move like one too. Years of restraining Grayson had taken their toll, and there was barely a moment that I wasn't in pain.

So when Ben, my new trainer, asked me to do box jumps, I looked at him like he was out of his gourd. My feet hadn't simultaneously left the ground since my college volleyball days, and I saw no reason to shake things up now. But Ben didn't care. He didn't see me as old or frail. He only saw a thirty-six-year-old body in need of being whipped into shape. And whip me into shape he did. He pushed me harder than I'd ever been pushed, even as a college athlete. His high-intensity workouts left me shaking and nauseous, uncertain whether I could make it to the car or crank the steering wheel enough times to get home.

But within weeks, my body began changing, as did my confidence. If I could make it through one of Ben's workouts, I could do anything, I began to believe.

One month into my training sessions, Arin came along to watch. More than anything, I think he wanted to look Ben in the eyes to ensure he wasn't a pervert. He studied Ben more than me that day, and the few times I snuck a peek at my husband, I saw an expression I hadn't witnessed for years.

Was that jealousy flickering across his face? I incredulously wondered. Right or wrong, I was exhilarated. My husband still desired me enough to feel jealous!

That October, Arin whisked me away for a quick weekend in South Dakota; it was our first time alone together in I-had-no-idea-how-long. A spark had been reignited, and we spent the weekend enraptured with each other.

We laughed our way through an anti-gravity tourist trap house, visited Mount Rushmore for the first time, and researched its history. Then we tried our hand at the hotel slot machines and spent our profits on an amazing steak dinner.

For once, Arin's dinging phone went unchecked.

Six months later, I cut off twelve inches of hair.

Years ago, Arin had shared that he was grateful for his father's death, for without it, we never would have met.

Similarly, I had uncovered the silver lining in Arin's prolonged absence. Without it, I would never have learned to stand on my own two feet.

His praise and adoration would have forever remained an intravenous drip line—infusing, sustaining, and giving me life.

But in the end, he could never have fully given the happiness that was mine to claim for myself—although he assuredly would have gladly died trying.

25

Reassessing

Only when we are brave enough to explore the darkness
will we discover the infinite power of our light.

—Brené Brown, *The Gifts of Imperfection*

April 24, 2015. I never knew how much peace was in death. Watching the signs and progression, I feel an odd sense of anticipation, almost like awaiting a birth. So many tears intermingled with laughter and then more tears.

A nod from Arin's mom, then a whisper to my dad. A sinking realization. Then three, maybe four more breaths, and she's gone. Absolute silence. Then my dad sobbing. But such a sweet sense of freedom and release. The yellow waxiness immediately consumes the hands I'd spent hours of my childhood studying—the blue, tunneled veins, the deep ridges on her fingernails, her Oil of Olay softened skin. Joy and laughter fill the room as stories are shared. Then Reagan is climbing up on Gramma's bed, taking charge of her lifeless arm—pulling it naturally across her body to lay beneath it. No fear. Just comfort, so much love, and the peace I've been missing. The kind that starts on the inside and radiates out. The kind that changes one's countenance and soothes a hurting heart. There is the feeling of her aliveness, the sense that she is not dead or gone but somehow more alive than ever. I know she's gone, but she's also not. And in her death, she continues to give. A departing gift of peace, light, and joy.

Exactly three weeks after my gramma's death, I awoke in the middle of the night inordinately *desperate* to reread my old journals from start to finish, almost as if she had poked me awake from beyond the grave.

My gramma was my everything. Besides regular childhood sleepovers, I worked at my grandparents' sod farm throughout high school and then lived there during our second year of marriage. As a teenager, besides working in the office, my summer job entailed driving my gramma anywhere she needed to go, which always included somewhere of benefit to me—my favorite store at the mall, a gas station, or Orange Julius for hot dogs and smoothies. When we weren't out gallivanting, she had a home-cooked meal ready every day at eleven. She regaled me with tales of her childhood and mine, and I shared my fears and insecurities that, by and large, went unspoken. These she dismissed with a wave of her arm. I was perfect in her mind, and anything wrong with me was—quite humorously—always somebody else's fault.

The day she died, I lost my biggest fan, closest confidante, and the most treasured link to my heritage and history. But her death stoked an internal fire and reminded me of the temporality of life and the urgent need to live my one life well.

Yet after rereading my journals from beginning to end, I slumped back in my chair, entirely discouraged. An overarching theme had emerged— one that did not make me proud.

Page after nauseating page referenced my redundant lifelong struggles—my self-hatred, anger, irritability, loneliness, and insecurities.

On paper, it was obvious that I was not a happy person. Well-intentioned? Yes. Striving and seeking? Absolutely. But happy? Definitely not. There were seasons of happiness, to be sure, but from a bird's-eye view of my journals, no one would have ever accused me of being on par with the jolly Dalai Lama.

To be fair, the concept had been discouraged my whole Christian life. *Joy* was a godly trait, affiliated with internal peace regardless of external surroundings. But *happiness* was shallow, stemming from transient material goods. If you were happy, you were most likely pursuing the wrong things in life. It had been burned into my brain that "God doesn't care about your happiness; He wants you to be joyful" or "Seek joy, not happiness. One is eternal; the other is fleeting." To some degree, I understood and still do. Millions of humans have pursued happiness through fame, wealth, or power and have died entirely broken, lonely, and miserable.

But *that* wasn't the kind of happiness I was seeking.

At the time, I was reading *The Gifts of Imperfection* by Brené Brown. In it, she writes:

> *People may call what happens at midlife "a crisis," but it's not. It's an unraveling—a time when you feel a desperate pull to live the life you want to live, not the one you're "supposed" to live. The unraveling is a time when you are challenged by the universe to let go of who you think you are supposed to be and to embrace who you are.*[1]

She goes on to say:

> *Wholehearted living is about engaging with our lives from a place of worthiness. It means cultivating the courage, compassion, and connection to wake up in the morning and think, No matter what gets done and how much is left undone, I am enough. It's going to bed at night thinking, Yes, I am imperfect and vulnerable and sometimes afraid, but that doesn't change the truth that I am also brave and worthy of love and belonging.*[2]

And *that* was the kind of happiness I *was* seeking.

I sat in my chair for a long while. Thinking. Thinking very hard. I had learned to accept the struggles of life. I could have even said I was content. But I wasn't happy. I concluded that, for me, happiness was a step above contentment and one I needed to pursue.

Years later, Arin and I would get into a heated debate. His highest life goal was contentment, while mine was happiness. He would quip that chasing happiness seemed a shallow goal, and I would launch into an emotional tirade explaining how my happiness was anything *but* superficial. Rather, it was the spoils of a battle hard-fought and hard-won. After seeing things from my point of view, he would concede, and then we would giggle over my impassioned emotional outburst.

All that to say, happiness, to me, is anything but shallow.

As I continued reading *The Gifts of Imperfection*, I felt the urge to create two lists. I labeled the first *Wholehearted Living*. On this list, I described my best life. It included *sitting, smiling, music, reading, candles, praying, stillness, gratefulness, happiness, laughing, wine, creating, pondering, relaxing, fluid, being (me),* and *light.*

The second list I titled *Empty Living*, and it included words like *angry, stressed, rushed, moving, comparing, perfection, striving, numb, exhausted, tuned out, escaping, chasing, doing, heavy,* and *dark.*

After completing both lists, I continued writing: *I live so much in the second category. So much empty living. But* how *do I make the leap from one list to the other? So many years programmed into me. It all seems impossible. I have been so lost for so long.*

Finally, I made a third list. Brené had written herself a "permission slip" when she went on the *Oprah Winfrey Show* that granted her the freedom to stop being so serious and afraid and to have a little fun. I figured if it was good enough for her, it was surely good enough for me. My permission slip read: *I give myself permission to sit, laugh, smile, do nothing, be alone, not lecture, let things go, laugh instead of getting angry, be thankful instead of complaining, play, have fun, clean or not clean, be happy, take a nap, and go to bed early—guilt-free!*

I concluded: *Somehow, giving myself "permission" feels so much more effective than the old to-do lists. It implies that the good I am striving to do already exists within me (as I am learning it does), as opposed to trying to create a good habit I don't yet possess.*

I closed my journal entry with a last-minute thought surrounded by clouds of heavily inked asterisks: **Perhaps doing the things on my permission slip will help me get from one list to the other!**

I had spent the last eight months tending to my material, fleeting body. I had trained hard at the gym, eaten well, met with friends, and napped whenever I felt tired—all of which might be considered overly indulgent by certain fundamental religious groups.

Yet even the Bible questions, "If a brother or sister is poorly clothed and lacking in daily food, and one of you says to them, 'Go in peace, be warmed and filled,' without giving them the things needed for the body, what good is that?"[3]

Truly, our physical needs must be acknowledged before tending to our ethereal souls.

Therefore, after eight months of caring for my body, I finally felt physically capable to survive my own life. My muscles no longer burned with exhaustion when restraining Grayson. The daily stress relief led to an increase in patience, and my boosted energy sufficiently sustained my long days.

At last, I was starting to understand the interconnectedness between body, mind, and soul. I could not tend to one without caring for the other two, and the inverse was also true—I could not neglect one without neglecting all three.

Finally, I felt prepared to nurture my soul.

Ten days into pursuing wholehearted living, I wrote a new entry in my journal: *I know for certain that if "all" I do with my life is be a wife and a mother, yet a* happy *one, this will be* enough. *Indeed, in the pursuit of happiness, I find* God *and* peace *and* light.

I find it ironic that I described my grandmother's parting gift almost identically as "peace, light, and joy."

After fifteen days of wholehearted living, I wrote:

> *After watching videos of when the kids were babies, I notice how much less I now play and sit with them. Back then, it*

was a necessity. Now, it's a choice, but one still just as neces-
sary. Life with Grayson has worn me down yet somehow left
me with sharper edges.

At the same time, I know I was not "happy" back then.
My quietness was not a true peace but a panicked striving
to be what I thought I should be—submissive, cheerful, and
peaceful. There are so many things I don't remember, so much
time spent in robotic survival mode, so many days not spent
in genuine honesty or self-reflection. But I do remember the
emptiness and despair that were ever present. Indeed, that
time was like Plato's "Allegory of the Cave." I lived in the
shadow of reality but was absent from its fullness.

So what do I want for my next fifteen years? To develop
true joy, peace, and stillness, to soften, be happy, to live with
both eyes fully open and anchored in reality, and to focus on
genuine and natural beauty—not as the world dictates but as
I decide—an inner radiance.

Weeks later, Grayson had a massively public restraint session with the
police. I had originally told him I'd pick him up from school, but when
plans changed, I called his teacher and asked her to have him ride the
bus. He had been doing so well I didn't even consider how the sudden
shift might affect his behavior. But when his bus arrived, he suddenly
bolted down the sidewalk and off the school property. He made it six
blocks before his teachers caught up with him at a fairly busy intersection. Thankfully, he stopped and didn't rush headlong into traffic. But by
the time I arrived, he was being restrained by several police officers and
was literally frothing at the mouth. It took nearly thirty minutes to calm
him down, and the officers were on the verge of ordering an ambulance
for sedation and transport. Almost every child and parent in our small
town passed by that intersection on their way home from school. My
kids heard about the event long before they ever reached home.

Anger and despair always seemed to kick in three days after a traumatic episode, and this time was no exception. Right on cue, the typical heaviness began settling in my chest, along with a seething, boiling rage.

I'm a terrible mother, I wrote. *I'm so impatient, irritable, and angry. What is wrong with me?*

But then, I remembered my commitment to wholehearted living. I had given myself permission to be compassionate instead of judgmental—even, and especially, toward myself.

I turned to a new page in my journal and uncharacteristically wrote myself a letter in the third person:

> *Sweet girl, you are a good mom. It's been a hard week. Be patient with yourself. Grayson is tough. These big episodes deplete you, and it takes time to get back to level ground. You're more impatient and irritable because you're exhausted. Of course, this affects the rest of your parenting. Be easy on the other kids when you're feeling this way. Don't take it out on them. Spend more time sitting and enjoying them. Give God your pain. Stay home. Clean. You'll feel better in an organized environment. Read a book. Drink a glass of wine. Or two.*

Tears streamed down my face as I wrote this letter to myself. It had never occurred to me to care for myself through the act of compassion, and this tender deed elicited a pure form of self-love in return.

The terrible episode came and went. It burned like fire, but I was beginning to understand how to emerge less scorched.

I always expected that a journey to my soul's core would result in disappointment, uncovering the root of evil, or a cold, black void. I never thought I would find *light* and *goodness* and *beauty*.

I had spent years scanning the horizon, searching for signs of an evasive

God somewhere far-off in the distance. It never occurred to me to go inward or that I might begin finding Him within the fibers of my very being.

I remembered the husband of my youth and his words from long ago: "I want you to know I see God in you."

I laughed and dismissed him as crazy.

Never in my wildest dreams did I imagine he might be right.

PART TWO

Painful Beauty

26

Piercing

Everywhere is to be found the reflection of eternal light,
so that the light in the human spirit
may find its splendor and become entirely light.

—GREGORY NAZIANZEN, *Dogmatic Poems*

There was an experience.

Whether it occurred in a second or over the course of several weeks, I don't know. That sounds ridiculous, of course. How could I not grasp the details of something so significant, something that happened, nonetheless, to me?

Even so, I don't know.

All I know is that one morning in the fall of 2017, I was driving Grayson to his new middle school and happened to glance at a cornfield off to my right. In that moment, I was instantly and wholly enraptured, for the cornfield *was* light. It was not bathed in light or ablaze with light; it was somehow light itself. It was not a light that came from the slanting morning sun, though it most certainly could have been. But *that* light I knew, and *this* light was different. It seemed to have no point of origin; rather, it came from within, as if every stalk was somehow alight with its own luminosity. Time disappeared, and I do not say that figuratively, as if it merely slowed or stopped. It simply became irrelevant, as if it never even existed.

By some means, I could observe every cornstalk swaying independently in the breeze and yet simultaneously behold their movement as a unified whole. And the colors! They were unlike anything I'd ever seen. The green was perfectly *true*, like the original mold that all greens must have most certainly been cast from, and its intensity was so pure and vibrant that it penetrated my heart like a clean shard of glass.

I experienced a pain I had never before known. Not physical or even emotional, it tore me open from the inside-out and made me long to weep for the agony of the world, although in that instant, there were no tears to be shed.

I wondered: *What is this beauty so sharp it's perceived as pain?*

Whether on that day or another, I do not know, but while passing the same cornfield, an image appeared and embedded itself in my mind. Even now, I can close my eyes and conjure the image. Reminiscent of Michelangelo's *Creation of Adam*, its *feel* was entirely different. A hand was reaching through the clouds toward the cornfields, index finger extended straight. The hand of Adam was nowhere in sight, and a word came to me, although I am not certain how—certainly not with my ears. *Piercing.* My heart lurched at the word. It made no logical sense, yet it resonated profoundly within my soul. Pain and beauty, joy and sorrow, broken and whole—terms usually held in strict opposition—swirled together to become one and the same. PainfulBeauty. JoyfulSorrow. BrokenWholeness. And somehow, a place deep inside of me felt spacious enough to contain their newly compounded forms. I lost all sense of my location in space, as if I existed everywhere and nowhere, yet the feeling did not alarm me for I felt more found than ever. I felt suspended and cradled, shattered and renewed, pierced and also mended.

For days, or perhaps weeks, I followed the same routine. I dropped Grayson off at school and drove for hours on end. I followed dirt roads anywhere they led—over hills, past sheep farms, between waving fields of golden grain—and everywhere I looked, beauty pierced my soul and made me weep. The colors were too bright, the lines achingly crisp, the air overly pristine. Tears fell effortlessly from my eyes and cleansed me like a gently trickling stream whose source knew no end.

Yet no matter how hard I tried, I could not absorb or retain any remnant of beauty. It poured through me like water through a hole-filled bucket. Still, I longed to take the earth inside of myself, consume it, and *become* the beauty I beheld. I longed to unite myself with its otherworldliness, and the presence of tears mourned my separate otherness.

No matter how long I drove, it was never enough.

Like Christ on the cross, I had been pierced and wounded, and now suffered from an insatiable thirst that refused to be quenched. I knew not what I craved—only that this desire was unlike anything I'd ever known, and it expressed itself through my tears.

For weeks, I cried over sunsets, sunrises, flowers, even weeds. Books came to life; their words leaped from the page, interacting with my unspoken thoughts as if in direct response. Everything around me was ebbing and flowing, giving and taking, and for once, I was not a mere observer but an active participant. The surrounding world felt so vibrantly *alive* that I could scarcely take it all in.

I make no claims to understand my experience. All I know is that for three years after, I felt *acutely* aware of God's presence, sometimes as palpably as if He were sitting in the chair next to me, and I *never*, not for a single second, felt alone. I felt *infused*, as if my piercing had somehow resulted in an influx of energy. I was still *me*, but more *truly* me, like the green on the corn.

I can only say that whatever happened was a gift. Just as Newton's law states, "For every action, there is an equal and opposite reaction," so the depth of our suffering over the next three years would rival the blessing of encountering God's tangible presence.

In the rapidly encroaching years, we would find ourselves involved in several court battles. We would purchase a new home, only to have it nearly destroyed. Grayson would be expelled from his first year of middle school after multiple physical encounters with the police and a forced hospitalization. We would uncover our oldest son's cocaine and alcohol abuse and then leave him in the Arizona desert with twenty pairs of underwear and nothing more. A single phone call would instantly change our lives, and the image of an upside-down flattened truck would be forever seared in my brain. We would have surgeries, infections, and three fractured backs in one year.

But the destruction would force us to rebuild in every way possible. We would be ripped from our shallow soil only to be replanted on the other side where roots could grow deep in fertile, freshly churned earth.

Of course, I knew none of that then. All I knew was that I had perceived beauty as pain.

I would soon find that the inverse could also be true.

Breath-taking, soul-crushing, heart-wrenching pain could also be experienced as sublime light and beauty.

When Caleb fishes, he becomes *light*. Rivers and lakes are his natural environment. Out there, he melds with the earth, embraced by a belonging he's rarely found elsewhere. His dark skin is the color of rich dirt, and his eyes break through the water's surface to behold a world unseeable to my untrained eye. His rod is a mere extension of his arm and does exactly as he wishes, every time without fail. With a controlled flick of his wrist, he lays his line in crevices far too small. Already, he possesses the precision of a lifelong fisherman. He recalls the line and, in perfect cadence, sends it flying once more. It whips through the air, snakes across the water's surface beneath low-hanging branches, and then lands in the predetermined hollow—no snags, no tangles. Now, he makes it hop back to him, like a frog skipping across water, and I marvel at his skill. Back and forth, his line arcs and waves, and he is a craftsman weaving living lines of poetry. He joins the flow of the river, and his soul dances the slow dance of peace. Within him, I see all potential and fullness. He fishes for hours on end, from sunup to sundown, without remembering to eat. When he fishes, I know he is happy. I know he is held. I know he is safe.

Caleb and Rylee, ready for the homecoming dance, fall 2017

Caleb quit fishing the fall of 2017, and the light went out from his sixteen-year-old eyes. He slept and slept and could not be roused. Not for his junior year of school. Not even for fishing. A thieving darkness had settled in—or more likely, had long been present. Caleb finally wearied of fighting it and succumbed instead to sleep.

Rylee is all fire and all ice. When enflamed, she emanates love with every ounce of her being, and anything in her path, consenting or not, *will* be loved and consumed, whether frog, fish, lizard, baby bird, chinchilla, chicken . . . or boy. There is a perpetual innocence and childlike wonder about her, and she's continuously enamored by the universe. To me, this sets her apart in a cloud of holiness, but others see it and scoff, leaving her rightly confused and indignant. Her heart is too large to be contained, so she wears its excess on her sleeve. She absorbs the pain of the world and makes it her own, whether concerns of global warming, dying dolphins in Thailand, or the homeless man on the corner.

Everything hurts her, and she often grows saturated with grief. It's hard for her to seek good when she perceives suffering at every turn. She does not know how to love any less than wholly, and her greatest strength is also her greatest weakness. When her heart gets wounded, it extinguishes her flame and wraps her in a thick, protective sheet of ice. Love is withdrawn, and she inflicts pain to avoid feeling it. She is like a wild mustang, full of strength and beauty, who, although unbridled, has not yet learned what it means to be truly free. I think she will settle when she feels safe enough to love in abundance. The restraining of love makes her wild. Setting it loose will quiet her soul, and then she will run, unencumbered as God intended.

The fall of 2017 found Rylee huddled in a bathroom corner, clutching a handful of pills that conveyed the desperation her words could not. At just fourteen years old, she had naively searched for love where love could not be found and had prematurely been introduced to the world's cruel double standards where boys are praised and girls are shamed. Her loving flame turned into white-hot rage, and a hateful venom spewed continuously in my direction. She felt worthless and broken beyond repair.

Jacob is a silent healer. Wherever he goes, he leaves the world a better place. He spreads happiness through sparkling eyes that narrow into moon slivers whenever he smiles. Like Rylee, he senses the brokenness around him, but instead of absorbing it, he shoulders it and assumes it as his to repair. Being the middle child, he is the perpetual protector of peace and tries to heal his environment by never making a mistake. *Perfect.* It has long been the worst insult his siblings can think to hurl. He tolerates it with downcast eyes and says nothing.

He is frequently speechless and sneaks around behind the scenes without needing recognition. I listen as Grayson's agitation increases. Time and again, Jacob interjects and suggests the trampoline. "Let Mom rest. I'll play with you." He whispers it privately, so no one else hears. Other times, I emerge from one of Grayson's violent fits to find the kitchen miraculously clean and Jacob nowhere to be found. As much as I try to hide my post-fit red eyes, he still detects them, and I receive wordless hugs the rest of the day. He swallows his siblings' secrets and locks them tightly away unless doing so would lead to greater harm. After partaking in what he considers "snitching," he castigates himself for causing problems. At school, he is always respectful and works hard for good grades. He strives not for himself but to compensate for the shortcomings of his older siblings. When he struggles or does poorly, he berates himself for adding to our worry. He constantly carries a load that is not his to bear. Occasionally, he gets in trouble for doing something boyishly stupid, like squirting dish soap on the science lab floor and ice-skating circles around the bubbly slime. When we question him—a trace of laughter still lingering on our lips—he stares sheepishly at the ground in shame. Jacob cannot handle making mistakes.

Similar to Rylee, Jacob's greatest strength is also his greatest weakness. He would do anything to make anyone happy, even hide his own pain, much like the mound of Starburst wrappers I found crammed beneath his mattress when he was young. He would rather bury his problems than be the cause of our disappointment or concern.

In the fall of 2017, Jacob was *perfect*. He was a quarterback on the eighth-grade football team and had the sweetest group of friends. He was

Arin and Jacob with the dirt bike, fall 2017

always happy and agreeable and never complained or got in trouble. Jacob careened through the year problem-free, politely creating room for us to deal with other, more pressing issues. Like a gentleman, he waited his turn, and only years later, after everyone went first, would he finally crumble and acknowledge *his* pain.

Reagan's name means "little ruler," and if born in a different time, a regal queen she would be. For someone so young, she carries herself with a noble dignity that is both self-contained and largely untouchable, although she is yet unaware of the grace, strength, and beauty she possesses. A lifetime of living beneath Grayson has made her fair, merciful, and serious and has bequeathed her with a quiet but stolid firmness disproportionate to her age. She does not bend, buckle, or act contrary to her nature, and to those with less fortitude, she may be perceived as aloof. Her very aura seems to casually suggest, "Take me as I am or leave me be." While she recognizes that her unwillingness to conform may lead to solitude, she would rather be friendless than coupled with hypocrisy.

She is wise beyond her years and could become anything she wanted. But she's also old beyond her years and therefore perfectly content to curl up with her cat while listening to Willie Nelson on her vintage record player. She belongs anywhere and everywhere, whether castle, cattle ranch, or eras of old. Yet this internal diversity causes her to believe she belongs nowhere at all. This assumption grows loudest among her peers. Their pre-adolescent silliness is gibberish to her, and I mentally concede that life thrust her into an unripened maturity when she was just fresh from the cradle. She bypassed the normal stages of childhood development—fun and girlish giddiness included. I often watch her shoulders wilt into a remorseful slump. While she rarely feels the need to defend her choices, she's constantly apologizing for *herself.* One day, she will come face-to-face with her own glory, and it will be more terrifying than the sum of her perceived flaws. Then she will stand erect, with shoulders back and head held high, and will rule over any domain she pleases.

Reagan and me at my parents' cabin, fall 2017

In the fall of 2017, I studied Reagan's eyes. Something caught my attention and struck me as odd. Upon closer examination, I noticed that half her eyelashes were missing, plucked out one by one until whole sections were cleared. The discovery knifed my soul. What kind of heartache causes a fifth-grade girl to harvest her eyelashes one at a time?

I know now—it's the kind that comes from hiding under desks, alone and afraid, as wine bottles hurl through the air and explode like Molotov cocktails, and angry screams penetrate and rattle both walls and nerves. When Caleb wasn't sleeping, he was raging, and the fighting had grown loud and intense, especially between him and Arin. Our household could be a scary place for a ten-year-old girl, so she coped by narrowing her focus. She escaped the ear-splitting, verbal bloodshed by creating a mini-kingdom beneath a desk, where she felt safe and in control. From the privacy of her fortress, she comforted her stuffed animals, possessed by a grit unknown to her child-self. Drawing from her newfound courage, which felt more like fear, she honored herself by discreetly revealing her pain, normally too small and unimportant. In silent solitude, she pushed back chaos and bravely found a way to cry out for help.

And all this was accomplished—one eyelash at a time.

27

Begging

It was the helplessness that scared the both of us.

—Lois Lowry, *A Summer to Die*

Fall 2017. The time had come for sixth grade—for Grayson to venture beyond the safety of the SOAR walls and join a "real" school with passing periods, loads of students, and a different teacher for every class.

He performed flawlessly the first three days. Then he decided he'd had enough. He was finished with middle school. And every day thereafter was a chore.

It's so warm in the car, he'd say, and outside was so cold. Couldn't he sit five minutes more? Three? Just one? Couldn't he skip one tiny day of school? Half a day? One hour? At last, when all his suggestions ran dry, he'd slip one arm through a backpack strap, then the other, and slowly ooze from the car one body part at a time like a giant blob of slime. He'd shut the door inch by inch, giving me ample opportunity to reconsider, and then suddenly jerk it back open, enlightened with a new reason why he should be allowed back home. The cycle repeated itself ad nauseam:

Grayson, fall 2017

Slooowly shuuut. Jerk back open. Interject new idea. Shuuut. Open. Shuuut. Open.

"Enough!"

My loud explosion and the sudden slamming of my hands against the steering wheel finally broke his redundant cycle. Attending school was a nonnegotiable, I informed him, and something he'd simply have to learn to manage.

At long last, Grayson would close the door for good and then firmly affix his gaze on the ground. He would turn, walk dejectedly toward the school without ever looking back, and then disappear into the building he hated more than he'd ever hated anything before.

I should have considered why, but I didn't.

Twelve days into middle school, Grayson threatened to put a staple through his finger. Mrs. Ballard, his new special-ed teacher and a new teacher in general, immediately called for help. Then, she and her backup team instantly moved into a full restraint.

In all my prior experiences, restraints were always the last resort, never the first.

I arrived at the school six minutes later, where I was greeted by the *new* secretary and escorted down the *new* hall to Grayson's *new* classroom, where I encountered the most downcast group of women I'd ever beheld. Six or seven pairs of red-rimmed, teary eyes looked anywhere but at me. Several hands dabbed bleeding wounds with damp paper towels, and sniffles could be heard all around the semicircle of teachers and aides just inside the door.

Unlike the stalwart, take-charge SOAR teachers, this doe-eyed bunch of women skittishly shuffled sideways to make space as I entered the room, and I distinctly recall feeling like they had been awaiting my arrival to receive further instructions.

Suddenly, they broke their silence. One after another, they began relaying their personal experiences: "Grayson hit me. He bit me. He headbutted Ms. Something-or-other; I think she's getting checked for a concussion."

This barrage of information nearly bowled me over, and I stepped back to allow their forceful words room to dissipate. I instantly felt like a recess monitor sifting through mounds of middle-school tattling. Only this time, the bully was my son.

I began apologizing profusely, ashamed that I'd given birth to someone so capable of causing such mass destruction. Still, the teachers' energy remained frenzied, and they chattered among themselves, comparing notes even as we migrated down the long hall to the conference room.

Upon arriving, I was shocked to find a sheriff's deputy seated at one end of the long, formidable table. Straightaway, he bluntly inquired whether anyone in the room desired to press assault charges against my eleven-year-old autistic son. I briskly scanned the faces on my left and then my right, desperate to connect with anyone who found the question as ludicrous as I did.

But everyone was business as usual—shuffling papers, filling out forms, neatly arranging pens in straight rows—so I sat back in my chair and resigned myself to our new reality.

I had known the day was coming when Grayson could legally be charged as an adult; I just didn't expect it would happen so soon.

One by one, the teachers answered out loud. Most replied definitively and incredulously, "No, I do *not* wish to press charges." But a few stared at the table and almost imperceptibly shook their heads *no*, and I got the impression they might have answered differently had I not been present.

When everything was said and done, the deputy wrapped up the meeting by instructing me to expect a phone call from the Department of Health Services, Colorado's agency for children's well-being. He didn't expect a lengthy investigation. If we were lucky, a phone call would suffice.

Fortunately, we were lucky. That time.

Grayson received his first in-school suspension (ISS) on October 26, 2017, for threatening Mrs. Ballard. He spent the entire following day, his twelfth birthday, in the principal's office. Another suspension was issued two weeks later for a similar offense.

Much to my embarrassment, it was only then that I realized Grayson was taking *eight straight academic classes—every single day*. While all the "regular" students had schedules interspersed with elective classes like PE, art, and music, Grayson's teacher and guidance counselor instead had signed him up for double math and language art classes—one special education and one general ed.

They assumed he might be more motivated to behave if they required him to "earn" his electives. Therefore, they expected my son, who could barely sit still or understand a mere fraction of what was being taught, to sit through eight academic classes without reprieve. The administration then had the audacity to suspend him for poor behavior.

Immediately, I requested that he be enrolled in PE and a 3D printing class I felt certain he'd enjoy.

But as usual, things would have to get significantly worse before they got better.

The day before Thanksgiving, I coyly suggested dinner with Arin and the kids at one of our favorite restaurants. I'd been working on Arin's Christmas present for weeks and could not stand waiting any longer. A large manilla envelope contained several smaller white ones, and the main letter read something that loosely paraphrased Andy Dufresne, one of Arin's favorite characters in *The Shawshank Redemption*: "Get busy living or get busy dying."

In my letter, I told Arin that I was no longer content living separate lives and invited him on a trip down memory lane to revisit where we'd come from and reenvision where we were heading. Inside each white envelope were five separate one-day itineraries for a trip I'd planned to California. We would fly into Palm Springs to watch Willie Nelson in concert and then take a road trip up the Pacific Coast Highway all the way to San Francisco. Stops along the way included our college in Riverside where we'd first met; the nearby Mission Inn (where a security guard once caught us making out); the Mexican restaurant on the Santa Monica Pier, where we'd had our first date; the deserted Maricopa land where he grew up; and a special pit stop near Pismo Beach to visit his father's grave.

Rylee captured Arin's face on camera as it contorted every which way in failed attempts to suppress his tears. With a long, passionate kiss right in the middle of the restaurant, he agreed to accompany me to California and "get busy living."

On January 5, 2018, we closed the deal on a ranch-style house on five acres, and by January 8, Arin and I were cruising top-down in a convertible from Palm Springs to San Francisco.

We had started talking about moving the day Grayson slipped away on his bike unnoticed and made it nearly ten miles down busy roads before one of Rylee's friends spotted him and called to alert us. Grayson needed more space, we had determined. *We* needed more space, we'd emphatically resolved.

Shortly after, we made an offer on a forty-year-old house out in the country.

Within one hour of assuming possession, we, my whole extended family, and Sean, our new contractor, descended on the new home to begin demolition.

It was originally painted salmon pink and was chock-full of yellow oak, green Formica countertops, and looping beige Berber carpet. But, by then, I had fully learned I could change anything I didn't like, and besides, it sat on five glorious, private acres surrounded by mature and stately trees. Additionally, the subdivision's HOA policy was relatively lax, which meant Rylee and Reagan could finally have chickens (and, they prayed, a few horses), and the boys could ride dirt bikes as recklessly as their worrywart mother would allow.

Within three days, we had that house torn apart, all the way down to the studs in some places. I ordered new cabinets, appliances, doors, railings, and flooring, and upon returning from our California trip, I spent every hour of every school day working alongside Sean.

That was one reason I chose him; he didn't mind me working on-site and underfoot and even took the time to teach me skills I'd never learned, like installing lights and hanging sheetrock. He, his wife, Rachel, and their five young children were new to the area, and I felt confident I could help get his construction business underway by introducing him to the local subcontractors and vendors I'd met during my few short years in the design industry.

Being that both of us had large families, we had a certain camaraderie and an unspoken level of flexibility. He brought his kids to the house when his wife was sick, and I picked up supplies and pizza to save him time. Soon enough, Rachel and I developed a friendship, and she occasionally kept me company while I painted and amused me with funny stories about Sean and her kids.

Despite Grayson's tumultuous struggles at school, my time at our new house was blissful. Sean was an agreeable work partner, and for seven hours each day, my world grew as small as the paint stroke before me. Strains of Norah Jones echoed lyrically through the house, and the productive sound of Sean's tools confirmed that our country house would be complete in no time.

I was standing on the top rung of a ladder painting when my phone lit up with a call from Grayson's school. It was 1:45 p.m. on February 20. Grayson had run away. Again. I hung up the phone, slowly descended the ladder, and calmly let Sean know I'd return as soon as possible.

The school's official report read:

> *On the way to his classroom, Grayson opened an outside door and said, "I'm out of here." Nan said, "No." Once in the classroom, he began grabbing things. Mandy told Grayson "he knows the rules," meaning he couldn't do that. He grabbed his jacket and ran out of her room, down the hall, and out the back door of the cafeteria. Nan followed, he stopped and hid behind the dumpster and threw snowballs at her, then ran across the road after jumping in front of two cars. He then ran further west into the field and hid between the feed bags. Once Brett and Nan caught up to him, he fled north over the fence into another field and hid in a shed. Gary and Amanda (from an SUV) told Grayson, "Mom is on her way. You need to make better choices," as he was running out of the shed to the other field. He started walking back to the car and Gary said, "Your mom is looking for you." Grayson got in the car, and everyone rode back to school together. The sheriff was on the road when we headed back to school and followed us. Brett told Grayson he needed to get out of the car and walk straight to the office. The officer, Nan, Brett, Gary, and Dwight walked into the building with Grayson. He stopped walking in the breezeway before entering the office. He hesitated, then went outside when he didn't see mom. He then picked up a rock and postured to throw it. The officer said he wasn't in trouble*

but would be if he continued. Grayson then slammed down the rock and told the officer to "Shut the fuck up and get the fuck away from me." He then hit and shoved the officer, and the officer restrained him to the ground. Mom pulled up and started to talk to Grayson and calmed him down. Once restrained, Grayson said, "Kill me, just kill me. I want to die." At this point, the sheriff took over, and the ambulance was called. Paramedics arrived to take vitals, and the sheriff insisted he go to the hospital for a psych. eval.

Everything happened as the school said. But there was more.

I arrived and calmed Grayson down, as reported. The deputy had promised Grayson could come home with me if I assuaged him—which I did. But then he called for an ambulance anyway—just to be safe—and Grayson panicked, flew into another rage, screamed that he wanted to die, and started dashing his head against the cement.

In return, the deputy ordered a seventy-two-hour suicide hold to be placed on my son.

Instantly, my thoughts grew still and silent as the winter air. I noted the frozen remnants of smeared tears and snot that crackled across Grayson's ruddy cheeks in a thin, white film and the dark blue veins pulsating through his red, chilled arms in the absence of a coat. I felt the reverberation in my knees as his bare feet hammered the cold concrete, and I grew acutely aware of the six staff members towering above us in a closed circle as if we were a caged exhibit at the zoo.

Tread lightly, an inner voice cautioned. *If you push this deputy, he will shove back ten times harder—just because he can.*

"Sir," I began pleading, hot tears streaming down my already burning cheeks, "my son is autistic, not suicidal. He says all kinds of crazy things when he's mad. Please don't transport him in the ambulance; he'll be terrified."

I turned to the six towering staff members for validation, but not a single one met my eyes or spoke on our behalf.

The deputy's rigid posture remained as unyielding as his decision, and he firmly informed me that whenever anyone threatened personal bodily harm, it was his duty to take them seriously and respond accordingly.

Growing frantically desperate, I began groveling, shamelessly pleading for the deputy to not take my son.

Still, no one spoke.

All too quickly, the ambulance arrived. A fresh wave of terror washed over Grayson, and I had to practically lie on top of him to keep him pinned to the ground. Suddenly, as the ambulance driver stopped the vehicle, Grayson's face blanched, and—petrified—he turned stock-still. Pulling him stiffly to his feet, I asked the deputy if, at the very least, I could be the one to transport him. We would go to the hospital, I swore. I would check him in and do anything he told me; I just wanted to be able to drive Grayson myself and prepare him for whatever might ensue.

Even then, the deputy refused. Policy was policy, after all.

But a kindhearted ambulance driver reassuringly winked at me from behind the deputy's back. Overriding the deputy's decision, he claimed he saw no reason for Grayson to ride in the ambulance as he was now perfectly calm.

Surprisingly, the deputy relented.

Grayson got into my car without a word, buckled his seat belt, reclined his seat, and instantly fell asleep. I spent the entire twenty-minute drive to the emergency room trying to calm my pounding heart and continuously sneaking peeks in my rearview mirror at the deputy, who was following closely behind. I felt sure that if I went one mile over the speed limit or broke a single law, the deputy would gladly make an example of *my* reckless deeds.

Upon arriving at the hospital, Grayson trudged through the sliding doors, entirely defeated. After ensuring we would be taken to a room, the deputy pulled the doctor aside and ordered the seventy-two-hour suicide hold.

Meanwhile, I was in the exam room, trying to keep Grayson from once again losing his mind. The nurse requested the white Cassio watch he never, ever removed. I asked her to make an exception, and thankfully she obliged. A new nurse came in with a scratchy pair of cotton scrubs. Grayson outright refused to wear them, and once more, I asked that he be allowed to remain in his street clothes until seen by a doctor. Again, the new nurse agreed. Next someone from the lab arrived, carrying a plastic cup. Grayson practically climbed to the top of my head and made it abundantly clear there was no way he'd ever urinate in a cup. The lab technician graciously relented.

I began preparing myself for the worst; I envisioned him alone in a hospital for three days, being inundated with his first non-gluten-free, non-egg-free, and non-dairy-free food in years, and I shuddered at the havoc I knew it would wreak on his system. Grayson had never been without us unless he was with my family, and I knew by his growing agitation that we were quickly approaching another massive blowup.

Fortunately, a competent psychologist soon arrived to examine Grayson and immediately recognized the debilitating limitations of his autism and the trauma that would be unduly inflicted by seventy-two hours alone in the hospital. She released him to return home five hours after we'd arrived, despite the sheriff's orders.

But the damage was already done.

I now knew how quickly and easily someone in authority could take my son from me, and as long as I live, I will never forget the humiliation and terror of having to beg to keep my child.

When I left the hospital that day, the world looked different, darker somehow. For the first time in my life, all the people I'd been taught to trust—teachers, principals, counselors, police officers, and to a lesser degree, doctors—had betrayed me. I felt like I had been exposed to a dirty little secret: that all the people I once believed to be good were, in fact, not so good at all.

I wrapped my coat around me high and tight to block out all of them and then intentionally sped all the way home to the only safe haven I knew.

28

———

Demolishing

We are threatened with suffering from three directions:
from our own body, . . . from the external world, . . .
and finally from our relations with other men.
The suffering which comes from this last source is perhaps
more painful to us than any other.

—Sigmund Freud, *Civilization and Its Discontents*

O ut in the country, our remodel slowed to a crawl. Sean always had
reasons for any delays—supply shortages, missing tools, wiring
issues—and I didn't think much of it till I started noticing little clues.
There was the lone vodka bottle in the bottom of the dumpster, then an
empty shooter poking out from the insulation between the studs, and
finally, the skinny brown bag crumpled in the back of a bathroom cabinet.

Feasibly, it could have been anyone—the plumber, the drywaller, or
even one of my kids, as Sean pointed out. But the pit in my stomach suggested otherwise.

One time, I entered the house late at night to check on Sean's progress. He had recently started arriving later in the day—purportedly to help with his kids—and then staying until nearly midnight to make up for lost time. I admired his dedication to his family and ours. He had committed to finishing our house by summer, and I appreciated his willingness to work overtime to keep his word. Besides, we were still living in our old house while the new one was under construction, so Sean's late nights were irrelevant to Arin and me.

That night, although Sean's truck was parked outside, the inside of the house was pitch-black and silent, save for a few dim basement lights. There were no banging hammers or whining drills, so I crept warily downstairs, calling Sean's name the whole way. Rounding the corner, I encountered him sleeping on the lone piece of furniture in the basement. He jumped up, ashamed, and apologized repetitively for sleeping on the job, promising it would never happen again.

I supposed I was pushing him rather hard to meet my summer deadline and sent him home without giving the occurrence a second thought.

On a different late night, I entered the house after Sean had left, only to hear the faint trickle of running water. By the time I descended the basement stairs, the trickling had turned into a gushing, and a waterfall was streaming from a ceiling vent.

Sean's explanation was simple, as was his solution. A valve had been left open while the water was off, with a bucket underneath. Before leaving, he had turned the water back on, but the bucket apparently muffled the sound of running water. After he left, the bucket clearly overflowed and poured down the nearest vent, flooding the basement. He would repair the drywall, he assured me, and luckily, the basement flooring hadn't been laid, so no damage there.

I chalked up that episode to a careless mistake.

I did find it strange that his wife or assistant drove him to work every day and that he never answered his phone on the weekends. It was also curious that his young children anxiously plastered themselves to my dining room window while awaiting his return on the one night he asked to borrow my car to run to the hardware store. Never mind that it was ten o'clock at night and the store was closed, or the fact he came back an hour later empty-handed. I had neither the time nor energy to manage Sean. He was a grown man, the father of five, and I was juggling enough plates of my own.

On May 1, four months after the start of demolition, I found myself racing to the bathroom after neglecting my natural urge all day long. I was going to quickly spring a leak of my own if I didn't get there soon.

My phone was pressed tightly to my ear in anticipation. Grayson had run away from school. Again. Police had been called. Again. Being so over the school's incompetent staff, I asked Arin to go in my stead, even though he'd never personally handled one of Grayson's school emergencies.

Besides, Sean had been missing for more than forty-five minutes, and I needed to keep things moving at the house.

"They've got Grayson," Arin informed me over the phone in a tight, controlled voice, "but I'm not sure whether they're going to release him to come home. Hold on a minute; I'm still negotiating with the police."

In the meantime, having finally arrived at my newly hung bathroom door, I frantically slammed my hand down against the lever. But to my surprise, it didn't budge. I knocked on the door and called Sean's name, but no one answered. Arin's muffled voice was still speaking in the background of my earpiece. Exasperated, I figured one of my kids had pranked me. Swiping my fingers across the top of the door jamb, I found the key and hurriedly unlocked the door.

It swung halfway open before colliding with the softness of a body.

There was Sean on my bathroom floor, curled around the toilet in a fetal position. I threw my body against the door to force it open and then nudged him awake. He reeked of vodka, his eyes were blood-red, and his hair was poking every which way but down.

Still, I had to ask.

"Sean, what's wrong?" I demanded, shaking his shoulders. "Are you drunk? Oh, God. Don't do this to me, Sean. I can't handle this right now."

Suddenly, I realized Arin had been talking in my left ear. "Yes, yes, I can hear you. Sorry, there's a lot going on over here. They're releasing Grayson to come home? Okay, that's great. Yeah, see you soon."

Sean was now falling asleep in my arms.

"*Sean! Wake up!*" I screamed in his face. "Arin will be home in *six minutes!* You can't do this to me. You're a good man. Your family needs you. I need you. I need you to finish my house; the kids get out of school in *ten days!* I need to get my life in order. I need you to be sober! *Please, just get up and finish!*"

By then, Sean and I were on our knees next to my toilet—forehead to forehead—and both of us were sobbing.

"It's bad," he was crying. "It's so bad."

Ignoring him, I forced him to stand. In my absolute desperation, I illogically began begging the drunk man who had just been passed out on my toilet floor to get busy remodeling my beloved country house.

All I could picture was Arin walking through our freshly painted front door, taking stock of the situation, and then picking up Sean—who was practically half his height—and pitching him into our bright pink construction dumpster.

If Sean was not up and moving in less than six minutes, we would *all* be dealing with an entirely different sort of mess.

I met Arin on the front porch, partially to create physical distance between him and Sean and partly to discuss the afternoon's events privately. Six months prior, Arin had started his own oil field business, intent on being more present at home. But after Grayson's first year of middle school, I seriously wondered whether his old position might appear more alluring.

From our weathered, gray Adirondack chairs, I watched Arin's truck roll into the driveway. It crept to a stop, and I craned my neck to witness Grayson silently slipping from the truck toward the garage door; he didn't want to see me any more than I wanted to see him. Slowly, Arin slid out of his truck. Trudging toward the porch, he dragged his heavy, steel-toed boots down our long sidewalk as if they were still filled with oily sludge. Letting out a long, exasperated sigh, he plopped down in his chair, and I instantly regretted asking him to attend to Grayson's emergency. He was new to the game and cold off the bench, whereas I had years of experience and had developed a certain amount of immunity that somewhat helped me survive.

Arin's face was drained of all color, and his eyes were sunken and black. He melted into the cracks of the chair like he hadn't a bone in his body and stared blankly into space.

Bit by bit, his voice flat, he brought me up to speed.

The school report read: "After asking for a break in the wrestling room, Grayson instead ran outside and began throwing rocks at Ms. Harrison and Mrs. Wallace, hitting one in the leg and the other in the hand. Shortly after, the dad arrived in the parking lot and Grayson entered the truck."

Once again, the report was accurate. But again, there was so much more.

With Grayson sitting in the truck, a new deputy instructed Arin to wait while he spoke with the involved teacher and aide. Ms. Harrison was fine, the deputy said, but Mrs. Wallace had a "minor abrasion" on her leg, and he needed to check whether or not she intended to press charges.

After several long minutes—which in hindsight coincided with my discovery of Sean lying wrapped around our toilet—the deputy returned.

"I tried my best to discourage her," he confided to Arin, "but she's insistent on pressing charges. Unfortunately, I'm going to have to take your son into custody, where he will remain until a court date can be set."

Then it was Arin's turn to beg, and this he literally did from bended knee.

The thought of my massive, bearded oil field husband groveling was nearly more than I could bear. He was such a strong, proud, and mighty man, and I wondered what it cost him to beg in such a way.

Assuredly, it's the invisible things we take for granted—security, power, control, and the unshakeable confidence our children will return home every night.

For nearly five minutes, Arin pleaded to take Grayson home, fervently trying to reassure the deputy that his son did *not* belong in juvenile hall. He was *autistic*, not a *criminal.*

Again, the deputy held fast to his position while Arin swore up and down he would have Grayson at court at any time on any day and we would accept each and every allocated consequence. But, he continued, to arrest him would only result in horror for everyone involved.

"Look," pressed Arin, "as of now, Grayson is calmly seated in my truck. The second you pull out your cuffs, he'll go ballistic. He *will* try to escape, grab for your gun, and try to attack you. He'll be terrified. Right now, you have within your power the opportunity to send him home, where he *feels* safe and *will be* safe, and I promise to have him in court any time you say. If you take him to juvenile hall, he'll be a cornered animal. It will be bad for them and worse for him."

He reasoned on and on until, finally, Arin sensed a slight softening and wavering within the deputy. For a brief moment, they saw eye to eye, and titles like *citizen* and *deputy* fell away, leaving behind only two men.

After a long, silent pause, the deputy reluctantly agreed to release Grayson to Arin's care. In return, Arin gave his solemn vow that we would appear in court with Grayson the following day.

Back on the porch, I quickly slipped in that I had found Sean passed out on our bathroom floor. A fire sparked in Arin's eyes, and he rose immediately to terminate Sean's employment. Sitting him back down, I reasoned with him that we needed our house to be finished. It was so close to being done, and it would take so much work to find someone new. Besides, didn't we have other, more critical issues to deal with?

Surrendering to my suggestion, Arin immediately forgot about Sean and then disappeared into the house and buried himself in a heap of lively phone conversations.

To this day, I regret not allowing Arin to follow through on his instinct.

29

Litigating

It was then that Hook bit him. Not the pain of
this but its unfairness was what dazed Peter. It made him
quite helpless. He could only stare, horrified. . . .
No one ever gets over the first unfairness.

—James Matthew Barrie, *Peter and Wendy*

The following day, our group filled two rows at the courthouse. Mr. Roth, Grayson's SOAR teacher and respite provider, had dropped everything to be present. Eric, our new lawyer, had been sent by Arin's business partner in support of our family at no cost to us, and sitting beside Arin, Grayson, and me were our four other children dressed in their Sunday best. We had spoken earnestly with them the night prior and informed them their attendance was nonnegotiable. When times get tough, family steps up. This they did beautifully (of course, skipping school was a bonus), and for one day, all bad attitudes, dark depressions, and raging tempers were set aside to support Grayson. Arin and I were desperate to prove to the judge that Grayson had a loving family and a solid support system and that he did *not* belong in juvenile hall. We stopped just shy of dragging my entire extended family to court—only because doing so would have entirely overwhelmed Grayson.

Before entering the courtroom, Eric took a moment to prep Grayson. He was a meek, quiet man who knew nothing about autism. But he addressed Grayson directly when speaking and treated him as respectfully as he would any high-paying client. For that, Arin and I adored him. He explained that Grayson would be required to stand before the judge, speak his name loudly and clearly, and then assert whether or not he understood the third-degree assault charges. Third-degree assault, he let us know, was a Class 1 misdemeanor, committed when a person either knowingly or recklessly causes bodily injury to another by use of a deadly weapon. He then asked Grayson to sign his name on a document.

Grayson printed only his first name. The letters were large and misshapen and could have been better written by most five-year-olds. He was twelve and still could not write his last name without asking how to spell it.

My child, who could barely write his name, much less *sign* it, was being tried as an *adult*—for assault in the third degree. The absurdity was beyond comprehension.

As court commenced, one juvenile after another was brought in from a holding room through a door on the left. Each wore an orange or green jumpsuit, and a few were handcuffed at both wrists and ankles. All were ushered in by an officer and had been transported from juvenile hall. I shuddered to imagine Grayson's response to such itchy uniforms and whispered a silent prayer of gratitude that he had been allowed to spend the night at home surrounded by family and could appear before the judge in his fuzzy black sweatpants and a broken-in cotton T-shirt.

Eric had requested that Grayson go last so fewer people would be present. The downside was that we first had to sit through fifteen to twenty cases, and Grayson was already on the verge.

The proceedings commenced, and as the judge entered the courtroom, Grayson crawled under the bench and hid instead of standing.

A nine-year-old girl took the stand for shoplifting, and Grayson found a pencil and started pantomiming stabbing himself. A police officer turned his head at the commotion, but I quickly swiped the pencil from Grayson's hand and pinned his arm to his side.

Next, a seventeen-year-old boy was brought in for stealing his mother's car. She was fed up with his behavior and, through tears, requested the maximum punishment the judge would allow. At this, Grayson wriggled free from my grasp, looked the officer square in the face, and pretended to slit his own throat. Fortunately, the officer's attention was diverted, and I again assumed control of Grayson's problematic arms. He then began inquiring about the officers' guns and what they would do if he tried to escape.

A thirteen-year-old girl came before the judge. Her expression was smug, her demeanor cocky. She had assaulted her best friend, who she claimed "deserved it," and, in doing so, had violated her prior restraining order. The judge issued a harsh sentence, and her father erupted loudly in tears, exclaiming, "My baby!" Squeezing roughly past the others in his row, he stormed through the back doors, ranting the entire way.

Never one to miss an opportunity, Grayson followed hot on his heels and headed straight for the elevator.

Every elevator button was glowing by the time I caught up with him. The girl's father was still hollering in the lobby, which, lucky for us, consumed the officers' attention. Grayson was practically hopping from foot to foot, anticipating the moving box that would soon dash him away from such madness to freedom. The elevator was still on the lowest floor, and I sincerely prayed it would stay there. I explained what would happen if he ran away, confident he would unlikely avoid arrest yet again.

After a long, tense moment, Grayson agreed to return to the courtroom; I don't even want to imagine what would have happened had those elevator doors opened.

Two hours later, we were the last family left, and the judge called Grayson's name. Arin and I flanked him to keep him in place and took our predetermined seats at the table. Eric stood to our right.

I had no idea what Grayson would do. I envisioned him rising abruptly, flipping the table, clearing the podium, and attacking the judge. He was deathly still, which was the one mannerism I could never interpret. We waited anxiously in the eye of the storm, waiting to see which way it would blow.

Yet, when requested, he stood and articulated his name loudly and clearly. He replied politely to the judge as we'd instructed, "Yes, sir," and shockingly presented better than every child who had spoken prior.

For a brief moment, we felt an unexpected burst of pride. There stood our son, who could barely write his name. He'd been thrust into a horrid situation, yet there he was, tall and erect, addressing the judge clearly and respectfully.

It was always the smallest moments that infused us with strength.

Eric spoke on Grayson's behalf and explained that he understood *why* he was there and had acknowledged his actions were wrong. However, he did not fully comprehend his charges or what was at stake.

Grayson then "signed" a restraining order, agreeing to avoid Mrs. Wallace (which would no longer be an issue once the school expelled him).

The bailiff set a new court date, and court was adjourned.

Grayson was mute and stiff as a board the whole elevator ride and didn't say a word while walking through the lower lobby. But the moment we stepped into the fresh air, he ran wild, as if ignited on fire, and let loose with torrential screams and angry cuss words long repressed.

Arin was back in the courthouse, still debriefing with Eric, so I managed to corral Grayson to my car. After shutting both doors, I let him scream and scream until he had nothing left to expel. I stared straight through the windshield and—chin quivering—*dared* a police officer to approach my car in rebuke.

When Grayson was done expelling all the rage and frustration within him, his body went limp, and he collapsed into my arms and allowed me to hold him. We cried together until our tears ran dry and then drove to Red Robin to celebrate the grandest act of courage I'd ever beheld.

The following Sunday, Mrs. Wallace reportedly showed up to her church on crutches—her "minor abrasion" wrapped in a thick ACE bandage. This we heard from one of my children's friends who attended the same church. The friend said Mrs. Wallace and her husband were bragging to her and an encircled group of friends that they were going to teach "that little punk who hit her with a rock" a lesson.

I called the school the next day and politely requested their staff members keep our family business private.

A year or two later, I spotted Mrs. Wallace in the grocery store. My muscles tensed and twitched, itching for the fight they never got, and I had to seriously resist my impulse to get a running start from the end of the aisle and challenge her to a game of grocery-cart chicken. I imagined the satisfying crunch of metal, her groceries spiraling through the air, and plowing all the way through the cart into her legs, which I fully intended to send flying over her head. Raging, I began salivating in anticipation and gripped the handlebar of my cart so tightly my hands shook.

Then I parked my cart—half-full of groceries—and walked out of the store. I did nothing noble that day. I did not pray for my enemies or bless those who had persecuted us.

But I also didn't kill Mrs. Wallace, and I figured that counted for something.

Several years after the near grocery store encounter, Reagan was in the same math class as Mrs. Wallace's daughter. From her desk, Reagan overheard the daughter laughing and sharing about "the psycho kid" her mom had taken to court to teach a lesson.

I called the principal and asked her to ensure my daughter would never have to endure such humiliation at school. Then I closed my eyes, took a deep breath, and cut Mrs. Wallace loose from my thoughts. I don't know whether that was the same as forgiveness, but my anger dissipated, and the woman never again crossed my mind.

Grayson was expelled from school one month before the school year officially ended. Now, I could work on my house *and* monitor Sean with Grayson in tow, as well as figure out how to wrap up the other major design projects I'd been overseeing. There was my mom's century-old Craftsman house we had completely gutted; a multigenerational farmhouse that needed not only gutting but a new addition; our church, which was receiving a massive facelift; and approximately four other smaller-scale jobs.

My phone rang nonstop. If it wasn't one thing, it was another. Additionally, Grayson had two upcoming court dates, and we had sold our old house and were officially living in an active construction zone.

I walked into the kitchen late one night after the kids were finally sleeping. The sink was still full of dinner dishes, and my following day was jam-packed. Summoning my last bit of energy, I pulled up my sleeves and turned on the water. Nothing. No water streamed forth from my faucet. *Fabulous.*

Sean had been working on something earlier that required the water to be shut off, I reminded myself. He must have forgotten to turn it back on. Irritated, I stomped down the basement stairs and opened the main supply.

Instantly, I heard loud, gushing water. Frantic, I traced the source to the girls' bathroom, where water was forcefully spraying out from behind the toilet and had already soaked clean through the drywall to flood their new floor. I twisted the lever behind the toilet to shut off the water. Still, it shot out like a horizontal geyser. Racing back to the mechanical room, I shut off the main water supply once more.

I called Sean to fix the leak and requested that once finished, he never again set foot in our new but already broken house.

My nightmares grew worse after he left. For months, I rarely slept through the night without jolting awake in a cold sweat. I dreamed of black smoke pouring out of attic vents, my children still trapped inside, and no matter how hard I tried to shake the nightmares, they still came in droves. Finally, I gathered enough energy to hire a licensed plumber and electrician.

The electrician found more than *fifty* exposed live wires in my attic—some within a quarter-inch of one another and others buried in pink insulation. I had electricity running through my bathroom faucet, which I inadvertently discovered when I touched my face to the metal and received a sharp zap. And once, when Rylee bumped the ceiling with her volleyball, all the lights on the main floor went dark.

Almost every toilet and new shower fixture had been leaking behind the walls. The hot faucet ran cold water, and my steam dryer had been vented straight into the attic instead of properly through the roof. After one Colorado summer, my entire attic would have been full of mold and mildew. Grout had been flushed down multiple toilets straight into our septic system, and we were frequently without hot water, as the plumber discovered our brand-new hot water heater brimming with drywall dust.

Even awake, my mind still imagined the worst. The sound of dripping water nearly gave me a heart attack, and I was constantly smelling wafts of natural gas, though no one else could ever detect it. I avoided bathing; our new tub groaned the few times I stepped into it, and I envisioned myself crash-landing in the basement—naked in a full tub of water. I decided Grayson's shower would have to suffice. I avoided the creaky kitchen tiles, certain the floor would collapse. And I couldn't even begin thinking about completing everything that had been left unfinished, simply because I couldn't stomach the thought of allowing another contractor in my already ailing home.

My idyllic house in the country had become a bottomless money pit and a millstone around my neck. The one place in the world that previously seemed safe now felt like a ticking time bomb. I felt robbed not only of my security but of my creativity, love for design, and desire to help people.

Still, there was one silver living in that very dark year.

Two or three court dates later, Grayson was set to receive his sentence. We had been prepping him for weeks regarding any potential outcomes. But truthfully, we were just as scared as he was. We had lost faith in a system intended to serve the public and had no idea which way Grayson's consequences would go.

The day before his sentencing, we received a call from the district attorney. He was calling to inform us that Grayson's court appointment had been canceled. Charges had suddenly been dropped, and any record of them had been ordered to be permanently expunged. All requirements were deemed to have been met, and the case was simply closed.

I can't say what happened for sure, but I have a pretty strong hunch. Arin's dear friend had a high-ranking father-in-law who sat in an elected position and carried some serious clout. While speaking highly of our family to his father-in-law, Arin's friend *might* have mentioned Grayson's court case. Coincidentally, a few short days later, Grayson's charges were dropped, and his record expunged.

I suspect that district attorney might have received a phone call from someone in a much higher position than his.

But all that, of course, is just speculation.

30

Slowing

The soul moves with a circular motion when it enters into
itself and turns away from the outside world; when it gathers
together its capacities of understanding, and unifies them
in a concentration that saves it from all bewilderment; when it
distances itself from the multiplicity of external objects, so as
to concentrate on itself. When it has reached interior unity . . .
it is led toward the Beautiful-and-Good.

—DIONYSIUS THE AREOPAGITE, *Divine Names*

Summertime. What was once a childhood luxury of lengthened days, ice-cream trucks, and games of neighborhood tag had evolved over the years into three months of steady despair. I began dreading summer on the first day of December. December meant a long holiday break; a long holiday break signaled Christmas, and Christmas officially marked the halfway point of the school year. The halfway point to the end of life as I knew it.

No matter how many years I practiced, I never discovered a graceful way of gliding through summer. It was always a fat man's bellyflop—ugly, painful to watch, and even more agonizing and embarrassing to endure.

No, adult summers were for coming unraveled, unglued, for bursting open at the seams. And school years were simply allotted seasons for repairs.

Such had become my natural life rhythm. Such was what I had come to expect.

Therefore, by the summer of 2018, my body was fully riddled with chaos. Within the last year, we had moved, undergone a horrific school year and a nightmare home remodel, and navigated our way—for the first time—through lawsuits and police-mandated suicide holds.

Before summer ever started, I was already exhausted.

July 17, 2018. It was Caleb's seventeenth birthday and the midpoint of summer. He didn't want to celebrate—and really didn't want to have anything to do with us—so I spent the night alone in the basement, torturing myself by watching old home movies. Arin was upstairs in bed, not yet ready to acknowledge the sting of Caleb's rejection.

On-screen, a younger, thinner version of me exited a basement bedroom at my parent's house. Four-year-old Caleb was wrapped around my legs and trying to climb his way up my body. His eyes were red and swollen, and my subconscious regurgitated the painful memory: He was crying because I had just spanked him. The walls of my throat began closing in, and I covered my eyes with one hand as if watching a horror flick.

Back on-screen, young me folded gracefully to the floor and extended lean and unwearied arms to welcome Caleb onto my lap. He plopped down, curled into a ball, and buried his head in my chest. I stroked his face and comforted him, encircling his body in my arms. I drew him closer, and we became one, just like when I carried him inside. Witnessing the love we shared lessened my guilt, if only slightly.

Yet seeing him desperate for me, clawing and clambering for my affection, shocked me and made hot tears spring to my eyes. I suddenly realized just how long it had been since I had caught sight of *that* Caleb, of *my* Caleb. I had forgotten how sweet and beautiful his spirit was. The stranger that roamed my house was nothing like that precious little boy.

Newly seventeen-year-old Caleb was nocturnal, vaporous in his waking hours, moody, and mean. Lately, he had reached an abnormal level of spite and only spoke to me when he wanted a late-night sandwich. If I dared refuse, he unleashed a torrent of insults and let me know just how worthless he believed me to be. "Why don't you have any food in the house?" he demanded. "Isn't your only job to care for this family? What's your purpose as a woman, if not cooking?" His face contorted with black hatred as he hurled various combinations of demeaning, hurtful words.

Simply avoiding him became the safest way to cope. Not a single family member remained unscathed by his raging darkness.

I had waited so long to not be needed every second of every day, to have independent children, to reclaim some space for myself. But with Caleb approaching his senior year, I started experiencing a strange new sadness over not being needed. A sadness that had been heavily masked by my anger.

The unexpected pain of seeing him on-screen—small, loving me, and clamoring for me—unleashed a flood of insecurities and pent-up emotions; I no longer knew how he felt toward me or whether he wanted anything to do with me or ever would. I could no longer even hold a civilized conversation with one who opened my womb, with the child who first called me "Mommy."

Then there was Rylee, who was constantly dumping her pain on me in the form of screaming hysterics and couldn't seem to refrain from sneaking out her bedroom window in the middle of the night; she was the sole reason we installed a security system. On the other hand, Reagan rarely left her room at all and avoided speaking to anyone besides her stuffed animals. Jacob seemed perfect except for the dark spells that randomly overtook him and sent him diving beneath his covers midday, and Grayson was, well, Grayson. Always Grayson. Unrelenting, energy-sapping Grayson.

Along with all the roller-coaster emotions, or lack thereof, was the steady supply of vape pens, shooters, and empty vodka and beer bottles I was constantly discovering in old suitcases, backpacks, shoes, coat pockets—anywhere anything could be stuffed. Ironically, they never belonged to anyone. Not Caleb or Jacob or Rylee, and certainly never to Arin.

Everything was slipping—always slipping—further and further from my outstretched, raking hand. My children's grades were plummeting faster than I could catch them. Flaming red "Fs" and notes from teachers were flying at me so rapidly that I quit responding to them at all.

If only I could somehow capture whatever was missing, falling, and failing, I could trap the ever evasive "it" in my clenched fist, manage "it," contain "it." Yet whatever "it" was kept slipping further and further away.

I sobbed that night, alone in the basement. I finally admitted that my firstborn son was far beyond my reach. I had lost him and was in the process of losing the rest. He was gone; they were going. Most likely, I conceded, this losing battle started long ago.

I plodded upstairs to bed, where Arin was assuredly already sleeping, first detouring by my office to jot down one eerily foreshadowing line: *May God grant me enough time for a new beginning.*

On July 25, 2018, I wrote in my journal:

> *Regarding the abstract art toward which I naturally gravitate, it is the lack of definitiveness that resonates. Nonsensical, undefined, jumbled messes captured on canvas, in time, and in space for all to behold.*
>
> *This is my life. I don't understand people, parties, traveling, or scheduling activities day in and day out. How do people survive their own lives when I can hardly make it through a single day? Is it normal to struggle like this all the time? To forever fight against this never-ending fear? I don't know if I'm happy or sad, doing acceptably or poorly; I scarcely have a second to think.*

My brain is still when I drink or create, or on the rare occasion I find myself alone. Why can I not just be straight-forward, like "normal" art? An apple tree. A spotted dog. A black horse.

But I am abstract. Unidentifiable to even me.

Flatlining again. I catch a whiff of joy . . . and then it is gone, leaving me alone to constantly wonder what's wrong.

Coffee in the morning, wine at night, emotionally satisfying yet horribly unhealthy food in between—cheap substitutes for true satiation yet the only things that offer a momentary reprieve.

Always trying to stick a Band-Aid on some unidentifiable wound.

Welcome to summertime at the Hatfields.

Being that the school district was legally obligated to place Grayson in a new school post-expulsion, they presented two options. Both required a referral to enroll, which essentially meant kids had to get "bad" enough before being considered for attendance.

One school's website advertised having "served Colorado's most neglected, abused, and traumatized children since 1904." That school was over an hour away, I was told, and Grayson would be accompanied by a security guard the whole bus ride. I imagined people told me these things to reassure me; I just never found them very helpful.

The other school was twenty minutes away and serviced children in our immediate area. Their front door was locked with a code, and once again, all their teachers were trained in restraint.

I supposed the second option was better. Still, I wasn't so sure.

Fortunately, a spot opened up that summer in the school closest to home.

When I visited it, the building itself appeared suspicious. It was old, dilapidated, musty, and wreaked of bad cafeteria food. Fist-sized chunks of missing drywall lined the halls. But the staff's refusal to acknowledge the holes, much less apologize for them, set my heart at ease and hinted that they might be extraordinarily adept at thriving amid high levels of chaos.

While touring the school, an episode took place that required restraint. I stepped aside as the staff slipped effortlessly into hyperdrive. They moved in unison with the fluidity of a well-oiled machine. Teachers filed out of classrooms while others stepped in to fill their places, and those involved in the restraint maneuvered with the skill and precision of a choreographed WWE wrestling match, eventually escorting the child to a private room to problem-solve with several teachers. Those who were no longer needed returned to their classrooms, smiling and smoothing their clothes as if strolling into church. I detected no remnants of frustration, no hints of bitterness, and no expressed need to be recompensed for their undue duress.

Contrarily, every staff member I spoke to that day was glowing, and their radiance transformed that ramshackle building into an elite institution where I could clearly envision sending my son.

On the first day of school that fall, despite the coded, locked door, Grayson snuck out behind a teacher, crossed the street, and ran away. The staff alerted the police department that a student was running but informed them no assistance was currently required. They chased him down, escorted him back to school, sorted through the situation, and then continued with their day—100 percent free of police intervention. They called me *after the fact* only to confirm his safety, not to request my assistance.

Later that week, Grayson again tested the waters by angrily hurling his shoe across the room. The shoe unintentionally connected with the secretary's face and broke her nose. The headmaster mentioned this in passing, as casually as if Grayson had come down with a cold.

But I knew it was just a matter of time until I'd receive a phone call from the police letting me know that the secretary did, in fact, intend to press charges.

The following afternoon, while waiting for Grayson in the school parking lot, I caught sight of the secretary talking to a teacher. (The looping black raccoon rings beneath her eyes and her hooked, swollen nose were telltale signs.) I was certain she was retelling the story of the "little punk" who broke her nose and obviously boasting of her upcoming plan to "teach him his lesson." Both adults were unaware of my presence, so I slunk down in my seat and tried to disappear.

Catching myself in this childish act, I summoned my courage and opened my car door. Sheepishly, I walked up to the secretary, introduced myself, and apologized for the excessive damage caused by my son. She greeted me warmly through puffy, squinting eyes as if we were old friends, and then dismissed my apology with a flick of her wrist. "Oh, it's just a hazard of the job," she said. "I've had fingers and hands broken and plenty of other injuries. The kids don't mean to do it. They're such great kids, and Grayson seems like such a sweet boy!"

I scraped my jaw off the asphalt and lugged it back to my car, shaking my head incredulously the whole way. What kind of twilight zone had we landed in? And how could we arrange to stay there and never, ever leave?

Grayson settled quickly and peacefully into his new school, and for the first time in an entire year, I felt confident leaving him, knowing he'd be safe and cared for the whole day long.

I returned home after dropping him off, where I was deliciously alone in our new country house for the first time ever.

Intent on pursuing the passive act of regeneration, I collapsed into my favorite herringbone chair with a steaming cup of coffee and my new book, *The Roots of Christian Mysticism*. Between paragraphs, I stared out the window and let my eyes wander aimlessly across acre after acre of waving fields and towering trees. The sun had barely begun her daily climb, and I had nothing but time.

At last, I could address my bone-deep fatigue. Finally, I could once again tend to my body and soul.

Not so ironically, an intense need for silence and solitude emerged. The mere thought of speaking a single word during school hours fatigued me, yet despite my relief over finally being alone, I felt surprisingly heavy, sober, and emotional.

Seventeen years prior, I had delivered Caleb naturally without drugs. I didn't shed a tear until the whole process was finished—until I'd fed him for the first time and the nurses had whisked him away for his testing. Alone, I finally cried, allowing myself to let down after performing one of the hardest tasks of my young life.

So it was with summer. Only when all the children were back in school would I finally allow myself to sit, to breathe, to cry.

Each and every summer was the new hardest task of my life.

For two solid months that fall, I made a beeline for my chair after leaving Grayson at school, and, for two solid months, I sat in silence, stared out the window, read my book, and cried.

On August 23, I journaled:

> *A similar feeling as in the corn fields last year—heaviness, sobriety, a crushing awareness of God's presence pressing in to fill. Overwhelming but not bad, emotional but not sad. The same PainfulBeauty. Colors so bright they practically hurt. My tears and the silence sustain and fulfill me. The only way to comprehend this is through the words of another.*

I then copied a quote by John Cassian, an Orthodox monk:

> *Sometimes . . . the whole soul descends and lies hidden in abysses of silence. The suddenness of the light stupefies it and robs it of speech. All its senses remain withdrawn in its inmost depths or completely suspended. . . . Sometimes, finally, it is so swollen with a sorrowful tenderness that only tears can give it consolation.*[1]

His words perfectly summarized my indescribable feelings.

I had once sought prayer in the pages of a little blue book, yet I had never succeeded in making the words my own. But in my current extended moments of wordless silence, I encountered the meaning of authentic prayer. On some minuscule level, I began to understand—not how to recite a prayer—but how to become it, embody it, and abide in a lasting posture of prayer.

Like a toddler with upraised arms, beseeching her father's help, sustenance, comfort, and guidance, I sat in my chair exposing my weary failing heart—imploring my Father's help, sustenance, comfort, and guidance. And for weeks, gently trickling tears washed away the summer's chaos and restored my internal equilibrium.

By then, I had finally learned that I couldn't care for my soul without concurrently tending to my body. So, alongside my morning hours of soul-restoration, I also committed to eating whole, organic foods, drinking plenty of water, and cutting back on coffee and wine (some things are never meant to be entirely eradicated). I went for long, rambling walks, scheduled weekly acupuncture to release my trapped emotions, and took daily afternoon naps. In between, I thumbed through farmhouse cookbooks—perusing the introductions and studying the gorgeous, detailed photographs—and I took great delight in cooking hearty and healthy meals for my family.

Slowly, I was becoming the mother I had long desired to be. My goals were to be home, healed, and available to my family. To these things, I committed as much time as my body required.

That October, I had a dream. Arin, the kids, and I all lived in a carnival with a Big Top Circus and carousel music that played round the clock. We spent our days in pure delight, eating hot dogs and cotton candy and repeatedly riding the Ferris wheel. In every fragmented scene, Arin and I were laughing with our children, touching, embracing, and enjoying one another's presence. It was abundantly clear we were living our best lives when suddenly, the carnival went dark.

All the rides disappeared, and scraps of trash now littered the ground. I saw myself lying on a mound of churned-up dirt where the Ferris wheel once stood, clutching a torn-up piece of grassy earth in my hand—the last remains of what was. The pile in my hand was slowly dwindling as bits of soil slipped through my clenched fingers. I squeezed tighter, attempting to preserve the last dissolving granules of our previously glorious life. The boys were gone, Arin was leaving me, and interestingly, only the girls remained to comfort me in my mourning. Running water was leaking from somewhere, and my losses felt simply devastating.

I awoke crying, a deep grief still reverberating in my heart.

Instantly I understood. As crazy as my life felt, I had everything I needed. Everything I had ever wanted. Yet I could lose it all tomorrow. *What matters right now?* I wondered and then immediately answered my own question: *I cannot afford to waste time. I must become the woman I need to be, the woman my family needs. They are the one investment I will never regret.*

I had dreamed of a crumbling world, and within my dream was a warning. Lying in bed that night, I perceived an urgency requiring change and was determined to do everything within my power to prevent it from becoming a reality.

But when I curiously examined this compelling impression, I realized it called for inaction. Instead of *doing*, it demanded my *being*—deceleration rather than speed.

My children were unraveling, and Arin was knee-deep in his new business. The worst thing I could do would be to add more frenetic energy to our family's already swirling momentum.

I concluded that my family didn't need me to bring home more money. They needed me to be their *anchor*.

The following morning, I made a firm decision: I would shut down my design business. For the time being, I would clear my schedule, immerse myself in my family, and attempt to make up for lost time.

Starting immediately, I rooted myself in the kitchen and spent more time preparing food than all the years prior. It's obvious that teenagers inhale love through food, so I spent many late nights at my stove, serving endless rounds of grilled ham-and-cheese sandwiches.

I began offering before Caleb demanded, thereby turning triangulated quadrants of bread, ham, and melted cheese into a love offering rather than my bitter pacification. His friends would sit around our kitchen island, tell me about their friends whom Caleb had never mentioned, and then thank me profusely while clearing their plates. Meanwhile, Caleb stared wordlessly at the counter, ate his food, and then walked out the door with his friends— his dish still sitting on the table. I cleared it with an exasperated sigh and reminded myself to be patient. After all, Rome wasn't built in a day.

Instead of retreating to my room when Jacob's and Rylee's friends came over, I lingered in the kitchen, the new heart of our house, serving late-night snacks and asking probing questions about their lives. Typical one-word answers soon blossomed into full-blown conversations, and before long, our kitchen had evolved into a local gathering place. Teenage boys and girls hopped up on countertops, scooped dip into chips, and shared high-school gossip over robust laughter.

Although my actions were routine for so many parents, I was practicing them for the first time. These deafening, boisterous moments filled my heart every bit as much as the silent morning ones spent in solitude. They were the bridges I never had time to build. The bonds I had historically lacked the energy to strengthen. By taking care of myself during the day, I had leftover energy for my big kids at night.

While my design business had been a wonderful creative outlet and had fulfilled a deep-rooted longing, a new yearning was beginning to surface— one that had always been present but perhaps had gotten lost in the shuffle.

In my heart of hearts, I wanted to be *home* with my children and *available* for my family. To do that, I would need to be *healed* and *whole*. I couldn't be who I wanted to be if I was constantly exhausted.

If I am to give my life as an offering to others, I journaled, *I must first ensure I am full. Whether or not I ever design another house, the potential for beauty lies within. It is not something I do, but something I can* embody *and* possess.

At last, the beauty that once seemed so uncontainable was within my reach. Yet it would not be confined and controlled by raking, grasping, clutching fingers but, rather, be infused in silent moments of solitude that were at once both empty and full.

31

Mooching

Many men go fishing all of their lives without
knowing that it is not fish they are after.

—ATTRIBUTED TO HENRY DAVID THOREAU

The last week of October, Caleb decided he needed to have his senior
portraits taken. All year, he had adamantly refused. Photographs
were stupid; besides, he didn't want to remember anything about the year
anyway. Yet suddenly, one week before the deadline, he changed his mind.

I grabbed my Fuji camera, and we bounced down back dirt roads in his
silver Dodge. He wanted to take pictures with his truck in front of an oil
derrick. He wore a Carhartt vest, a plaid flannel shirt, Wranglers, cowboy
boots, and his Freedom Drilling hat.[1] For someone who wanted so little to
do with his father, Caleb looked as though he'd raided Arin's closet.

The day was picture-perfect, with white clouds drifting lazily across a
cobalt sky and crisp fall air that smelled like burning leaves. It could have
been a milestone moment shared between a mother and her son. Instead,
the day was one of my worst.

I did my amateur best to position him for a photograph and then looked down the lens and zoomed in on his face. "Smile, Caleb!" *Click.* I looked at the picture on the screen and frowned. Something wasn't right. "Try again!" *Click.* Still not right. "Caleb, you have to smile. I know you think you're smiling, but you're actually not. *Smile!*" *Click.* "I don't know what's going on with your face."

The corners of his mouth turned upward, but he appeared to simply be showing his teeth. His lips were correctly shaped, but the rest of his face was not participating, and he looked like he was either grimacing or sneering. I distinctly remember feeling like he had forgotten how to smile.

As I continued to focus on him through the narrow scope, I realized I was studying him more closely than I had in a long while. The young man sitting on the fence post was my son—but he also wasn't. He was there but somehow not. There was a hollowness to him, a dimness as if all the light had gone out from his eyes.

His eyes! Suddenly, it dawned on me. Something was wrong with his eyes. I looked closer. They were so dark and empty, like bottomless orbs of blackness, and something about them scared me and bristled the hair on my neck.

In the end, only a few photographs were acceptable enough to print. Although Caleb was bodily present in every frame, his soul seemed missing. It must have escaped through the dark holes in his eyes.

The following Friday, November 2, he was at a party and had planned to spend the night at a friend's house. At 11:00 p.m., I was lying in bed wide awake, unable to shake the feeling that something was seriously wrong.

Despite the battle I knew would ensue, I called to tell him he needed to come home, even though I had previously promised otherwise. After multiple attempts, he still had not answered my calls or texts, so I called his best friend instead.

"Uh, Caleb can't talk right now," Dylan stammered, groping for words. "He's uh . . . sick."

"Sick or drunk?" I pressed him. "Give me the address. I'll be there in fifteen minutes."

As I pulled up to the house, Caleb stumbled down the front steps and then threw up in the bushes. We barely made it out of the neighborhood before pulling over for another puke break. It was obvious he'd had too much to drink, but something about that night felt different. Darker.

His head was resting on my window, his eyes closed, and I softly asked him, "What's going on, Caleb? Why are you doing this to yourself?"

Then the tears started, and the words he could never speak, the silent pain he'd been holding close to his heart, came tumbling out. "I'm hurting, Mom. I'm hurting so bad. I'm doing bad things, and I can't stop."

My eyes welled with his pain, and my heart started racing. Deep inside, I knew what he meant. I continued in a low, quiet voice, "What kind of things? Are you doing drugs? What kind of drugs are you doing?"

"All kinds," he sobbed.

He was doing all kinds. But mostly, and frequently—cocaine.

At last, I understood the blackness in his eyes.

He tripped and fell while getting out of the car. Arin opened the door at midnight to see his son sprawled out on the garage floor. His first impulse was to stifle a laugh. While he disapproved, he also remembered his high school years. He compassionately bent and hoisted Caleb to a standing position, and Caleb draped a limp arm across Arin's broad shoulders.

"You're gonna be okay, buddy. Let's get you to bed."

He was barely through the door before I whispered, "Arin, there's more . . . ."

After tucking Caleb into bed and observing him for a while, Arin and I transitioned to the living room, where I filled him in on the details. His spine stiffened as soon as the word *cocaine* slipped from my lips, and his every muscle went taut. He seemed to me then as brittle and fragile as a thin sheet of glass, and I imagined that had I but tapped him with the smallest of hammers, he'd have shattered into millions of pieces.

We immediately called our dear friend Brian, who, in years prior, had struggled with a long-term methamphetamine addiction. He worked nights as a caregiver, and we knew he'd still be awake. When the phone began ringing, Arin put it on speaker and laid it on the coffee table between us. The lilt in Brian's voice confirmed his questioning concern; he immediately understood we weren't calling for a friendly midnight chat.

"Brian, it's Caleb," Arin began. His tone was inordinately smooth and level as he began speaking, but words flew from his mouth in a barely restrained panic. "We just found out he's been using quite a few drugs. Mostly cocaine. But we don't know anything about that world. What should we do?"

Now, it was Brian's turn for questions.

"What other drugs has he used?" Brian asked matter-of-factly. "And how long has he been using? Needles or snorting? Do you know if he's ever tried meth?"

Brian was more amped up than I'd expected. I had imagined he'd set our hearts at ease by offering a few trite clichés like, "Oh, it's just a phase. Don't worry. This, too, shall pass."

Instead, he was saying forceful things like, "You have to act swiftly, firmly, and in unified strength" and "You need to call a rehab center immediately! Tomorrow! Check Caleb into the first open bed!"

Brian had struggled with his addiction from age sixteen, well into adulthood. I knew that he knew.

Even so, I doubted.

Tilting my moss-green ottoman forward to press the soft spot of my knees against the cold, black metal edge of the coffee table, I wondered: *What if Brian was wrong? He's never even met Caleb. What if he's responding to his experience rather than ours?*

I watched with inordinate interest as my indented flesh paled into a perfectly straight line of white and then blossomed outward into a bloody shade of pink. Plopping the ottoman loudly back on the floor, my soft knee-spots resumed their usual color. My eyes met Arin's, and he imperceptibly shook his head.

"How did we even get here?" his bewildered gesture asked.

Arin and I stayed awake long into the morning hours, in shock and researching potential rehabilitation centers. When Caleb finally rolled out of bed the following afternoon, we told him we needed to talk. We offered to take him to lunch, hoping a good meal might loosen his tongue. But his reeling stomach revolted at the thought of food. So instead, we went for a drive.

We traversed country dirt roads, past the cornfield of PainfulBeauty and the golden wheat fields that once made me cry. They were no longer beautiful, I observed. Rather, they were brown, dry, and dull. I glumly wondered how I could have ever thought otherwise.

The portal of communication from the night prior—the one that had opened briefly enough to permit Caleb's free-falling tears and painful confessions—had again been resealed. Once more, Arin and I were on the receiving end of empty, black-holed stares, and answers that came in the form of disyllabic grunts.

We spoke as if to ourselves and informed Caleb that doing nothing was not a choice. His situation required our response, and he could either contribute to a possible solution, or we would make the decision for him. Caleb's eyes remained dull, and I twisted in my seat to study him while he continued ignoring me.

After a long silent lapse, his eyes slightly brightened.

"I know what I need to do," he blurted suddenly. "I want to go to Seattle and see Father Tom."

While I loved Father Tom dearly, I was equally delighted and puzzled by Caleb's response. Although Father Tom had greatly helped me through my depression, Caleb had only briefly spent time with him.

Roughly seven years prior, we visited Carol's house for brunch, where Father Tom was staying as her guest. He opened the door very un-priestlike—barefoot and in shorts—then greeted my kids with a warm, welcoming smile. Before introductions had even been properly made, he instructed ten-year-old Caleb to run upstairs, dig through his suitcase, and fetch his boxing gloves. Interest piqued, Caleb instantly complied, and the moment his feet hit the bottom stair, Father Tom commanded him to gear up for a fight. Caleb looked at me and then back to Father Tom, obviously confused. Surely, he wouldn't be allowed to spar with a fifty-six-year-old priest? But spar they did, and not only that—they went outside to play football when they were finished.

I barely saw my kids that morning. They were far too busy following

Father Tom around like little ducklings. Yet from that simple experience, seventeen-year-old Caleb felt safe enough to seek out an Orthodox priest amid his struggles with cocaine.

The hair on my arms prickled with Caleb's proclamation, for I knew something Arin and Caleb didn't. Besides being an excellent priest, Father Tom was a licensed marriage and family therapist. He had also started a Give-Back Group, a support group intended to help addicts and their parents support one another through their pain. Peace settled over me then, and I knew that some deep part of Caleb was still capable of making good decisions.

Four days later, we found ourselves in the Denver airport, waiting to board a plane to Seattle. Caleb slouched low in a leather-slung seat off to my left and had again receded into a moody silence. He stared incessantly at his phone as if it was his best and only friend while Arin sat immediately to my right, watching the flashing screen on his phone. Between the three of us, no words were spoken.

Just beyond Caleb, a young mother was sitting on the floor with her toddler son. Her diaper bag bulged with toys and snacks, and she read to her son in a cheery, enthusiastic voice. I acutely remembered being a young mother as if it were just yesterday, and the thought of holding a young child on my lap filled me with longing and nearly drove me to tears. At the same time, those experiences seemed one-million light-years away, and I could scarcely remember the feeling. That had been a different life, and I a different woman.

Once, I, too, had known that mother's sparkling excitement and exuberance, but sitting at the airport now, I suddenly felt old, tattered, and fatigued. Within my line of sight, I could observe both her and her child, as well as my son, who was most likely hungover and soon to be graduating from high school. (With that thought, I mentally knocked on wood.)

The juxtaposition felt insufferable. Where had the time gone, and what had happened to us all?

Caleb was sleeping before we even pushed back from the tarmac. I stared at his hands for a long while, wondering what would happen if I reached out and held one. They looked exactly the same as when he was young, except a bit more dirty and a lot more calloused. His hands were the first thing I noticed when he was placed on my belly, fresh from the womb. His fingers were surprisingly long and graceful, nail beds were short and squared, cuticles caked in fresh blood. From my airplane seat, I snapped a quick photo for posterity's sake; although the image was already so burned in my brain, I could have picked him out of a lineup solely by his hands.

I started and finished a book en route to Seattle: *Beautiful Boy* by David Sheff. It's a father's memoir about his son's meth addiction. The movie was soon to be released, and I would watch that, too. With both eyes wide open, I needed to know all the gory details—the needle tracks, stolen cash, turned tricks, homelessness, and possible overdoses. I wanted to understand every nuance of what we could be facing. Prepare myself for what was potentially still to come.

Meanwhile, Arin slept soundly in the seat next to me. It took all my strength to let him be. I wanted to read every page aloud, to shake him awake and make him understand what we could be facing. But he wasn't interested. He didn't want to know what lay ahead. He was content with not knowing. Why worry about something that might never happen?

Such were our responses to crises. I revved up, while Arin shut down. We had yet to learn how to grieve together.

Perhaps grieving was never intended to be a joint effort.

We would spend our first night in Seattle at a hotel. I wanted some time alone as a half-family before meeting with Father Tom. Besides, I had chartered a private fishing boat the following day. It was embarrassingly expensive, and from the moment I booked the reservation, guilt perched on my shoulder and never ceased to remind me of my extravagant frivolity. *Such a waste! Couldn't you find a better use for your husband's hard-earned money?*

But I was desperate to do something good for Caleb, frantic to show him how much we cared. And above all else, I needed to know whether the light could come back to his eyes, and fishing was the only light switch I knew how to flip.

That night, we went to a well-reviewed steak and seafood restaurant on the water. My sister, Jenna, had preemptively sent a generous gift card that made me tear up with gratitude. Once again, it was the little things that pulled us through. At the dining table, Caleb and Arin sat on one side and I on the other. I looked out the window at the lights reflecting off the water. As my vision retracted from the harbor, the outside image melded with our own: a mother, father, and son all sitting down to a nice dinner, none talking, none remembering how, the parents searching the young man's face for traces of their son.

How had it happened? How had they become strangers with the child that came from his loin and her womb? When had they lost him?

The mother had an idea. She had written out his life's timeline several nights prior.

The father had left for the oil field right as the boy's autistic brother truly started acting out. In that sense, the little boy lost both parents within the same year. One year later, that disoriented and lonely boy started lashing out at school, and his parents were called into a meeting. They chastised and corrected but failed to listen. Around the same time, that little boy met sweet Father Tom, who boxed and played football with him—things he used to do with his hardworking father. His mother took him to see their priest, to better understand his fits of rage. And when Father Evan asked if he missed his dad, a lone tear spoke the truth that his words could not: "No, I don't care. I know that he has to work."

But the mother and father did not treasure his tear. They barely even noticed. There were bills to be paid and an irate brother to restrain.

I recalled my mind from the past and reentered the present. My eyes settled on my son's handsome, emotionless face. It was true; we had lost Caleb years ago.

As we scoured the menus, we told him to order anything he wanted. The special for the night was a Kobe Wagyu steak, which we had heard of by reputation only. It was listed at market price, which upon inquiring, we discovered to be a whopping $150. We all locked eyes in disbelief, and a shocked laugh rippled forth from each of us. The warm reverberations slightly thawed the awkward tension. Arin ordered it for him regardless, and I don't know whose eyes grew wider—mine or Caleb's.

Conversation flowed easier then, as we googled facts about *Wagyu beef* and our mouths began watering in anticipation. When the food arrived, Arin cut into his ribeye first. It was well-marbled and perfectly cooked. He passed bites around, and we scoffed: How could anything possibly be better? But then Caleb cut into his Kobe Wagyu steak. He giggled like a little boy as his knife slipped effortlessly through the meat. He took a bite, and his whole face lit up as the steak melted in his mouth. Apparently, there *was* something better than a ribeye.

Perhaps that steak was a blood offering to appease our burning shame. Maybe the money spent was wasteful and could have fed hundreds of starving children. But by the same token, perhaps our offering was received in the spirit we intended. Maybe a boy who felt forlorn and forgotten accepted our gift, and the significance of an expensive cut of meat was not lost on him. Perhaps he felt noticed and loved in a way long forgotten. I don't know. Maybe I never will; the line between love and guilt is quite fine.

Early the next morning, our little fishing boat sputtered slowly through the Puget Sound harbor. However, once clear of the wake-free zone, it roared to life and skimmed across the surface of the glassy water. Looking backward, I could perceive superficially that the land was beautiful, but the emotional strain on board would not allow beauty to penetrate my soul.

The damp northwestern cold, however, sliced through my multiple layers like an obsidian blade, and before we had even reached our first fishing spot, my teeth were chattering so hard I feared they might crack.

We had been forewarned. Our captain agreed to take us out but refused to guarantee our success. Salmon season was over, and anything we caught would have to be released. He informed us that we had planned our "vacation" at the wrong time of year. If we were lucky, we might catch a few.

Salmon fishing was new to all of us, even Caleb, and the captain was going to teach us how to fish with an interactive method called "mooching." We were to drop (not cast) our baited lines down to the proper depth—where the graphs showed little squiggles that were supposed to be fish—then reel in our lines fast and steady. You would know if you caught a fish as it neared the surface. Apparently, salmon put up a good fight.

We neared our first spot, dropped the anchor, and then our lines. Nothing. Second spot. Absolutely nothing. Not even a nibble.

Although the skies were clear, the surrounding air felt thick and lethargic, as if the world above and below the water was still sleeping, or perhaps, just uncaring. We were the wrong people at the wrong place at the wrong time. Everything about us was just wrong. The biting chill of the day seemed to both predict and ensure our unavoidable lack of success.

Caleb's shoulders drooped low as his mood, and his overcast face made the day even gloomier. I supposed our Washington fishing trip would go down in history as another epic mom-failure.

Through chattering teeth, I whispered a silent, fervent prayer: *Please, God. We need a miracle. Just give us this one day.* By then, my knees were knocking uncontrollably, and I was sure I would lose several toes to frostbite.

On the way to our third spot, the captain pointed out the magnificent curve of a humpback whale and, later, another's spouting blow. They shadowed us at a distance for a while, and Caleb stood up with interest flickering across his face the same way hope was fluttering across mine. But then the whales dove beneath the surface and disappeared. The moment passed, and Caleb returned to his wordless silence. Why was I so quick to hope? The day needed so much more than two measly whales.

I was cold enough that I was quickly ready to call it a day. Obviously, we weren't going to catch anything, so we might as well be warm. After docking across the way for a quick refuel and hot cup of coffee, we determined to try one more spot before finally heading back.

We dropped our lines once last time, just to say we tried, and lo and behold, we each caught a fish—and then another, and another, and another. Honest to goodness, God as my witness, from that point on, nearly every time we dropped our line, we hooked a fish. At one point, we each had a fish in tow and had to dance and maneuver over and under one another to avoid tangling our lines. Eventually, even the captain could no longer refrain. He grabbed a rod, ordered us never to tell a living soul, and dropped in a line of his own.

Caleb's face came to life as we caught fish after fish, and he began emoting like a human being instead of a robot. He hollered and stomped his feet when he lost a big one, beamed with pride when he landed another, laughed at the sight of me struggling to keep my balance, and roared when Arin fumbled, sputtered, and then lost the massive fish he appropriately dubbed "Fat Bastard."

We caught *more than seventy-five fish* that morning. The captain said he had never in all his years seen anything like it. When I asked him how often he'd experienced something similar, his face grew earnest and deadpan serious. He responded in a firm and steady voice, "Zero. Absolutely zero. You guys must be good luck."

When, at last, our time was up, the captain turned the boat around to head back to shore. Caleb plopped heavily into his seat, and again his shoulders dangled limply. But instead of sagging beneath the weight of defeat, they rounded softly with the relaxed contour of success. Exhaling a satisfied sigh, he uttered the words I will never forget, "Thank you, Mom and Dad. That was really fun."

I willed myself to look into his eyes. They were bright and full of light, and in them, I saw my *son*. Caleb was there, behind the black holes. And I knew at that moment I would do whatever it took to keep him from disappearing.

A calm settled over me as we docked the boat, and quiet words entered my mind.

"In the darkness, I am there."

I noticed my teeth were no longer chattering.

32

Imbibing

She was saying goodbye and she didn't even know it.
—MARKUS ZUSAK, *The Book Thief*

That night, I wheeled my suitcase into Father Tom's guest bedroom, my heart full of hope. Our fishing excursion had set the bar high. Fish had practically thrown themselves into our boat, begging to be caught. Surely the salmon were foreshadowing an extraordinary and miraculous visit.

But Caleb was largely silent—and so was Arin.

While driving with Father Tom to the Give-Back Group meeting, Caleb shared a few fragmented thoughts in short, clunky sentences. Yet when Father Tom walked through the door with shrugged shoulders and upraised palms, I knew he hadn't uncovered anything worth sharing.

The following morning, we met as a family in Father Tom's counseling office. Caleb responded to questions in grunts and single-word answers; I shared my opinions, and Arin sat silently listening. After a while, Father Tom observed that Caleb seemed resentful toward Arin, while Arin's anger toward Caleb seemed to bubble only slightly below his emotional surface. Both required only a sideways glance to be sparked into full-blown flames. Just beginning to understand the relational dynamics between him and his son, Arin offered Caleb a genuine but generic apology for any way he'd potentially contributed to his pain and anger. Caleb shrugged unemotionally, and Arin quickly retracted his extended vulnerability and refortified his typically guarded walls.

As for me, I might as well have stayed home; Caleb completely ignored my presence. Anything I asked went unanswered, and on the rare occasion Caleb did speak, he directed his words toward anyone but me. Father Tom later privately commented, "It's strange. Caleb doesn't address you. It's as if you're not even there."

I ended our three-day trip feeling less confident than ever. How could I help my struggling son who refused to acknowledge my very existence?

Caleb slept the entire plane ride back and said nothing for most of our hour-long drive home. But in the last fifteen minutes of our entire trip, he finally opened his mouth and started speaking.

"This modern generation is all depressed and suicidal," he remarked offhandedly, not really to Arin and certainly not to me. "Guys are doing all the big drugs, and a girl is usually at the root of his problems. Kids today don't see a point in living, and music plays a big part; all the songs about are drugs, alcohol, and dying."

I was ecstatic that he was conversing and sharing his thoughts, and I felt desperate to keep him engaged. But as usual, he ignored my questions.

Then Arin joined in, equally confused and irritated. "What's so hard about kids' lives today that they feel the need to *off* themselves? All you kids have to do is go to school and sleep.

"Back when I was a kid . . ."

Arin's voice rose as Caleb's once again fell silent, and I began my customary dance of intervening and interpreting.

By the time we got home, doors were slamming, and both males were marching off to their separate corners to lick their inflamed wounds. I trailed behind, lugging my cumbersome suitcase up the garage stairs. It caught on the lip of every step, reluctant as I to enter the house. With one last heave, I hoisted it over the top step and through the doorway, and in an instant, our miraculous Puget Sound fishing trip became nothing more than a distant memory.

The door swung shut behind me, and its wall-shaking slam shattered an even louder silence.

"Welcome home," it seemed to say. "You're trapped."

Caleb started drinking again immediately after Seattle. I suspected, but could never prove, that he also promptly resumed his routine drug usage. I continuously found large empty vodka bottles stashed beneath his bed. Rumor had it he chugged a full liter each time he sat down to drink.

I began preparing myself for disaster, just like years ago when little Grayson had stood on the wrong side of the railing, threatening to jump. Each time my hand touched Caleb's cold metal doorknob, a question popped into my mind: *How will you handle it when this happens?*

Once again, horrific scenes would flash before my eyes. I imagined myself entering Caleb's room, cautiously calling his name to no reply and then wading through a sea of empty liquor bottles to extend a hesitant arm. I envisioned ripping off his covers all at once like a bandage—as if the pain might somehow hurt less—only to behold Caleb's stiff and lifeless body. Remnants of cocaine rimmed his breathless nostrils, and an empty vodka bottle lay entombed in his slack, waxy hand.

Eventually, I would take a deep breath, force myself to open his door, and attempt to rouse him. I never allowed myself to touch him. The barrier between us was too great if he was just sleeping, and if he wasn't, I never wanted to remember the coldness of his flesh. So I just stood in the doorway and yelled his name.

It often took many tries, and the in-between seconds of silence throbbed louder than my pounding heart. Eventually, his tired, scratchy voice would scream at me from beneath his blankets, "Get out and leave me alone!" And his angry cries were like a symphony of angels, and I found myself again free to breathe and return to feeling highly irritated.

Sometimes, I was too afraid, and I let him sleep through school rather than wake him. If he was asleep, he was safe—or at least that's what I allowed myself to believe.

I later discovered this on my computer, written on an unknown date:

> *This child that I grew cell by cell in my womb—blood of my blood and flesh of my flesh—now stands staring down the barrel of a loaded gun, alcohol being his weapon of choice. He presses his forehead white against the bottle as, through tormented lips, he bears his teeth, daring his demons to pull the trigger. What he consumes in one day would send me to my grave, but for him, it's a normal dose—a slow but steady death sentence.*
>
> *Occasionally, I encounter my grown man-child sitting on the bathroom floor in his underwear—legs sticking out straight like a toddler. He retches and pukes out what poisons him and then curls up in a ball, drooling and crying. "It was a bad night, Mom. Just a bad night."*
>
> *The liquid courage he's consumed opens his heart. He speaks freely of the hurt, the darkness, and the loneliness. He lets me rub his back, hold him, and sit with him as he purges his pain and flushes it down the toilet. In my eyes, he's flushing away his honesty, bravery, and vulnerability. I know his walls will be back up by morning, but I'll remember the night prior with tenderness, remembering what it felt like to be his up-close mom instead of the faraway one he keeps locked out of his life.*

One-and-a-half months later, we were packing our bags for yet another trip, this time to Mexico. I had been too exhausted to shop for Christmas presents, so Arin and I opted for a family vacation instead. Caleb was a senior, and we recognized our time as a whole unit was approaching its end. We would celebrate Christmas 2018 in Riviera Maya.

The day before our scheduled departure, a churning ball of stress awoke me while it was still dark. I curled up in my favorite chair and began journaling:

> The reality of Christmas is that I am awake at 3:30 a.m., not to fill stockings and put presents under the tree for excited kids, but rather because the pit in my stomach won't let me to sleep. Advent, baby Jesus, church—all unreachable, unfathomable, and not for me this year. Instead, I grieve for my child.
>
> The one that was is no more. Any light in his eyes is long gone, and I feel so saddened, hurt, and angered by what remains. The reality of Christmas this year is that it is one more opportunity to feel like a failure, like a waste, like my whole life "career" has been for naught. All the stories read, the time spent, the good intentions—they ended up being wrong, not good enough, like always.

There I sat on Christmas morning, drowning in a sea of teenage moods, ungratefulness, and behaviors I'd worked my whole life to correct. Rather than feeling excited for a tropical family vacation, I felt only dread over being stuck in a hotel for six days with my own children.

Even so, our week went more smoothly than anticipated. Upon arriving at the hotel, we changed into our swimsuits and headed straight for the beach. Within minutes, Caleb was hoisting little Reagan over large, rolling waves, where she nearly died of surprise; I couldn't remember the last time Caleb acknowledged her presence. Over the following days, we jumped off rickety wooden structures into bottomless *Cenotes* (natural sinkholes filled with water), swam with the dolphins, snorkeled until our backsides burned, scuba-dived alongside sea turtles, and lay on the beach sipping bright pink drinks with paper umbrellas. Both Caleb and Grayson were equally amiable, and for a brief moment, our family felt like any other *normal* family just vacationing in Mexico over Christmas break.

On the final night of our vacation, we all lingered at the dinner table, each of us unready to return to reality. Grayson impressed the staff with magic tricks while several of us looked on and laughed. Caleb and Arin were deep in conversation, excitedly discussing their future joint business plans, and I quickly snapped a picture for posterity's sake. Both sets of arms were folded the same, their opposing legs crossed one over the other, and their heads were bowed close, forming a mirror image of father and son. All traces of animosity had been washed down by a few shots of tequila.

At that very moment, I recalled an image I had pictured—yet immediately forgotten—just before traveling to Seattle. It was a double helix, a molecule where two strands held together by opposing bonds wind around each other like a twisted ladder. A crystal-clear thought was attached to the image weeks prior and reentered my mind once more: *Arin's and Caleb's healing will be tightly intertwined, each highly dependent on the other.*

On one level, this idea calmed me, for I accepted it as a promise and believed it to be true. But it also stirred up my insides. For if my perception was correct, I remained the ignored and irrelevant third wheel. There was little for me to do and even less to control.

Still, there was one thing.

In an instant, I made up my mind. I told Arin he could follow the other kids to the hotel rooms and I'd be along shortly. Then turning toward our waiter, I ordered two shots of tequila, one for Caleb, who was finally addressing me for the first time in ages, and one for me. We toasted each other and giggled, and then we ordered another, and possibly another. After that, I lost count.

If I got nothing else for Christmas, I sure as hell was going to gift myself one good night with my son. Who knew how many were left? I admitted in my tequila-infused haze that, on some subconscious level, I had planned our Mexico vacation as one last hurrah, a week of good memories—in case there were no more.

The shots slipped down one after another, and before long, we were laughing and carrying on like best friends.

Suddenly, Caleb impulsively jumped up onstage and started singing karaoke and dancing. When the DJ asked who he was with, he pointed me out with pride instead of his usual scorn and shouted, "*That's* my mom!"

"Your mamí es muy bonita!" proclaimed the DJ.

"Sí!" Caleb enthusiastically agreed. "My mommy is muy bonita!"

After finishing his singing debut, Caleb descended the stage. Walking away from the amphitheater, he draped his arm around my shoulder as if it were the most natural thing in the world, and I cautiously looped my arm behind his broad back. I couldn't remember the last time I had been allowed to touch him, and despite my inebriated state, I found the wherewithal to savor the moment.

While returning to our rooms, Caleb abruptly stopped some fellow vacationers and handed them his phone. Completely out of character, he blurted, "Can you take a picture of me and my mom?"

We posed on the steps of a white gazebo as a stranger snapped photos—my best and worst moment frozen in time. Who orders tequila for their substance-abusing son?

I leaned my head on his shoulder and whispered, "I love you, Caleb."

"I love you too, Mom," he replied.

And with those five simple words, my guilt up and disappeared. I would deal with my conscience later. All that mattered then was that Caleb said he loved me and allowed me to hold him close. For just those five words, I would have consumed my weight in tequila, jumped from the highest platform into the deepest *Cenoté*, and endured one-million sunburnt backsides.

Caleb, Grayson, Jacob, Arin, me, Reagan, and Rylee in Mexico, Christmas 2018

I would cope with my irresponsible decision later, but for one careless and beautiful night, I allowed my cup to runneth over. I had my moment—my single, solitary, blissful moment that would remain forever frozen in time. I had hugged my son and told him I loved him, and he had offered the same in return. I made peace and said my goodbyes—in case there was no other chance.

By the next morning, the enchanted Caleb had turned back into a grumpy pumpkin, and I was just "plain old mom." We were each severely hungover, and Caleb was once again raging. By the time we arrived back home, we had all returned to our angry, frustrated selves.

I never saw our photos from that night. Caleb never allowed me to see them. Not then and not ever. No matter how many times I asked, he outright refused or conveniently forgot to send them.

My other children have never let me live that night down. It was the only time they've ever seen me stumbling drunk. I still blush whenever they tease me; I don't think I'll ever get over the embarrassment of my indiscretion.

Yet, I wonder, would I change anything if I had a do-over? Probably not. If it meant missing the weight of Caleb's arm wrapped around my shoulder, definitely not. Some choices we make may never be justifiable.

But they also might be the best we ever make.

33

Deserting

We have found that no modern prescriptions heal the human
heart so fully or so well as the prescription of the Ancient
Ones. "To the hills," they would say. To which we would add,
"To the trees, the valleys, and the streams, as well."
For there is a power in nature that man has ignored.
And the result has been heartache and pain.

—ANASAZI FOUNDATION, *The Seven Paths*

One month after Mexico, Arin and I found ourselves seated on the
outdoor patio of an Arizona restaurant. Although the February air
was already as warm as a Colorado summer, I drew my sweater tightly
around me, unable to keep myself from shivering.

The glowing Phoenix sun was slowly sinking into a wavy mirage of hot
pink and orange as if a tropical mai tai had been splashed across an otherwise barren desert. Less than twelve hours before, we had boarded a plane
with iced-over wings, and here we sat, preparing for a late-night dinner

with no children in sight. Drinks and appetizers had been ordered, and the only place we had to go was back to our hotel room. Alone.

But our churning stomachs kept us firmly tethered to our reason for being there in the first place.

Our spinach and artichoke dip sat untouched on our table. Neither of us spoke, until, finally, my stifled giggle broke the silence, and my eyes jumped at the chance. Desperate for any excuse, my tears swelled and overflowed beneath the socially acceptable guise of humor.

"I was just imagining," I explained, wiping my eyes, "what Caleb will say when his counselors hand him a pack of dehydrated food and inform him that's all he'll be eating for the next seven weeks."

My words caught Arin off guard, and white IPA foam nearly spewed from his nose. "No, no, no, what about *this*," he countered, picking up my game and dabbing his nostrils. "What do you think he'll do when they hand him a branch and instruct him to carve his own spoon?"

I slapped a palm to my cringing brow and peeked at Arin through parted fingers.

"Oh my gosh!" I exclaimed. "He's going to be livid! What about when they give him a tarp and some rope and tell him to make his own tent?"

Envisioning the scene, I felt relieved that, for once, I was not the one dealing with Caleb's explosive anger. Relaxing, I allowed my arm to slowly slide to the table.

"Oh man," Arin said, snickering, "picture his face when he gets cold and his TrailWalker hands him two sticks and some string and tells him he can have a fire when he learns how to make it."

That last image tipped the scales, and our repressed emotions erupted in a geyser of giggles. Our laughter billowed high into the neon sky with the force of Old Faithful, and our nervous energy slowly dissipated with the fading heat of the day. As our laughter thinned to intermittent chuckles and then further dissolved into softening smiles, at last we simmered down enough to ask the serious questions we were at first too distraught to utter.

Leaning in toward each other, we spoke in low, reverential tones: "Do you think Caleb will hate us forever? Is he scared or lonely? Will he ever forgive us?"

I prayed to God we made the right choice.

Shortly before our Mexico vacation, I was getting dressed in our closet early one Saturday morning when I heard a strange shuffling sound behind me. I whipped around, still pulling up my pants, and an involuntary scream escaped from my lungs. A stocky young man with shaggy brown hair stood less than three feet away. He was staring blankly into the space that had just been occupied by my bare derrière. Slowly, he lifted his lingering gaze to meet my eyes and extended his hand for a friendly shake, as if we were meeting for the first time at a summer barbecue and not in my walk-in closet.

"Hi, I'm Jaxon," he murmured sleepily through thick, lazy lips and a barely moving tongue. "I spent the night, and when I went to leave, I got lost in your house. It's nice to meet you, though. How are you?"

I awkwardly shook his hand and then waited for him to apologize or slink off in mortified shame. But he did neither. Instead, he stood motionless, staring at me through glassy, vacant eyes. Because of Grayson (and my naïveté), I wondered whether he had special needs. I was too shocked to be scared and too confused to consider him a threat.

"Can you wait in the kitchen?" I asked calmly and then finished getting dressed. Only when I overheard him talking to Grayson did his drug-induced stupor finally dawn on me.

Meanwhile, ecstatic to find a captive audience sitting at our kitchen island, Grayson was taking every opportunity to showcase his magic tricks. I overheard Jaxon's drawled-out response from my closet, oozing like cold molasses into Grayson's childlike ears, "*Duuuude*, you are *fuuuccckkkinnng aaaawwesooomme* at *maaaagiiic*."

I immediately roused Caleb to escort Jaxon from our house before Arin made it home from work. Afterward, we made it very plain—no drugs or paraphernalia, or anyone under their influence, including Caleb, would be tolerated in our home. If Caleb could not agree to abide by our rules, he was no longer welcome to live there.

The precipitating event that led to our hasty Arizona departure occurred four days prior to boarding the plane.

Arin and I were reading in bed, ready to call it a night, when Jacob suddenly appeared at our bedroom door, white as a ghost. His freshman body was shirtless, gangly, and coltish—he had grown to the height of a man, but not yet the breadth—and his ribs were heaving, struggling to breathe. His lanky limbs jerked spastically about like the rusted tin man of Oz, and as he sat beside me on our bed, his uncontrollable tremors spiraled through the mattress coils straight into my questioning body.

Arin abruptly sat up and began hurling questions. But when Jacob opened his mouth in response, only wheezy, panicked breaths squeaked out.

Eventually, he calmed down enough to rasp in choppy bursts, "Caleb, he—he asked me . . . I held a flashlight for him. He was cutting, like, chopping up a pill. I told him I was worried, and he—he pinned me against the wall and said he'd kill me if I ever said anything like that again or ratted him out. But I—I had to tell you. I'm really, really worried."

We pressed him for details as he sat wringing his hands and continuously checking over his shoulder: "What did the pill look like? What color was it? What shape?"

It was a long, tan bar with two or three scored lines. A quick google search informed us that Caleb had been cutting a bar of Xanax, better known by high schoolers as a "Zanny." A potent benzodiazepine, Xanax is a sedative normally used to treat anxiety, and when combined with alcohol, it can quickly turn fatal because of the resulting respiratory failure.

Arin rose from our bed, and I met his narrowed eyes. My wavering maternal heart searched Arin's firm-set jaw to determine whether he might renege. Could we really kick our seventeen-year-old son out of the house? But with a single, determined stride, Arin expelled any lingering questions—Caleb would receive no second chance.

From the basement, the low rumble of Arin's steady voice traveled through the floor, followed by the high-pitched vibrations of Caleb's irate response. He yelled and argued, ranted and raved. We were crazy. Jacob was lying. We were all conspiring to get rid of him. But never once did he refuse to leave.

The following morning, he slipped from the house without a word. I watched from the kitchen window as his silver Dodge backed down our long driveway. He straightened out his truck; then, with a puff of black smoke, he was gone. My heart, while heavy, was far from sad. Caleb's volatile temper had exhausted my sadness long ago, and all that remained was a defeated sense of resignation.

My firstborn son was hell-bent on destroying the life I imparted, and he was adamant—there was nothing Arin, I, or anyone else could do to stop him. It was his life to live as he pleased.

We didn't speak to him for three days, though I knew where he was staying and kept in touch with his friend's parents. Finally, on the third day, he reluctantly called home. His flat, monotonous voice made it abundantly clear that I was the last person on earth with whom he wished to speak.

"All right, what do I have to do to come home?" he mumbled, hoping his three-day absence had served sufficient penance.

I closed my eyes and summoned my courage. "I'm sorry, Caleb," I said and then exhaled, my speech well-rehearsed. "You can't come home. Not yet. But we'll happily pay for rehab, and we're willing to accompany you first thing tomorrow. You'd be gone for seven weeks and miss the end of your senior year. But that's the only way you'll be allowed back home."

I stopped breathing and steeled myself for his anticipated fury. Instead, I was met with a long, silent pause.

"I need to think. I'll call you back." And then the line went dead.

Thirty minutes later, my phone rang again. Caleb's voice, no longer flat, shook with contempt. "Fine. I'll go. But I have only one thing to say. *Fuck you and fuck Dad!*"

Twenty-four hours later, Arin and I found ourselves seated on that outdoor patio, semi-humorously envisioning Caleb's responses and seriously wondering whether he'd ever speak to us again.

We had dropped him off at the main office several hours prior. Caleb hadn't wanted to know anything about where he was going or what he'd be doing. Everything about his upcoming wilderness adventure would come as a surprise. Caleb knew nothing of the hundreds of all-terrain miles he would hike with just the pack on his back or his three-day Primitive, where he would survive on only plants and roots that could be foraged high in the Arizona mountains. He knew nothing of the Anasazi name his ShadowWalker counselor would bestow or that he'd one day symbolically tattoo a falcon on his arm in fond remembrance. Above all, he knew nothing about why I'd selected that particular program.

I had narrowed my search to a ranch in Montana, but at the last minute, a mother I'd contacted for a referral returned my call. She said one of the owners was on a strange power trip and demanded nothing less than instant obedience from the boys. I immediately crossed that ranch off my list.

As a last and desperate resort, I called the Anasazi Foundation in Phoenix. I had read multiple positive reviews about their program, but I knew Caleb would balk at the Native American references.

Lori, the receptionist, answered my call immediately and spent well over thirty minutes answering my questions. She had personally been through the program, as had her husband and numerous other staff members.

After learning about the program's general structure, I asked my most pressing question: "What do you do if a camper runs away?" I envisioned Grayson sprinting through cornfields, surrounded by deputies and screaming teachers with waving arms. I'd had my fill of police involvement and unnecessary restraints.

Lori breezed through my question like it was the easiest one in the world, and I could hear the smile presumably dancing on her lips. "Oh, we just run with them. Eventually, they wear themselves out."

Then, she launched into a story, and I knew we had found our people.

"One time," she started, "We had a little thirteen-year-old girl entering the program. Her parents had warned us she might run, so we were ready when she arrived. As soon as their car pulled into the lot, that little girl jumped out and took off down the street, followed by two of our counselors. But in her rush, she forgot her shoes. It was 120 degrees that day and the cement was practically scalding. As she sprinted down a sidewalk in the middle of Phoenix, one of the counselors remarked, 'Your feet must be on fire. Do you want my shoes?' When she stubbornly refused, both counselors took off *their* shoes in an act of solidarity. When they finally limped back into the parking lot, all of their feet were blistered and scorched. That's the Anasazi way. We just run alongside the kids for as long as they need."

When we pulled into that same parking lot on February 11, 2019, we were met by two outdoorsy-looking men who appeared to be fresh (or perhaps not-so-fresh) off the trail. The two counselors, or TrailWalkers as they're called, introduced themselves. Arin and I shook their hands while Caleb hung back and did nothing. They motioned him up the stairs to be outfitted for his journey; he was grumpy, hungover, coming off of some unknown substance, and had refused food all day long. Caleb headed toward them without a backward glance, and Arin and I quickly called out our parting words. In quivering voices, we told him we loved him and would see him again soon.

Caleb's only response was the back of his hand—and a lone middle finger waving goodbye.

34

Corresponding

I cried so much you'll find that my Dover Thrift
Edition is waterlogged. Methinks I have grown soft in my
middle age. But me-also-thinks my latter-day reaction
speaks to the necessity of encountering stories at precisely
the right time in our lives.

—GABRIELLE ZEVIN, *The Storied Life of A. J. Fikry*

February 14, 2019. My journal reads:

> *Three days after dropping Caleb off at Anasazi, I am back
> home in tears, broken. But as always, never in the way I expect.
> I cannot shake the feeling that we are exactly where we need to
> be at precisely the right time. Ironically, on Valentine's Day, I
> am consumed by God's indescribable love and care. Everything
> is so beautiful; we are so blessed with family and friends.*
>
> *"The necessity of encountering stories at precisely the right
> times in our lives . . ."*

This is the right time, the right place, and the right peo-
ple, and we were led here by some invisible thread.
I am undone.

Anasazi isn't just for troubled teenagers; it's also for their parents. The following morning after dropping off Caleb, Arin and I began an intensive day-and-a-half of classes. We would have several books to read over the next few weeks, including *The Anatomy of Peace* by the Arbinger Institute and *The Seven Paths* written by the Anasazi Foundation,[1] and we were required to write Caleb weekly letters. In return, he would, we hoped, reply.

So began the outworking of the double helix I'd envisioned months before: Caleb's and Arin's intertwined healing.

February 16, from Arin:

How did I hurt you? How much did I hurt you? These are the questions I've been wrestling with for the last week. They weren't the questions I had before Anasazi. Those questions were, unfortunately, selfish regarding how I felt slighted by you. They were the wrong ones.

I came to Anasazi like you, Caleb. I knew little to nothing about the program. Your mother showed it to me, and I was desperate enough to agree. I didn't expect what the program had in store for your mother and me.

The day after we dropped you off, we met with a man named Michael. My goal was to help you, but the class was aimed more toward us. Throughout the day, we felt an awakening in our spirit and a conviction of soul as we realized how our actions and dispositions might have invited within you the very things we were warring against. I am responsible for your pain and alienation; I have been distant and unavailable, and I am sorry. Know that I am wandering in my own wilderness and doing everything within my power to meet you in a far different mindset in seven weeks.

February 20, from Caleb:

I want to apologize for our goodbye. I just couldn't bring myself to say anything. My first two days here were hell. I have never been more depressed and alone. I think this program will help me for a few weeks, but after that, it will be pointless. I hope you'll consider letting me come home early to start my new life. The main thing I want you to know is that, after a while, this camp will be pointless, and I will get more depressed. Please think reasonably and let me come home.

March 4, from Arin:

My grandfather (your great-grandfather) died of liver failure because he was an alcoholic. I started asking myself, "Have I drank too much? Have I exposed myself to habits that are slowly killing me and vicariously influencing my children's attitudes?" The answer is yes. I drink to cope, manage my stress, and deal with my life. I don't want to be controlled by anything and have decided to make decisions that will help me become a better version of myself. I quit drinking the day we returned from Arizona—not because of you but because of me.

I am sorry for drinking too much, exposing you to a lie, and hoping you would make decisions different from mine. I cannot expect of you what I do not expect of myself. I love you, son, and I hope you are doing well.

March 6, from Caleb:

This has been a hard week. I'm tired of being here and want to come home. The hike this week was the longest I've done so far. We hiked straight up the creek and then camped in a spot where everything was covered in leaves. I've lost my fear of spiders because I wake up and there's always one on me. I am constantly seeing giant lizards and scorpions. I'm just glad I haven't seen a tarantula. They don't give me enough food. I'm trying not to come back with my ribs showing, but it's hard to ration my food.

Another thing, I hope you aren't even considering gifting me with more time here because that would be pretty terrible. Also, it would be dope if you could come a week early so I can have spring break with my friends.

Just wondering what's going to happen with my truck and phone when I get home?

March 10, from Arin:

When I started in the oil field in Rock Springs, Wyoming, I was driving an old Camry and wearing Levi's jeans and a pair of thirty-dollar boots from Walmart. I joined twelve new trainees in a classroom setting. I remember walking into that class. Man, did I feel out of place! Every guy there was like some character out of a Larry the Cable Guy TV special—big beards, bellies, trucks, and mouths full of chew! Little did I know that in a few short years, I'd find myself trying to fit that same bill.

After buying an old Ford truck, the next logical step was to start having a beer or two with these guys, and the relationships I made helped me advance my career. But somewhere along the way, I lost who I was.

Father Evan once told me, "No man can wear two masks. Disjointed lives always bleed over, infecting and destroying one or the other." So I decided to leave the oil field and start my own business. Why? Simply because I was not strong enough to remain a directional driller and be who I wanted to be.

You, too, will have to make the same decision. When you are alone in your sleeping bag (with the spiders) and being honest with yourself, who is it you are and want to become?

Caleb, I want to challenge you. Courage is a virtue that doesn't come easily or cheaply. It's admitting who you are and then deciding to remove your mask and reveal your true self to the world. This will not be easy, which is why so few people do it. Look into your heart and ask yourself: "Who do I want to be?"

Then courageously remove your mask.

March 13, from Caleb:

Anasazi taught me to be thankful for things at home. Then we had the Primitive—just a blanket and the clothes on our backs for two days. No pack, no nothing. We had to dig up food and eat roots and plants. The Primitive taught me to be thankful for Anasazi. I will never complain about food again.

Another random thing I've been thinking about is reinventing myself. It's been cool having a new start with people I don't know.

Mary, my therapist, has helped me to see that I can't keep apologizing and doing the same things. This is my new beginning.

I'm also learning a lot about myself and feel like our family relationships will be much better. I miss everyone, and my problem with drinking is apparent. I truly hope you'll join me in two weeks for Family Camp (and I'm not just saying that to get out of here).

In Dad's letter, he said to think about who I am. When I am lying awake, looking up at the stars or hiking and looking up at the mountains, I think of who I want to be. Hearing what other people say about how I act, I realize how much of a jerk I truly am—not just to people here but to my own family. This has gotten me down a lot thinking about this. How can I be so mean to the people who love me most?

March 14, from Arin:

Your eyes are so bright! Your mother and I have your latest photograph set as the screensaver on our phones. "There he is," we've said. "Look at his eyes! Look at his smile!" Seeing those pictures made me want to take you in my arms and tell you how sorry I am for not being the dad you needed and how proud I am of you.

Caleb, we have no desire to remember the past or return to the way things were. We avoided setting boundaries because we were afraid of confronting you. Fear is no way to parent and certainly not conducive to love.

We will be with you shortly at Family Camp. Know there is a house in Colorado waiting to receive you with open arms.

March 16, from Caleb:

Please let the whole family know I am genuinely sorry for how I've acted over the past few years. Even though I've had my own problems, I shouldn't have been so distant and rude. I treated you (Mom) really poorly. I was mean, I didn't listen, and most of all, I wasn't appreciative. And, Dad, I have had some of the best times of my life with you, but I feel like we were always fighting to see who was more "dominant." In the future, I picture being able to call you guys all the time and just talk.

To Dad: In your letter, you wrote about how you came to the oil field and all that stuff. I really related to this letter. Coming into high school, I didn't want to be a nerdy kid who sucked at football and who no one liked. So when I got to high school, I made it my goal to be popular.

March 20, from Caleb:

In the middle of my last letter, I started crying for the first time out here. I broke down and talked to Mary about everything— the changes I have gone through and all the stuff I want to do. I'm genuinely scared I'm putting in all this work and worried it will just go to waste and not get recognized.

April 1, last letter from Arin:

In your last letter, you mentioned that you do not want to be remembered as "the kid who did cocaine."

When we were in Arizona, your mother and I did a "blanket stepping" where Mary asked us what we wished to leave behind. I chose guilt. Guilt for not being the father you needed. Guilt for responding out of fear and treating you in ways that made you feel bullied. Guilt for being less than what God called me to be.

How will you respond when we are less than what we need to be? While seven weeks is a long time to be in the wilderness, it is not enough time for any of us to completely change. In the same way you don't want to be seen as the kid who did drugs, I don't want to be seen as his overbearing father. I will endeavor to not bring the past into the future and ask that you try and do the same.

You have gone into the wilderness and proven yourself in all the ways we hoped you would. You have accepted the challenge and emerged as a better version of yourself, which is all we desired. Our prayer now is that we can all continue working on what we've learned at Anasazi.

I want you to hear me say, Caleb, that I love you. I believe the best in you, and I know you will become the man you want to be.

Arin and I were reunited with Caleb the first week of April. When we saw him on the trail, it was readily apparent that our son was no longer a boy. He was deeply tanned, his arms were as giant as tree trunks from doing pull-ups on branches while wearing his pack, and his legs looked like he'd packed small boulders beneath his skin.

He wrapped us warmly in his man-arms for a hug and then immediately set down his pack and pulled out his "fire sticks." Arin and I were baffled. We were seeing our son for the first time in forty-nine days, and all he could think of was starting his fire?

"Son," pleaded Arin, "we just got here. The fire can wait till later. Besides, it's still mid-afternoon."

Caleb paused for a split second and then looked at us like we were crazy.

"Dad," he exclaimed, "I've been hiking all day. I'm starving! No fire, no food."

With that, he went back to twisting a worn-down stick back and forth in another notched-out plank of wood filled with dry kindling. After a few moments, there was the smallest spark, and Caleb scooped up his pile of kindling with his hands and blew ever-so-gently on his nest. Before long, smoke began rising from his bundle, and shortly after, Caleb was emptying his pack to cook us dinner over a full-fledged fire.

We literally ate for *hours* and sampled everything Caleb had learned to cook, although his methods were slightly less than appetizing. After a day on the trail, the last thing the campers wanted to do was waste time dicing dates, onions, or garlic. So they simply popped them in their mouths, "loved 'em up and spit 'em back out"—mincing done in a flash. Caleb made macaroni with powdered milk, "loved-up" garlic, and parmesan cheese, followed by lentils and rice seasoned with more "loved-up" seasonings and dried vegetables. Then, we ate "pop tarts"—kneaded flour and water, which he buried in the sand to cook and then filled with "loved-up" dates. He finished his masterpiece with "frosting," a pasty concoction of water, powdered milk, and Gatorade powder. Caleb scarfed down his campfire creations as if they were tastier than Wagyu beef. He ate and ate while Arin and I marveled. We went to bed starving every night, but Caleb went to sleep—for the first time in seven weeks—uncomfortably full.

By the end of Family Camp, Caleb would be the only kid in Anasazi history to finish a week's worth of food in slightly over two days.

For two nights, Arin and I slept in the sand next to Caleb and hiked with him during the day. We ate what he had eaten, heated rocks for the bottom of our sleeping bags when we grew cold, and experienced life as Caleb had known it for the past seven weeks.

Our son was a sight for sore eyes. He had grown resilient and independent in a few short weeks; he chopped down yucca stalks to whittle new fire sticks and pointed out all the edible plants and roots he'd eaten on his Primitive.

Three days later, we returned to Phoenix to fly home as a happy, reunited family. At the airport, Caleb mentioned that a few of his friends might meet us at the airport to say hi. Arin and I uneasily agreed.

In Denver, he mentioned the fact they might just drive him home. He hadn't seen them for over seven weeks, to be fair, and he promised to come straight home.

That night, he polished off a bottle of Vodka on the car ride home with his friends.

So disappointed I could hardly breathe, I asked him—through barely restrained tears—about everything he'd written in his letters.

Caleb looked at me, once again disgusted by my ignorance. "Everyone knows, Mom, that's just the 'Anasazi high.' It's just what you say when you're at camp. No one really means it."

35

―――――

Detaching

Detachment involves "present moment living"―living in
the here and now. We allow life to happen instead of forcing
and trying to control it. We relinquish regrets over the past and
fears about the future. We make the most of each day.

—MELODY BEATTIE, *Codependent No More*

Caleb's therapist, Mary, had warned us of an instant regression with
his first bit of freedom. "Hold the course," she had said. "Think
long-term, not just present moment."

But I didn't understand Caleb's regression. Hadn't I done everything
right?

I had sent Caleb heartfelt, honest letters every single week. As a matter of fact, I was constantly checking over Arin's shoulder to make sure *his*
letters were finished in time. The campers only received mail once a week,
and I wanted to ensure Caleb was never without something from both
Arin and me.

Beyond that, I kindly reminded Arin to do his weekly assignments and readings; even when he forgot, I still completed mine, and I read every book I encountered on addictions and setting boundaries. I invited Arin to read them with me and never nagged when he said "sure" but never followed through. I even kept tabs on his schedule so he didn't double book himself during our weekly sessions with Mary and three-way called him if he had to be working.

If I had to have a kid in rehab, by golly, I would be the best rehab mom ever!

I just couldn't comprehend why Arin didn't feel the same way.

Over the years, his running complaint was that I was controlling, although I'd never understood what he meant. It would have been far easier to rope the wind than control my husband; Arin did what he wanted when he wanted—and I never uttered a word.

But then, I stumbled across Melody Beattie's book *Codependent No More*. Without even knowing me, she somehow managed to splash my life and experiences across every single page. She wrote:

> *Detachment is based on the premises that each person is responsible for himself, that we can't solve problems that aren't ours to solve, and that worrying doesn't help. We adopt a policy of keeping our hands off other people's responsibilities and tend to our own instead. If people have created some disasters for themselves, we allow them to face their own proverbial music. We allow people to be who they are. We give them the freedom to be responsible and to grow. And we give ourselves that same freedom. We live our own lives to the best of our ability. We strive to ascertain what it is we can change and what we cannot change. Then we stop trying to change things we can't.*[1]

Oops. Well, *that* I obviously hadn't done.

In another chapter, she added:

People say codependents are controllers. We nag; lecture; scream; holler; cry; beg; bribe; coerce; hover over; protect; accuse; chase after . . . drag to counseling; drag out of counseling . . . bring home; keep home; lock out . . . look through pockets; peek in wallets; search dresser drawers; dig through glove boxes . . . punish; reward; almost give up on; then try even harder.[2]

And those I had definitely done.

Who else would ensure that my children came home on time and alive? Who else would keep my family from killing each other in arguments, wake them up for school, or allow them to sleep when sleeping seemed the safer option? Who else would calm the rage, prevent teenagers from impregnating or being impregnated, make sure all the alcohol was hidden, read the books, do the homework, smooth over fractured relationships, ensure apologies got made, and sort out every other messy detail of life?

The answer was *no one*! There was only me. If I didn't do it, no one else would, and since everything in my life was falling apart at the seams, apparently, even *I* wasn't performing my own job very well.

I didn't understand. *Arin* didn't get worked up like me; *he* wasn't running around trying to fix everything and everyone. *He* fell asleep just fine every night. Didn't that *obviously* indicate his lack of concern?

I had just read, "When should we detach? When we can't stop talking, thinking about, or worrying about someone or something. When our emotions are churning and boiling. . . . A good rule of thumb is: you need to detach most when it seems the least likely or possible thing to do."[3]

And there was my problem. There was *my* gaping wound in need of healing.

While Arin and Caleb had been resolving their issues over seven weeks of back-and-forth letters, my problem was that I couldn't get out of their way and simply *let* them. I had to have my hands in *everything*. I made it my job to ensure Arin's letters got written and that he completed his homework. I suggested topics for such letters, reminded him of deadlines, and covered for him by offering unasked-for explanations should he miss our weekly counseling sessions.

I was our family's self-appointed Public Relations Manager.

Arin was right. I was truly controlling.

Yet if that was the case, how could I fix that which I had so blatantly failed to observe?

I sat down at my computer, intent on printing several images that captured the concept of *detachment*. I needed to surround myself with quick and simple reminders of my current task at hand.

But when I googled the word, pictures of fluttering butterflies, drifting balloons, and lighter-than-air bubbles popped up.

I wrote in my journal: *Why is "letting go" depicted with things that effortlessly float away? True detachment is fist-clenching, gut-wrenching, mouth-covering, heart-pounding, finger-biting, head-holding, fearful, falling, dying, and killing.*

In my new journal, designated just for quotes and pictures of detachment, I taped photographs of an unclenched hand dangling limply and a woman releasing papers to blow in the wind while falling through the air. In others, a woman is exhaling bubbles underwater—the world above fading from view—and a silhouetted figure sits alone in an enclosed box, head clasped dejectedly in her hands. I also filled that journal with quotes from Melody Beattie and Dr. Reedy, a psychologist in Utah, who often spoke on detachment and boundaries. He spouted tidbits of wisdom such as "Maybe acknowledging the reality of a situation is not the same as condoning it," or "The right or wrong decision will not cause or stop substance abuse," or one of my favorites, "Embrace the wisdom of not knowing, so others can access their own resources."[4]

Midway through Caleb's desert journey, I became cognizant of how ardently I was trying to hold my life and my crumbling self together. Like Humpty Dumpty, I felt cracked from head to toe, as if my insides were continuously seeping through each of my cracks. Whole chunks of shell were breaking off, and my "yolk" was spilling onto the ground. But by the time I picked up one broken piece to replace it, another had fallen.

So was I spending my days—picking up shattered fragments while desperately trying to gather my liquified innards that simply refused to be gathered. The harder I tried, the more I disintegrated. I was angry with my family. Raging, in fact. I was mad at each and every one of them—even those who didn't deserve it. Everything everyone did felt like a slap in my face. My children, my life, and my emotions were entirely uncontrollable.

Finally, I read the words by Melody Beattie, "For each of us, there comes a time to let go. You will know when that time has come. When you have done all you can do, it's time to detach. Deal with your feelings. Face your fears about losing control. Gain control of yourself and your responsibilities. Free others to be who they are. In so doing, you will set yourself free."[5]

I had tried everything I knew to do, and nothing seemed to be working. I was spinning all four wheels on sheer ice.

Despite all the ways that detachment had previously felt gut-wrenching, head-holding, and fist-clenching, in a single moment of despair one morning, I simply opened my hands and . . . let go.

I had finally exhausted all energy to control that which was never mine to control. Even if it meant every piece of my outer shell breaking and crumbling or my innards spilling to the ground, at last I felt ready and willing.

Tearfully, I succumbed to my disintegrating world.

Slowly, as my stuffed emotions bled out, all the grief I'd stiff-armed came seeping in. The drugs, the drinking, the lost relationships, the failing grades . . . me never being enough.

Grieving the living is like a cracked and oozing egg, I concluded. It takes a long, long time for all the pain to drain out.

Mornings always found me in my favorite spot—my herringbone chair in the corner of my office. For years, it had been my habit to rise while it was still dark and savor a few moments (or hours) alone with a good book, my journal, and a steaming mug of coffee (or two).

As each family member arose, they would trickle into my office, drag themselves—still half asleep—straight to my chair, and then plop down on my footstool and lay their head in my lap. Depending on the person, I would either scratch their back, rub their head, play with their hair, or "spider" their arms.

Caleb was the only exception. He never came to my office unless he needed something, and if he did, it was never early in the morning.

But on Sunday, June 23, 2019, at 6:30 a.m., Caleb was the first to hesitantly peek his head in my office door. He was wearing his clothes from the day before and appeared to not have slept a wink.

"Mom," he whispered urgently, his voice shaking, "go wake Dad. We need to talk."

Arin trudged in a few minutes later, still wearing his flannel pajamas and wiping the sleep from his eyes. He settled in the chair adjacent to mine, and Caleb positioned himself at my desk.

"So I spent the night at Dylan's last night," he began, "and I've been talking to his parents all night. They told me I should talk to you, so here I am."

His hands fidgeted with anything in reach, and he bounced his knee so vigorously the room shook.

"I've been doing cocaine again—a lot," Caleb confessed, tears starting to stream down his face. "I've been on a three-week bender, and I'm scaring myself; I need to stop. I want to get clean. Today. Right now. I'll go to the cabin with Bop[6] and quit cold turkey."

Arin and I listened to all he had to say, and then I picked up the phone to call my dad.

Four hours later, I was sitting in a pew, listening to Father Evan's sermon. He was holding a five-gallon pickle bucket and an icon of Christ. In front of me, a mother shushed her young child for the five-billionth time. Doing so seemed to exhaust her, and I felt like leaning over and vindictively whispering, "Just wait. These are the easiest problems you'll ever face." In another row, two preteenagers rested their heads on their mother's shoulders, and she spread her arms around them in loving response.

I hated everyone that morning, from the cute little girls with bouncy ringlet pigtails to their smiling, approving parents. I loathed the older folks bobbing their head in agreement with Father Evan's sermon and despised anyone else who even dared appear remotely happy.

Up front, Father Evan extended his arm, holding the pickle bucket high.

"What would happen if I put a shirt in this pickle bucket?" he asked.

Little children called out their answers, giggling, "It would smell like pickles!"

"That's right," he replied energetically, "and if we put this icon in the bucket, it would smell like pickles too! In the same way, if we spend a lot of time around Christ, we begin to absorb the aroma of Heaven."

Steam practically started billowing from my ears. Five-gallon buckets, icons smelling like pickles—what did any of that have to do with anything? My son was doing *cocaine*, consuming copious amounts of alcohol, and God only knows what else! Not to mention my other children, who were coming unglued in ways of their own.

All of my children except Grayson were failing miserably in school. Rylee was in the process of recklessly destroying her life, and Jacob was experiencing long stretches of sleepless nights; he felt panicked for no perceivable reason. Furthermore, it had been brought to my attention that Reagan refused to wear shorts for fear of exposing the scarred-over slashes high on her thigh.

Our family had *real* problems, not cute little kiddie problems. Where was the God for *our* problems, "the Christ of burnt men," as Thomas Merton called Him? The Jesus who healed lepers and walked among the poor, depraved untouchables. Where was *that* God, and why didn't I hear about *Him* from the pulpit?

There was no pickle bucket large enough to contain *our* family that day. Everyone else's problems were too neat and tidy, and the church too squeaky and shiny. Besides, who wanted to smell like pickles or Heaven when you could walk around smelling like *shit*?

I left immediately after Communion and allowed my inward monologue to eke out.

"Arin," I began as soon as my car door closed, "remember the story of

Balaam, that guy in the Bible? He was doing something God didn't want him to do, and God placed an *angel* before him, an *angel*! Then He made Balaam's donkey talk. If God can do all that to get Balaam's attention, why won't He do the same for our son? Why won't God put a flaming angel in Caleb's way to stop him? Hell, for that matter, why doesn't He put a freaking talking donkey in his path? He *can* do it, so why doesn't He?"

I flopped back against my seat in a huff. Beneath my simmering rage, huge, gathering teardrops threatened to expose my breaking heart.

Four days later, a flaming angel appeared.

In just four short days, Caleb's truck would veer into oncoming traffic, spiral through the air, land upside down, and skid across the asphalt—dragging half his body beneath it.

36

Crashing

June 27? That was the day that I died.

—Caleb Hatfield

When Caleb returned from the cabin with my dad, his eyes were once again bright. He was "high" on being un-high and jumped back into life with two feet. To distract himself, he worked for Arin and fished—then he fished and fished and fished some more.

He also surrounded himself with supportive friends. On Thursday, June 27, he met Jeremy, a dear family friend and one of Arin's employees, for dinner. Afterward, he planned on attending the Greeley Stampede, a local rodeo, with his friend Xander.

Caleb was bursting with energy, proud of his good-for-once choices, and Arin and I were equally pleased.

On his way to dinner, Caleb rear-ended a car at the same intersection where Arin ironically happened to be stopped for a red light on his way home from work. The damage was negligible, a mere fender bender, and Arin, fortuitously, was present to help Caleb resolve his first traffic accident. Phone numbers were exchanged; Arin headed west for home, and Caleb resumed traveling eastward for dinner with Jeremy.

Afterward, he courteously texted to let us know they had a great time, and he was now heading back to meet Xander.

Arin and I started letting down our guard. When Caleb was happy, he was such a *joy.*

Finally, summer started feeling more like summer, and we began allowing ourselves to enjoy it. Windows were flung open, and the drifting evening breeze carried wafts of barbecuing meat. Arin, Reagan, Grayson, and I ate dinner on our covered porch, leaving the dishes piled high in the sink. Rylee was out with her friends, and Jacob was playing video games downstairs.

As dinner wrapped up, Arin announced that it seemed the perfect time to take our new, four-person side-by-side for a spin.

I jumped up to grab my flip-flops, while Grayson immediately began begging to drive. Everyone else had already driven, he argued. Even Reagan, who was smaller than him.

Fortunately for Grayson, Arin was still giddy over Caleb's good decisions, so he handed over the keys, and off we went—racing down the street at a whopping three miles per hour. Reagan was seated behind Grayson on the driver's side, and I was behind Arin, where we could still meet eyes in his side-view mirror.

After several long minutes and a few mad grabs for the steering wheel, we finally made it to the end of our short street where Grayson took a wide, wobbling right. Miraculously, he smoothly maneuvered onto the narrow two-mile dirt trail that wound its way around our neighborhood's perimeter.

My phone rang the second we pulled onto the dirt road. Thankfully, we were crawling at a snail's pace, or I never would have heard my phone ring. It was Rylee. Her voice was high-pitched and frantic, more full of gasping than words. I barely discerned the words "Mom, Caleb, and truck" before Xander's number uncharacteristically popped up on my screen.

For some crazy reason, I put Rylee on hold and switched over to Xander. Arin eyed me curiously in his mirror, and I casually shrugged before plugging my right ear to hear better.

"Hi, Mrs. Hatfield. It's Xander," he said hesitantly; it was the first time I'd ever heard him speak more than three words. "I'm just calling to check in on Caleb. He was supposed to meet me, and I haven't seen him yet. I heard he might have been in an accident."

Instantly, I relaxed. Surely, this was why Rylee was so mistakenly worked up.

"Yeah, Xander, he was in a little accident," I informed him. "But it was just a fender bender. He's fine. Did you try calling him?"

"I did," Xander replied, "but he didn't answer, and his location on Snapchat hasn't moved for a while. Someone said they saw him getting loaded up in an ambulance."

By this time, Arin had wearied of inching along. Despite Grayson's reluctance, they were walking opposite half-circles around the vehicle to switch places.

Meanwhile, my phone buzzed again. In typical Rylee fashion, she had grown tired of waiting and was incessantly demanding my attention. Knowing she'd keep trying until I finally acknowledged her, I denied her call, mentally reassuring myself I'd connect with her after Xander. But the second I rejected her call, another number popped up. Blake, another one of Caleb's friends, was calling. The idea that something might be wrong gradually started seeping into my brain, infusing it with a cloud of confusion.

At that moment, a blurry photo arrived from Rylee's phone number; it vaguely looked like Caleb's truck. I quickly glanced at it and then returned to my conversation with Xander, my confused brain still pondering Rylee's cryptic photograph.

Finally, an enlightened Xander suddenly blurted, "Wait—you don't know his truck is flipped over on 257, do you?"

With Xander's words, my world likewise inverts. My senses enter an alternative realm where I am no longer living my life but somehow standing outside of it. I observe Arin staring at me intently, silently motioning and demanding to know what's happening. Ignoring him, I robotically hang up on Xander and mechanically speed-dial my daughter.

"Mom! Mom! Why do you keep hanging up on me?" Rylee demands. And on some level, I realize she's sobbing—loudly—though I don't know how I detect this, for I'm not really hearing. "It's Caleb. His truck—it's crushed. Flat. I saw his blood—lots of it—and his red shoes, but no Caleb."

Arin is staring at me beneath his concerned, furrowed brow, and our eyes meet in his rearview mirror. This locked gaze might have lasted indefinitely, but eventually, I let it slip through my squinting, questioning eyes that something is indeed wrong. With the spell now broken, I soundlessly mouth, "Caleb's been in a crash." Still, I don't comprehend my own words.

Spinning my finger in a fast vertical circle, I signal Arin to turn around and head home. Instantly, he slams on the gas and yanks on the wheel. The back tires spin in place, kicking up dust clouds and gravel. The moment they finally catch, we take off like a jet. We are nearly airborne, and then suddenly, we are flying. On some level, I grow remotely aware that my unfeeling body is being dashed against the door of the side-by-side with every turbulent turn.

Within seconds, we're tearing back into our driveway. For some odd reason, Arin finds it imperative to run into the house and change pants. He's muttering something about them not being suitable for the hospital. Meanwhile, I load the little kids in the car and then turn from the front seat to prepare them.

"Guys, we have to go to the hospital," I tell them. "Caleb has been in an accident. We're going to have to drive right by the crash, and when we do, I want you to put your heads down. Don't look up—no matter what."

I hear my voice; it's inordinately calm, and I find myself wishing I could be this way always.

Reagan nods compliantly as Grayson speculates, blunt and out loud as always, "I wonder if he's dead."

For once, I don't correct him, for I, too, am wondering this very thing. I notice that—like Grayson—my wonder is simplistically curious rather than appropriately dread-filled, and even as I think this, I recognize it's bizarre.

Within two minutes, we are approaching the intersection where Xander claimed the accident occurred. He was not wrong.

Unbuckling, I lean forward to sit tall. Myriads of fire trucks, police cars, and ambulances are lining the street. Everywhere I look, blue-and-red flashes pulse like strobe lights, visually signifying to anyone hard of hearing that a disaster has occurred. I tuck this image away, intent on recalling it later. I feel certain I'm missing something I'm intended to grasp, and although time feels expansive, I recognize it's not expansive enough to perceive the ever elusive, ungraspable "something."

As we maneuver our way into the heart of the accident, I observe vehicles strewn helter-skelter as if dropped from a toddler's careless hand and then forgotten. Car doors are wide open; bikes remain wherever they skidded to a stop. People are milling about—I suppose frantically—but in my mind, the scene is eerily apocalyptic. Void of all movement and sound.

Despite the chaos I'm witnessing, in my head, everything is blissfully silent and still.

Off to my left, a three-wheeled motorcycle sits several feet away from what I assume to be its recently attached sidecar. The two units have been completely severed, and an elderly couple sits on the curb clutching motorcycle helmets and shaking their heads.

He's killed someone, I flatly presume, already knowing my son is at fault.

We pass two smaller, crushed cars and then a pickup. A fair distance away, I spot Caleb's truck. My eyesight is seemingly failing, and I blink my eyes; then I open them wider. The silver Dodge before me is nearly unrecognizable, so I strain to make sense of the scene.

Laid out diagonally across two lanes of traffic, Caleb's vehicle is, as Rylee said, upside down and nearly flat. The lifted truck, which once towered above me, now appears no taller than my waist. Perhaps, I briefly consider, it is simply slowly sinking into the endless sea of sparkling glass shards. The top must be partially buried, I conclude. For if not, Caleb's body would have certainly been crushed—an obvious impossibility.

Caleb's impounded truck after the accident

For some reason, I snap a picture of the scene just before Arin slams on his brakes. Parking in the middle of the road, he begins waving his arms at the advancing officer before even stepping one foot from the car.

"My son!" he yells frantically as I grow embarrassed by his agitation. "That's my son's truck! Where's my son?"

The officer raises both hands, attempting to calm Arin; then Arin steps forward to meet him in the empty space.

"Sir," the officer warns, "I'm going to need you to calm down."

"Calm down?" Arin blasts. "That's my son's truck, and you're telling *me* to calm down?"

"Sir, I'm not allowed to confirm where they've taken him," the officer stoically replies. "If I were you, I'd call all the local hospitals, starting with the big trauma one right off the freeway."

He adds, "But I can't let you drive in your current state."

With that, I step in between them.

"I'm calm enough to drive," I offer evenly as the officer assesses my disposition. He pauses, looks at me skeptically, and then nods.

Turning back toward our car, I notice two small heads and four very large eyes taking in everything I never wanted them to behold.

Arin flies around to the passenger side while I ease into my seat. Glancing in the rearview mirror, I witness the officer motioning to another, as if in slow motion. He indicates with two fingers, pointing first to his eyes and then toward us, that we are to be monitored and followed. A second officer nimbly hops into his car and pulls out after us. Once again, I drive precisely the speed limit, not wanting to test an officer's patience. He tails us all the way to the city's edge, and the minute he turns off, my arms and legs start spastically shaking.

Meanwhile, my phone rings again. We'd forgotten about Jacob. He's standing in an empty kitchen, wondering where everyone went. I instruct him to sit tight while Arin dials Jeremy. I inform Jacob that Jeremy will be along shortly to drive him to the hospital. There's been a small accident, I casually mention.

Ten minutes later, we are pulling up to the ER. Arin is jumping out of the car before it even stops rolling, and I'm trailing behind with our two youngest children.

For forty-five minutes, we don't know whether Caleb is dead or alive. No one with his description has checked in to the trauma hospital or any other hospital nearby.

The hospital staff escorts our growing bunch to the family room, where we wait for them to—hopefully—receive information about our son. My panic-stricken dad bursts—right arm and right leg first—through the ER metal detector. I think: *This is a strange way of walking, right arm synced with right leg,* and as I contemplate my dad's entry, Arin rushes forth to embrace him. Two grown men cling to each other, sobbing, heaving, and united by their fierce love for Caleb. Rylee is sitting in the waiting room with her friend Raelyn, and my mom is walking Grayson around the vending machines. Carol, her husband, Arlen, a few of Caleb's friends, their parents, and my sisters arrive.

Nearly everyone is crying, and I disperse tissues. I take note of everyone's presence and mentally note where they are sitting. This fact seems rather important; *I* must *remember where everyone is sitting,* I think, almost certain this information will come in handy at some unknown point down the road.

But for some odd reason, although I can cognitively identify everyone, I can't discern their faces. Instead, I see only white smudges surrounded by faint outcroppings of hair, as if someone has taken their thumb and smeared away any distinguishing features. I can recognize voices and link them to their owner, yet even then, I can't determine their source of origination.

Before long, Jeremy and a few of Arin's employees trickle in, but Jacob, I'm informed, is outside with his friends. Going to him, I rub his back and console him as we sit on a metal bench. Then I return to the waiting room, where a stranger is asking to pray with us. I plainly tell her no and escort her to the door.

Still, Arin and my dad sob and heave.

And then there is Grayson. His attention span is ticking like a time bomb, along with his appetite. How long until he needs something to eat? I'm constantly aware of his pacing and muttering, "I know Caleb is probably hurt bad or dead, but I was really looking forward to Elitch's[1] tomorrow. I hope this hospital thing doesn't take too long."

"Grayson," I patiently remind him for the umpteenth time, finding his words slightly amusing, "I'm guessing we're going to have to cancel tomorrow."

Simultaneously, I'm thinking there might still be a chance.

What would it be like, I wonder, to have the luxury of being singularly focused?

From an endlessly long white corridor, a nurse's voice tinkles like a bell.

"Mr. and Mrs. Hatfield?" she sings out, and Arin bolts from his seat.

With an unreadable expression, she informs us Caleb is alive. She continues, "He was awake but incoherent when the paramedics first arrived. It took the ambulance longer to get to the hospital because, in his hysterics, your son ripped out his breathing tube and IVs, and the paramedics had to pull over to re-intubate and stabilize him."

Later, the police would inform us that Caleb gradually drifted across his lane into stopped and oncoming traffic. He hit the first vehicle near the driver's rear tire. Then, his side mirror hit a motorcyclist's helmet, knocking it clean from his head. His contact with the motorcycle was forceful enough to separate it from its sidecar. Caleb's truck then ramped up the driver's side of a small SUV, peeling back its top like a can of sardines and forcing it backward into another truck. At that point, Caleb's vehicle became airborne, flipping nearly two hundred degrees in the air and partially ejecting Caleb's body before finally landing upside down. From there, his truck spun one-and-a-half rotations on its top. His legs were trapped in the cab while his torso was dragged behind on the asphalt.

Including Caleb's truck, five vehicles had been totaled.

"The police informed us that there were no brake or swerve marks," the nurse continues, "and onlookers reported that your son actually accelerated as he approached the other vehicles. They speculated he might have been suicidal."

"Was he?" she wants to know, and all we have to go on is his text telling us that "dinner was great."

"Caleb has a significant head injury," the nurse continues, "and it will take several hours to run him through tests and clean him up. As soon as we're finished, you can see him."

Right then, a police officer strides past. Although we are invisible to him, he's heavily shrouded in black (or perhaps it only feels that way) and carrying a small kit. The nurse follows our eyes and confirms: It *is* a toxicology kit, and the officer *will* be testing Caleb's blood for alcohol or "other substances."

The accident occurred at approximately 7:40 p.m., but it is well after 2:00 a.m. when a doctor comes to collect us.

In hushed tones, he informs us that our son has multiple fractures, including in several vertebrae, his nose, pelvis, scapula, and two places in his skull.

I fight off the urge to interrupt him and ask for a pen and some paper; I have a feeling he's spouting off the beginning of a very long list, which again seems imperative to remember.

Without acknowledging my unspoken need, the doctor continues, "Over half of Caleb's back and his right leg from hip to knee have been scraped away. Some areas are exposed all the way down to his muscles. His lungs are severely bruised, and he went into respiratory failure in the ambulance. The paramedics had to intubate him, and a ventilator is now doing his breathing.

"Most concerning," the doctor says gravely, "is Caleb's brain. It's swollen, and the swelling is still increasing. The nurses are watching his inflammation markers, but if they climb much higher, I'll have to immediately remove a piece of his skull to allow for expansion and prevent brain damage. A screw in his head is currently monitoring his bulging brain. Caleb undoubtedly has a brain injury—the question is, to what extent?"

When asked, the doctor says he's unable to predict any sort of prognosis. He has induced a medical coma so Caleb's body can rest, but he can in no way guarantee how or *if* he'll emerge. Before entering the trauma ward, he turns to offer one last thought. "The following seventy-two hours are absolutely critical."

Hand in hand, Arin and I follow the doctor through one, then two, locked doors. The trauma wing is cold and stone-silent, save the incessant beeping of machines keeping mutilated bodies alive. It suddenly strikes me that in one of the twelve or so darkened rooms . . . lies our son.

I pause at his door. Inside, darkness extends infinitely beyond and below. His bed seems to hover over a bottomless pit, and I shrink back lest its swirling vortex consume me. If I remain outside, life still exists as I know it. But the second I pass through his door, I inherently understand that I will be entering an alternative universe about which I know nothing.

Half-step by half-step, I draw near.

As I approach, I'm pleasantly surprised. A few clean stitches cross the bridge of Caleb's nose, still smeared with dried blood, and some staples hold a gash together near the screw in his partially shaved head. I inspect him inquisitively. His familiar nail beds are caked in old, brown blood, and a thin stream of fresh blood oozes from his left ear. I question the nurse monitoring the machines. It's probably from his fractured skull, she surmises; he might lose hearing in that ear.

But besides all that, Caleb appears to be peacefully sleeping.

Perhaps his doctor is prone to exaggeration, I muse.

The most bothersome sight, I decide, is the countless cords, wires, and tubes encapsulating my son. A line trails out the top of his gown, draining a pinkish-brown fluid, while another deposits some clear liquid into his body. Rubbery hoses snake into his nose and mouth, and a way-too-big, accordion-looking plastic hose has been jammed down his windpipe.

I swallow hard, imagining.

Everything together makes me feel slightly queasy.

But already, Arin is at Caleb's bedside—stroking the good side of his head and smothering him carelessly with kisses.

I, on the other hand, hesitate to reach out, frozen in place by my old fear that his flesh will be cold. Cautiously, I stretch out one arm and brush his cheek with the backs of my fingers. Quickly, I withdraw them, having learned all I need to know.

Caleb's flesh is still warm.

Around three in the morning, I drive Jacob home to sleep. It is pitch-black, and few other cars are on the road. An uncanny sense of peace settles over me as I drive, and a Bible verse from the book of Job comes to mind: "Though He slay me, yet will I trust Him."[2]

Somehow, I understand—though not with my mind—that whether Caleb lives or dies, everything will be all right. Somehow.

I pull into our long driveway, the moon reflecting off the hood of my car, and watch Jacob disappear into the house. It hits me then that I will never again hear the rumbling sound of Caleb's truck pulling down our drive.

A strange lump catches in my throat and sits there. Unmoving.

37

Thawing

I will give you a new heart and put a
new spirit in you; I will remove from you your heart
of stone and give you a heart of flesh.

—Ezekiel 36:26 (NIV)

Arin and I sat awake by Caleb's bedside for what little remained of that first night. For hours, we stared through gritty eyes at the fluctuating number that would determine whether Caleb's doctor removed part of his skull and constantly reminded us that his brain might be permanently damaged. It crept steadily toward the limit and then paused, plateaued, and slowly declined. So it continued for hours. Our panic rose with Caleb's inflation markers and settled as they lowered. We spoke little to each other. His body was obviously waging an invisible internal war, and all we could do was wait and pray. Accordingly, every minute felt like a day, and each hour felt like a year.

By the time the sun rose on June 28, Arin and I felt as though we had each aged a decade.

Mid-morning, our kids were allowed to see their brother for the first time. Grayson loudly let us know how disappointed he felt to have missed out on Elitch's, but the others tiptoed in silently and spoke in hushed, reverential tones. Guilt flickered across their faces as they lightly stroked his arm, for by that point, each had wished away his raging, domineering presence numerous times. The question looming behind each of their pinched faces was plain: *Did I somehow unwittingly will this to happen?*

Back in the family room, the mother of one of Caleb's friends had sent bagels, and three mothers of Jacob's friends had offered to bring lunch. Most of our extended family was present. Toddler nieces and nephews played hide-and-seek underneath and behind the few furniture pieces, delighted by their unexpected reunion. Little by little, Caleb's friends (most of whom I'd never met) began trickling in. When the room grew too crowded, they overflowed into the hallway. They brought coffee, played cards, and offered to order pizza for dinner. The friends Caleb had worked so hard to keep separate from his immediate family were now meeting his grandparents, uncles, aunts, and cousins.

For once, I was surrounded by a massive support system in the midst of a crisis, and although my son was fighting for his life, I couldn't help but feel overwhelmed with gratitude and a subtle joy. Arin's coworkers sent flowers, his employees stepped up to run the business, and someone from church called to arrange future meals. Gift cards to local restaurants began pouring in, Dylan offered to stay with our dogs, and perhaps for the first time ever, I imagined that our family might possibly be loved.

JoyfulSorrow.

PainfulBeauty.

By noon, I still hadn't brushed my teeth or changed clothes. I could have asked someone to bring something from home, but for some reason, it seemed absolutely essential that I select my own clothing. I rushed to Walmart—three miles away—to purchase a new outfit and toothbrush.

I picked out a bright-yellow T-shirt with flowers—which was odd because I rarely wore flowers, and I *never* wore yellow. I distinctly remember arguing with myself while studying the shirt. Half my brain thought the shirt was fantastically horrid; the other part thought it was simply fantastic. Next, I selected a dark pair of capri jeans; again, I rarely wore capris, and I *never* wore dark-washed denim. When I later had to hop up and down in the hospital restroom just to get the jeans over my hips, I would finally realize they were a full size too small. I would have to unfasten the top button just to breathe, and my love handles would squeeze over the top. But for some bizarre reason, I remember feeling genuinely pretty that morning, even though Arin raised a quizzical eyebrow the first time he witnessed my choice of clothing.

Regardless, my Walmart shopping spree was going along swimmingly until it came time to select new underwear. They were tangled together in pull-out bins, allegedly according to style and size. I dug through several bins before realizing I was doing nothing but shuffling around brightly colored underwear. Refocused, I started again, freshly intent on finding my size. I made it through *all* the bins that time before I caught myself entirely zoned out, wrist-deep in underwear. Now absolutely committed, I began staring intently at each tag. Still, I could not distinguish the words to find my size.

I had known this disorientation before and understood it would only get worse. Scanning the aisles, I tried to catch another woman's sympathetic eye, but I couldn't seem to differentiate the people from the racks. For the life of me, I didn't know how I was ever going to find the right-sized underwear, and at that very moment, finding the right size seemed the most critical task in the world.

Completely distraught, I sat down in the middle of the aisle and buried my face in my hands. Before long, tears were streaming down my face, and I was sobbing—not because my son's body lay broken in the hospital but because I couldn't find my size of underwear.

After a long (or perhaps short) while, I stood up, eventually tracked down an employee, and asked her to help me find underwear. She looked at me like I was crazy. I'm not sure she was wrong.

I've never felt so helpless in my life.

My parents graciously offered to pay for a hotel room for the week so anyone needing sleep could rest in a queen-sized bed rather than the "luxurious" hospital chairs. Mid-afternoon, Arin left for the hotel to catch a nap before his family arrived from Florida. Then he and my dad would take the night shift while I got a full night's sleep.

It was hard to believe that it had barely been twenty-four hours since Caleb's last meal with Jeremy. Since he was in a coma and incapable of eating, his nurse arrived carrying the equivalent of a protein shake and a large syringe. She positioned his bed upright and then suctioned half the liquid and injected it into a tube that ran directly into his stomach.

Within a few moments, Caleb started convulsing.

The heaving started from his belly and then seized his chest, neck, and head. Suddenly, cream-colored liquid was spewing from his mouth, followed by large chunks of undigested food from his dinner with Jeremy.

I froze. The massive volume filled Caleb's mouth and began pressing into his cheeks and leaking from his nose. The nurse scurried to empty his mouth with a suction wand, but the chunks of food were too large. She pressed a button for help, and I stepped back against the wall to create space. Nurses began pouring in as Caleb started involuntarily coughing. I watched, horrified, as he inhaled large food chunks through his corrugated tube. Soon he was neither coughing nor inhaling but simply convulsing, not breathing, and still entirely unconscious—suffocating before my very eyes.

As if reading my mind, Caleb's nurse whispered to the others, "He's asphyxiating," and then began using her fingers to sweep out his mouth.

After that, I recall nothing but blackness.

The following morning, June 29, the doctor informed us that the swelling in Caleb's brain had remarkably stabilized, and he felt comfortable removing the screw from Caleb's skull, despite the fact he had not yet crossed the seventy-two-hour benchmark. But instead of relief, Arin and I felt unnerved. How would we know if the swelling resumed?

The doctor casually replied, "You won't, but his body will tell you. He'll vomit, or his temperature or respirations might change. He might even have a seizure."

Acquiescing, we returned to the waiting room.

'Tis a strange thing entrusting your child's life to another.

After removing his screw, the doctor determined it was time to test whether Caleb was still "nonresponsive," as he'd been labeled upon admission. He informed us that he would incrementally dial back the medication that was keeping Caleb in a coma and then issue a simple command to check for compliance. Arin stood on one side of the bed, clutching Caleb's hand, and I took my place on the other.

"I'm dialing back the medicine now," said the doctor somberly. We waited expectantly . . . but nothing happened.

"Caleb," the doctor yelled loudly, "Can you hear me? Wiggle your right toes if you can hear my voice." With that, he gave Caleb's toes a little pinch.

Nothing.

"Buddy," Arin implored, "can you wiggle a few toes for your mom and me?"

Still nothing.

Arin and I exchanged nervous glances as the doctor dialed back the medication a bit more.

"Caleb, can you—" the doctor requested, leaning in. Suddenly, Caleb's right leg flew straight in the air with an exaggerated kick, missing the doctor's nose by mere inches.

My gaze met Arin's glistening eyes across the bed. Our son was in there and was literally alive and still kicking.

Even though Caleb had successfully responded to the doctor's commands, his medical team still opted to keep him in a medically induced coma as he remained entirely reliant on a ventilator. But the following day,

June 30, Caleb's doctor promised to remove the tube from his throat if he could prove himself capable of breathing independently.

Once again, Arin and I convened by Caleb's bedside. Barely breathing ourselves, we gripped the metal rails as the doctor slowly began turning down the ventilator.

After several long moments of silence, we were pleased to observe Caleb's oxygen levels holding steady. Still, his chest remained motionless. To our dismay, there was no rise or fall, no sudden gasping for air as I'd romantically envisioned.

I groped for Arin's hand as the doctor resumed lowering the machine, his expression pensive and grim. The clock on the wall pounded out the seconds, and we watched every flashing ventilator number like a pair of hawks, though we knew what none of them meant. We jumped at every beep, whirr, and cleared throat, until finally Caleb's doctor quietly proclaimed, "This is him. Your son is breathing—and he's doing it all on his own."

After several hours of successful, independent breathing, the next step was to wake Caleb from his coma. Once the supply of medicine was completely cut off, there was no telling how long it would take him to wake up, and for whatever reason, Arin and I were—temporarily—not allowed in his room.

Consequentially, we were gathered in the family room when a nurse cracked the door with a gleam in her eyes.

"Your son is awake and ready to see you," she shared. Then she pulled me aside as I lunged for the door. "I'm a mother too," she confided, "and I thought you should know that the first words out of Caleb's mouth were 'I want my mom.'"

Arin entered the room before me, and the second Caleb saw him, his eyes sparked, and he attempted a smile. Motioning with his hand—still tethered with cords and wires—he summoned Arin close. After being intubated and not speaking for three days, his voice was hoarse and raspy.

"Dad," Caleb whispered, his face clouding over with worry, "am I ever going to get better? Where are all my friends?"

"You're doing perfect, son," Arin reassured him. "Your friends have been here the whole time, and you'll be better before you know it."

Then it was my turn. Sitting down beside his bed, I scooted as close as the bedrails would allow.

"Hi, Mom," Caleb croaked almost sheepishly, reaching for my hand.

Then the world disappeared, just as it did when he was first placed on my belly, fresh from the womb. Once again, it was only my firstborn son and me. No longer hesitant, I grabbed his hand and cradled it gently between my two. Gathering it to my face, I repeatedly kissed it, beaming from ear to ear. Instantly exhausted, Caleb tucked my hand beneath his chin. Slumping toward me, he drew as close as the bedrails would allow and then once again fell deeply asleep.

I sat, as I did nearly eighteen years prior, not daring to move lest I wake him. I studied his beautiful face, long eyelashes, and short, stumpy nail beds, and only when he started softly snoring did I move. I gently stroked his thick dark hair, kissed his weathered cheeks, and loved him in a way he'd forbidden for years.

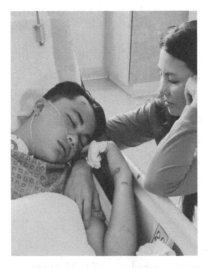

Caleb and me, moments after he came out of his coma and spoke for the first time

Slowly, I felt my heart thawing, and I allowed myself to remember what it was like to love my son—softly, compassionately, and tenderly—like his up-close mother. Fear gripped my heart, for in some ways, loving him hurt worse than everything. If I opened my heart to love, I risked losing him. Again. Yet there was also the chance that I might *find* him.

Later, Caleb would refer to June 27 as "the day that I died," and in many ways, he was right. A part of him perished in that accident, never again to return, while the rest of him was resurrected to new life. On that day, he became my twice-born firstborn, and his broken body cracked me open—once more—to love.

That night, Caleb spiked a high fever. A chest X-ray confirmed he had aspiration pneumonia. He spent his fourth night in the hospital literally packed on ice, while I once more stared at a screen, praying for numbers to lower.

38

Hallucinating

You are a falsehood, you are my illness, you are a ghost.
Only I do not know how to destroy you, and perceive that for a
certain time I must suffer you. You are a hallucination I am having.
You are the embodiment of myself, but only of one side of me.

—FYODOR DOSTOEVSKY, *The Brothers Karamazov*

Caleb's eyes were wild with fear, and his face was contorted in agony. His strong grip was crushing my hands, and his screams were practically intolerable.

"Stop, please stop," he whimpered deliriously, tears streaming uncontrollably down his face. Crouching by his bed, I attempted to look him straight in his rolled-back eyes.

"It will all be over soon," I consoled in a soothing voice. "You're doing great. Just keep breathing and try not to move."

The nurse gave me a warning glance and then picked up her sponge to resume the debridement. Over and over, her sponge—which reminded me of steel wool—audibly scraped Caleb's raw flesh, and its looped, wiry strands caught on bits of embedded asphalt and glass, ripping them from his back. For nearly twenty minutes, the nurse scrubbed, Caleb howled, and I attempted to comfort my son, who, in all reality, would remember neither the procedure nor my presence, thanks to his newly injected medication.

Morphine hadn't touched the pain of his road rash, which rivaled that of third-degree burns. So his doctor ordered ketamine, a drug with amnesic properties, to ensure Caleb would, at the very least, never recall such a painful procedure.

After the nurse finished, Caleb lay on his side, panting, and then instantly fell asleep, while I crept around his back for my first peek at his undressed wounds.

Nearly 75 percent of his backside was raw and pink as fresh meat. Black, linear gouges streaked his left flank as if a monster with thirty asphalt claws had tried to shred the flesh from his ribs. Bright red blood trickled from the deepest wounds, and on his right buttock and scapula, thick ribbons of skin had been stripped away, revealing the depths of his striated, yellow-oozing muscles.

Typically, I would have found such a sight revolting. But per my normal crisis mode, my head had detached from my body. I studied Caleb's wounds inquisitively as if I were a medical intern doing my rounds and he were merely a stranger. Likewise, for the entirety of Caleb's hospital stay and rehabilitation, I would robotically take copious notes, evenly ask rational questions, commit all my observations to memory, . . . and then dissolve in a heap weeks later.

But at that very moment, I was just grateful for the ketamine. If Caleb didn't remember the procedure, I could almost pretend it never happened.

Unfortunately, along with the drug's amnesic effects, ketamine can also cause hallucinations and flashbacks, which reportedly last less than an hour.

Caleb's hallucinations lasted all night.

Beckoning Arin's sister Joetta, who was also spending the night in the hospital, Caleb covertly whispered in her ear, inquiring whether she might be American. After she confirmed her citizenship with a giggle, he confided his top-secret plan. His bed was actually a boat, he divulged behind a cupped hand. If she would push, they could sail through the door, out of the hospital, and back to their home country.

When Joetta didn't comply, Caleb tried to rip off his bounteous tubes and wires and make his escape.

We pinned him to the bed with the help of his nurse, and I spoke in low, calming tones like I'd so often done with Grayson.

Then, just as he started drifting off to sleep, he bolted wide awake, suddenly sure that his oxygen mask was filled with narcotics. I was his friend, Adrian, and Joetta was Cody, Adrian's accomplice. Apparently, we were trying to poison him. Ripping the mask from his face, Caleb glared at us with black, hate-filled eyes and then screamed at us for not helping him stay sober. His flailing arms turned into angry face-seeking fists, and now, we had to try keeping his mask near his nose without getting decked. Still riddled with pneumonia, Caleb's oxygen levels dangerously plummeted to the low seventies without his oxygen mask. But with it, his paranoia skyrocketed.

We wrestled and restrained him for hours, untangled his cords, redressed his bandages, and reattached his monitoring pads, all while trying to keep his oxygen mask near his face.

After a long while, he settled down. But then his mask became a refreshing glass of cold water, and he suddenly grew so thirsty he thought he might die. Regardless of the ice chips his nurse provided, Caleb wanted water, which he was still incapable of swallowing. Refusing to wear his mask, Caleb now insisted on drinking from it, and when no ice-cold liquid spilled forth from his tipped-back "cup," he grew enraged that we were withholding the one thing he needed for survival. How could he survive the blistering Arizona desert without water? He demanded to know.

This continued for hours.

Finally, near 3:00 a.m., Caleb partially fell asleep. In the land between sleep and wakefulness, he fitfully murmured about thousands of cranes flying around a beautiful mountain, marijuana dabs, lines of cocaine, and a heroin delivery he'd be murdered for missing. He continuously asked for my phone to call his friends for a "hit," and incoherently rambled about all sorts of events I could only pray had never actually happened.

Although his toxicology report had come back clean, I felt confident his nurses would report him should they overhear his delusional rantings. Therefore, I shushed him and distracted them whenever they entered his room—for his protection and mine.

My heart was just beginning to soften toward him again, and I was entirely uncertain whether it could handle him returning to his old ways. Again.

Inwardly, I had greatly hoped that this accident would change him, that it might be the one thing, the flaming angel, that would restore Caleb to himself, restore him to us. Yet with every passing drug-related comment, my optimism crumbled.

By morning, my faith was gone. I felt certain I had peered into the darkness of his soul the night prior, and I had grown convinced that his battle with drugs would be never-ending. This accident, this major wake-up call, would pass by unheeded. Caleb would continue consuming drugs, and they would, in time, utterly consume him. I reluctantly conceded, *This will all be another wasted experience, another "Anasazi high."*

I felt deathly afraid to let myself love him.

On the Fourth of July, the pandemonium outside Caleb's door suggested a new trauma patient had arrived. Through paper-thin walls, I listened to what Caleb's room must have sounded like one week prior. A doctor was barking orders; machines were rolling and then beeping; nurses were flying around the room, speaking in heightened tones.

Through overheard conversations, I learned the new patient, a young man, had been tubing down the Poudre River in celebration of the holiday and had somehow fallen off his tube, broken his neck, and nearly drowned.

In time, his room fell silent.

Eventually, I heard hushed whispers. I could imagine his family encircling his bed, dabbing their eyes, taking in all the machines, wires, and cords. For hours, I heard soft comings and goings.

When it grew dark, I reclined in my hospital bed right next to Caleb. He had asked me to sleep nearby. Every time he startled or groaned, I rested my hand on his chest, and he settled. Twice he even murmured, "I love you, Mom."

At exactly 10:30 p.m., the piercing wail of what could have only been the young man's mother broke the silence and my heart. Her son had breathed his last while mine slept restlessly beneath my hand. At that very moment, explosions began shaking the hospital windows. Fireworks were going off, whistling and bursting in the air, commemorating our country's freedom.

Why? I immediately wrote in my journal. *Why are we so fortunate? My son is still a warm body. Still breathing, moving, speaking, reasoning . . . becoming. There are no words.*

I stayed awake a long time that night, scarcely daring to breathe.

It didn't seem right.

Nothing seemed right.

On July 5, eight days after the accident, Arin sat by Caleb's bed, trying his best to explain why Caleb was in the hospital. Once capable of speaking, Caleb had immediately began demanding that we release him from "rehab." He was nearly eighteen and *sober*; we couldn't force him to stay. Yet no matter how often we told him he was in the hospital and had been sober for the four days prior to his accident, his poor brain couldn't keep anything straight.

"Remember," Arin began, sitting beside Caleb's bed with his arm draped over the rail, "You had just gone to dinner with Jeremy and were headed to the rodeo with Xander."

Caleb's eyes, now purple and swollen, closed softly as he struggled to recall.

"We went, we went . . ." he started and then stopped, already forgetting his train of thought.

"You passed our house," Arin continued. "Then, right at that gas station, you had a terrible accident."

"Hmmm . . ." Caleb mused, "I don't remember that." He blinked repetitively and then stared off into space. After a while, he turned back toward Arin.

"Was the accident . . . was it my fault?" he inquired.

"Yeah, buddy, it was," Arin replied faintly.

Caleb pondered Arin's words momentarily and then immediately resumed attempting to convince us to check him out of "rehab."

"Yeah, but see, you can't just keep me here," he mumbled agitatedly through barely opened eyes. "You can't just say, 'You need to go, like, we're dropping you off here, we're taking you . . . like, go there.' Like, you guys can't just do that. It's more up to me now. I can see where it looks bad, like I already fu . . . messed up so bad, but you can't just keep me here."

Arin and I sighed—then relented. Stroking Caleb's forehead, Arin reassured him, "I know, buddy. You're perfect."

Two sweet nurses stood at the foot of Caleb's bed discussing his recovery and *actual* rehabilitation.

Besides his mental deficits, he still needed multiple nurses, a support belt, and a trailing wheelchair whenever he attempted to stand, walk, or use the toilet. He dragged his left leg behind him; he could wiggle his right toes but not his left, and he could wiggle his left leg but not his right. His chart read: "Patient is well below baseline with deficits in balance, strength, activity tolerance, and functional mobility."

Additionally, his pupils weren't responding to light, and he seemed incapable of hearing out of his left ear. His wounds weren't healing properly, and his doctor was considering a more intensive debridement that would require Caleb's full sedation. Miraculously, none of his fractures had displaced and would heal on their own over time. His doctor was recommending a long-term rehabilitation center that specialized in traumatic brain injuries (TBIs).

Suddenly, in the middle of our conversation, Caleb, who we'd all assumed to be sleeping, flung one arm from his covers to point straight at one nurse.

"You," he practically shouted without opening his eyes, "you have the single most annoying voice in the world. And you," he continued, flopping his arm toward the other nurse, "you have the second."

With that, he instantly fell back asleep.

Arin and I were appalled and profusely apologized to Caleb's undeserving nurses. But they laughed and told us far worse things had happened with TBI patients. Mattresses and IV machines had been hurled across the room along with the most horrible insults anyone could possibly endure.

It was typical, they informed us. Head-injury patients are literally out of their minds. Regardless of how "normal" they occasionally act, they lack discernment and abound in impulsivity. A bad combination, to be sure. What they think, they speak. What they crave, they eat; and any scheme they devise, they execute—which is why a high percentage of TBI patients are prone to serious reinjury.

Caleb had certainly validated his nurse's words by refusing to consume anything other than Watermelon Sour Patch Kids, Mountain Dew, cheeseburgers, chicken strips, and French fries since the time he relearned how to swallow. Anything remotely nutritious had to be coaxed into his mouth one bite at a time.

In so many ways, he had reverted to toddlerhood but with a much more extensive vocabulary. He referred to one nurse as a "bitch-whore" and told anyone he deemed incompetent exactly where they could "shove it."

Suddenly, his language rivaled a trucker's, and Arin, especially, was mortified.

Caleb's medical records somewhat humorously read: "Patient's father seemed particularly concerned about his rude behavior. Normalized to father that recovery is a process and ignoring rude behavior is best because Patient will most likely carry minimal if any memory of this time, so staff/family shouldn't take offense to what the Patient says or does."

The tricky thing was that, in so many ways, Caleb acted the same after his accident as he did before—the rudeness, bluntness, and food particularities—and it was hard to determine what behavior was "normal," what was the TBI, and what was just *Caleb*.

For example, before anyone knew he could stand independently, I was in the waiting room visiting with a friend while he slept.

Suddenly, I heard Caleb's irritated voice screaming from the end of the hall, "Mom! Mom! Where are you, Mom?"

I and his team of nurses simultaneously descended on Caleb. They chastised him for walking unsupported, led him back to bed, and reset the motion detector on his bed. The second they left, he let me have it.

"Why weren't you there when I woke up?" he demanded. "I couldn't find you." Then his face crinkled into a childish pout, and I sincerely thought he might cry. He added, "Besides, those nurses are *mean*. They *yelled* at me, and I didn't do anything wrong."

Then he was off to the races feeling on his head for what he called his "pike" or his "pole." Somewhere in his brain, he vaguely recalled the screw in his head—he just couldn't remember what to call it. He wanted to know where "the baby that lets me hold her" was, referring to my one-year-old niece. On and on, he rambled, and all I could think was *What in the world will home life be like with TBI Caleb* and *Grayson?*

God forgive me for thinking of myself, but aside from the thought of Caleb returning to drugs, my next biggest fear was that he would forever stay stuck in this amped-up, entirely dependent, childlike state. Already, the doctors were talking about house modifications that needed to be made and what type of in-home care he'd be eligible to receive.

So I did what I'd always done when life grew complicated: I started researching.

I read up on brain injuries, dug out a memoir I'd once read about a boy who had fallen down the stairs and permanently required full-time assistance. I called a mother whose grown son had toppled out of his college window and, after one year, was finally relearning to walk. I talked to Jeremy, who had been hit by a car and temporarily lost his ability to speak, and Arin's friend, Mark, who had experienced something similar. I learned as much as I could, arming myself with the protective sword of knowledge.

I had done this before, and I would do it again.

On July 9, twelve days after being admitted to the hospital, Caleb was released. A transport driver from the rehabilitation center rolled him out of the hospital in a wheelchair and loaded him up in a van.

Eight days later, on his eighteenth birthday, Caleb walked out of the rehabilitation center *on his own two feet.*

That night, he was out at the lake—fishing.

39

Unearthing

In one long glorious acknowledgment of failure,
he laid himself bare before God.

—John Grisham, *The Testament*

July 17—Caleb's birthday and homecoming. I wrote in my journal:

Caleb, when have you felt powerless? Why is control so important to you? When do you think you lost it? Do you feel emotions too much or too little?

Your physical damage is blaring. Your brain injury will take time to recognize. Understanding your long-term soul-brokenness feels practically impossible.

Who are you, Caleb Hatfield?

❖

My July 20 journal entry reads:

> *Caleb walked when he was nine months old before he ever crawled. He spoke in complete, multiple sentences before he turned two. By three, he was reading* The Chronicles of Narnia *with my mom.*
>
> *None of this seemed exceptional because I had no point of comparison.*
>
> *Three weeks and two days ago, Caleb was in an accident and placed in a medically induced coma. Within forty-eight hours, he was responding to commands—kicking his leg in defiance when asked to wiggle his toes, and by day three, he was speaking. He walked alone on the eleventh day, and nine days after that, he was back home and fishing.*
>
> *None of this seemed exceptional because I had no point of comparison.*
>
> *But since then, I have spoken to many others whose recovery took months or even years, others who lost their ability to speak, walk, and think. Now I know his recovery was miraculous.*
>
> *Still, I cannot fully grasp just how miraculous it truly was.*
>
> *There remains a bit of dullness in my head. The awe seems just beyond my reach. Truth be told, all my emotions seem evasive. I feel very matter-of-fact and unemotional about everything—as if it all happened outside of me and not to me. Disassociation or solely tolerable because I believe it was somehow necessary? God's grace or my delusion? Resilience or internal deadness?*

Caleb's trauma doctor intended to release him to Colorado's leading brain injury hospital for rehabilitation, but by the time he was cleared for transport, the rehab center no longer had an available bed, and Caleb had improved so rapidly that he no longer qualified for such a high level of care.

Instead, he was transferred to a local center fifteen minutes from our house.

The new center, traditionally accustomed to dealing with stroke and joint replacement patients, had nowhere for parents to sleep. So Arin and I tucked Caleb into bed and then—for the first time since his accident—wholly entrusted him to another's (we hoped) tender loving care.

Unfortunately, it was sorely neglectful.

The first night, a new CNA decided he "looked healthy enough" to walk himself to the bathroom, despite the fact that—unless sneaking out to find me—Caleb had yet to walk anywhere unaided. The nurses brought his pain medications hours late. He then convinced his speech therapist to cancel any further sessions (he deemed them unnecessary) and made mincemeat of the scrawny occupational therapist trying to teach him to walk without dragging his left leg.

I'm sure the staff would have been sufficient for senior citizens recovering from strokes, but for a headstrong teenage TBI patient, their services were severely lacking.

To be fair, caring for Caleb was no walk in the park. Nearly every conversation obsessively centered around getting out of rehab, leasing his own apartment, and "chillin'" with his friends. He was nearly eighteen, he belligerently reminded us, and nothing we could say would stop him; it was *his* choice now.

To complicate matters, although the security guards were supposed to regulate after-hour visitors, we came to find out that Caleb's friends often smuggled in forbidden "treasures" like chewing tobacco and vape pens—both excellent supplements for recovering brains.

One morning, I walked into his room a few minutes past eight. Already, he had called several times demanding to know why I was late and when I would arrive with his breakfast from "Doba" (by which he meant Qdoba Tex-Mex restaurant). He was *starving*, and despite his Anasazi vow to never complain about food, the cafeteria options were "extremely disgusting." Unfortunately, I couldn't disagree.

Although I had been there just the night before, five empty Sour Patch Kid packages littered his floor; empty milkshake, burger, and French

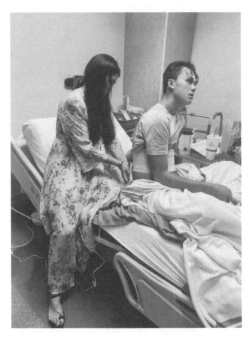

Me rubbing Caleb's back at the rehab center

fry containers were strewn across his tray; and no less than five crushed Mountain Dew cans were heaped in a pile—all compliments of his well-intentioned friends.

Comatose, he was glued to the TV he wasn't supposed to be watching and barely glanced my way when I entered. Grabbing his food from my hands, he returned to staring wordlessly at the television while removing his shirt.

"Rub my back, Mom," he pleaded. "It's itching so bad!"

Sighing, I sat down on the edge of his bed and began gingerly rubbing the tops of his bandages.

I have a photo of this very moment, though I don't remember anyone else being present. I've spent considerable time studying this picture. It's the only thing that makes me feel *something* about Caleb's accident.

There I am, sitting on his hospital bed wearing a long, pale blue, kimono-looking duster. My hair is blow-dried and straightened, and my makeup is fully applied. I'm wearing jewelry and the black sandals with chains that I only wore when dressing up, and I have a serene, contented look on my face.

The whole scene makes me want to scream.

Three years later, on November 1, 2022, I've turned off my phone and disconnected my computer from the Wi-Fi. Although no one is home, I've locked myself in my bedroom. I'm fuming for reasons unknown to me, and on some subconscious level, I know I can't even begin unpacking my rage unless I feel alone enough to be brutally honest.

After days of struggling to write this chapter, I want to strangle the "me" sitting on the bed that day. Why doesn't she look like *me* now? Here I am—three days of unwashed hair piled on my head in a messy bun, still wearing what I slept in last night. My pants are unbuttoned, my belly is hanging out, and I'm wearing black socks. Black socks that I hate! It's 12:45 p.m., and I still haven't brushed my teeth.

Why does the "me" in that photo not resemble me now? I demand, seething at that perfectly made-up woman I'm studying while downing a quick swig of whiskey. She had every right to unravel! Why has it taken her three years to feel the way she *should* have felt back then, during that time when her son nearly died?

Who does she think she is, looking so put together, manicured fingers trailing over gnarled scars that rippled beneath her son's skin like fat, burrowing earthworms? The fury is rising in my throat, choking me, only now I know better than to gulp it back down. Now, I welcome the pain. Let it flow.

Flaming accusations begin streaming forth like hot poison.

Doesn't that woman know it was *she* who failed her son, *she* who drove him to drink, *she* who ultimately caused him to crash? Doesn't she know everything was her fault? *She* was never enough. What right does she have to wear fancy black sandals, make-up, and jewelry? Damn her! Damn her. Damn her . . .

And here come the sobs, the deep, gut-wrenching sobs. If only she had been a better mother, nothing would have happened. If only she'd loved him like he'd needed and noticed his pain and his rage . . .

If only, if only, if only . . .

If only she could have felt what I'm feeling now.

But there she sits—smiling serenely.

Why couldn't she feel what I feel?

On July 27, exactly one month after Caleb's accident, I arrived at my parent's cabin and settled into an armchair near the window with a cup of coffee to watch the gently rolling river.

Lying on the table next to me were my journal and two books, *The Body Keeps the Score* by Bessel van Der Kolk and *In an Unspoken Voice* by Peter Levine. Between acupuncture, yoga, and chiropractics, I simplistically understood that our bodies can somehow retain that which our minds can't actively remember. But with the severity of Caleb's accident, it seemed imperative that I understand such concepts on a deeper level so that should he ever suffer from flashbacks or strange bodily sensations, I might better know how to help him.

After a long while of staring out the window, the river had sufficiently soothed my soul. It was time to begin my work.

I picked up a book and began reading.

"When we fight against and/or hide from unpleasant or painful sensations and feelings," Peter Levine wrote, "we generally make things worse. The more we avoid them, the greater is the power they exert upon our behavior and sense of well-being. What is not felt remains the same or is intensified, generating a cascade of virulent and corrosive emotions. This forces us to fortify our methods of defense, avoidance and control."[1]

In a different chapter, he continued:

> *[Her] body language reflects both distress and her "resistance."*
> *The resistance is there for a reason: it is the physical expression*

of how she is protecting herself. In part, [she] is defending herself as though from an outside "attack." However, she is protecting herself primarily from disowned sensations and feelings. Resistance needs to be worked with gently and indirectly.[2]

I underlined both quotes, using double lines in many places. Then I boxed them in and scribbled Caleb's name in the margins. Levine's words described him to a T.

For a long while, I stared out the window at nothing. Eventually, I had cried enough tears to overflow the river's banks.

Conceding to my God-honest truth, I crossed off Caleb's name and wrote: *me.*

I did not know it was me, I journaled as the river rolled on. *Levine's words describe me to a T.*

When have you felt powerless? Why is control so important to you? When do you think you lost it? Do you *feel* emotions too much or too little?

Your physical damage is complicated. Your wounds will take time to recognize. Understanding your long-term soul-brokenness feels practically impossible.

Who are you, Corey Hatfield?

PART THREE

Broken Wholeness

40

Confessing

Seeking what is true is not seeking what is desirable.

—ALBERT CAMUS, *The Myth of Sisyphus*

Too broken to work yet too healthy to lie in bed, Caleb passed many nights in a lawn chair at the far edge of our property, staring into space. From the back porch, my eyes couldn't perceive the vodka bottle dangling from his hand or the shimmering tears that so often streaked his cheeks. I certainly never detected a whiff of alcohol the singular time he plodded through the kitchen door, plopped down on a barstool, and asked me to talk.

"Mom," he started, with downcast eyes, "Do you think God punishes people?"

"I don't know," I answered honestly. "I don't think so. Do you?"

"I think I'd deserve it if He does," Caleb said remorsefully. "I've made a mess of my life."

After a long pause, he continued, "Hiking the other day reminded me of

Anasazi. Maybe one day, when I get everything sorted out, I'll go back and walk as a counselor. I really loved my time there; it was a great experience."

There was another long pause and then another tough question. "Mom, do you think depression is real? Do you think I was actually depressed in high school? I feel so overwhelmed by what I've done, and now I have nothing to do but sit outside every night and think about it. I can't control my mood swings, and I have no idea what to do with my life. Jeremy said I could work for Dad when I get better, but I don't want to work like that."

He turned to me then with misty eyes and quietly added, "Dad missed a few years of life, ya know?"

"Yeah. I know," I said sadly. "But he always did his best. He just wanted to give you guys the life he thought you deserved. I'm sorry. For everything you missed, for everything we truly failed to give you."

By the next morning, Caleb had again relapsed into silence.

After Caleb's accident, Rylee routinely awoke with terrible nightmares, most of which involved our entire family drowning or burning inside a car while she stood frozen in place, unable to save a soul. Many nights, she turned up at my bedside, her face dripping with tears. I would groggily open my covers to her, and—at sixteen years old—she would crawl in beside me and curl into my body like an infant. She shook and trembled, while I peeled the hair from her salt-soaked face and stroked her head until we fell back asleep. Sometimes, she'd silently return to her bed after a few hours. Other times, she'd wake with the sun and beg me to let her sleep through the start of school; I rarely denied her requests.

Roughly three months after Caleb's accident, I took Rylee to her first counseling appointment. On the therapist's couch, Rylee again reverted to a young child. She wiggled, swung her legs, fidgeted, and stared at the ground as she spoke, frequently looking to me for verification. She answered the counselor's questions in one or two words, and upon leaving, she stated the counselor was "weird" and that she felt uncomfortable talking about herself.

Yet late that night, Rylee appeared in my office and asked to talk. For once, confessions tumbled freely from her lips, and although they broke my heart, I remained expressionless so she wouldn't blame herself for my pain.

"Honestly, Mom," she began, "I don't have many happy childhood memories except playing with neighbors in the street. I was so stressed out by Grayson's problems, but then I felt bad because my problems were so small compared to his. At least I *had* friends. Mom, do you think Grayson will ever be *normal*?"

"I think Grayson is who he is, and while that may change and grow over the years, I think he'll always be uniquely himself," I replied.

She moved on to talking about her friends, specifically boys. "I don't know why, but around certain people, I feel like a dog on a leash—like I have no say and just have to do what I'm told."

"That's really sad, sweetie," I said, choosing a simplified adjective to describe my internal agony. "Do you think that if you liked, loved, and respected yourself more, you might be more inclined to do what was best for you?"

"Yeah, probably," she answered dejectedly. "I just feel like I have no control."

Despite talking for over thirty minutes, she mentioned nothing of her brother's accident.

After Rylee left, I made a mental note to schedule her next appointment with a new therapist and then sat awake for a long while, feeling crushed beneath the unbearable weight of five hurting children.

Just that afternoon, Grayson had slid into my car near tears.

Alarmed, I demanded to know why, instantly ready to raise a ruckus if any middle-school bully had dared mistreat my son.

"We were supposed to run with partners at cross country practice, and

I had no one to run with. I asked a few kids, but they all ignored me," Grayson replied, facing the window. "But it's fine. I just ran alone."

Then there was Reagan, who—at barely twelve years old—hid behind her locked bedroom door as much as humanly possible and refused to say much more than "I'm fine." Jacob couldn't drive by the scene of Caleb's accident without having flashbacks and breaking out in a cold sweat, and of course, there was Caleb, who slunk off every night to ponder his seemingly unforgivable errors.

Every one of my children needed help, therapy, something, anything . . . and it all seemed up to me to figure out what.

Before turning in for the night, I jotted a quote in my journal from one of my favorite books, *The Impact of God*: "He had been hauled beyond the threshold of his own resources, taken to those outer limits where the only alternatives are a Spirit that fills, or chaos. It was as if the normal anesthetic that normal life provides had worn off, his inner self had been scraped bare, and he now ached in a way he never had before for a God who was utterly beyond him."[1]

Prior to Rylee's first counseling appointment, I had awoken abruptly mid-sleep. My stomach was twisted in knots, I could barely breathe, and my heart was pounding. Always pounding. On a whim, I slipped into my office, pulled out my journal, and began listing every harrowing memory I could still *feel* in my body, breath, gut, and soul: *Mom picking up Grayson when I couldn't handle him, Grayson on the outside of the railings, him biting Reagan's toes, telling her to die, dashing into five lanes of traffic . . .*

My list continued for *eight pages*, and by the time I finished, I felt like I'd just ran the Boston Marathon. All of *that* was inside me. I could feel them and see them, even taste them—these memories still alive and unconstrained to the past. They made me shake, tingle, and feel numb and nauseated all at once.

Suddenly, I realized—in my quest to help Caleb and my other children process their traumas, *I had uncovered my own.*

I wrapped up my eight-page entry by stating: *Perhaps I am the one who needs help.*

᛭

September 10—EMDR session 1. I am sitting in a therapist's basement.[2] Cinda lives five minutes from my house, does eye movement desensitization and reprocessing (EMDR), and accepts our insurance, thereby checking off my basic, required boxes. I find it strange that she counsels from home, but after Caleb's accident, I'm willing to overlook almost anything for convenience's sake.

She's sitting directly across from me without even a coffee table of separation. It's just she and I, face-to-face, alone in her basement. Tall, willowy, and athletic-looking, I find her a little intimidating, mainly because she doesn't speak in a warm, fuzzy voice like the previous counselors I'd taken Rylee to see—the same ones to whom she's refused to return.

In an even-keel, no-nonsense voice, Cinda asks whether I know anything about EMDR therapy. I tell her that I knew of someone once, an orphan from Romania, who used it to help her "process her trauma." But my words are simply regurgitated and carry no meaning; I have no personal understanding of EMDR or even what it means to "process one's trauma."

"Well," Cinda continues, "you've heard of REM sleep, right? Rapid Eye Movement? Your eyes flicker quickly from left to right in this state, thereby reconnecting both hemispheres of your brain and attempting to make sense of your experiences. Traumatic events can cause thoughts or emotions to get 'stuck' in your brain or body, but by simulating REM, we can often access these 'stuck' events to better evaluate and work through them."

The whole thing sounds "weird," to use Rylee's word, but at the same time, I'm desperate for help. Besides, I'm the self-appointed canary in the coal mine; I need to determine whether EMDR therapy is good, dangerous, or pointless to better help my family, should anyone else agree to get counseling.

How do you even begin healing an entire family? The thought overwhelms me, but all I know to do is start with myself.

By this point, I've already chatted with Cinda once or twice, and she feels that I am stable enough to attempt EMDR without risking "re-trau-matization." She explains that she will slowly wave a metal "wand" back and forth. All I have to do is focus on the lighted tip and tell her what thoughts, emotions, or bodily sensations arise. It sounds easy enough, but I am skeptical about whether I am a good candidate. A good-sized portion of me thinks the best idea is to bolt up her basement stairs and drive away.

Back and forth the wand goes. All I feel is ridiculous; I'm sitting in someone's basement, watching a moving metal wand. My only thought is that this will never work, and my sole body sensation is the tightness in my chest, which has been my long-term on-again, off-again sidekick.

Today is an on-again day, so when the wand stops, I report that the only thing I notice is the tightness in my chest.

"Okay, just pay attention to that feeling," says Cinda, "and this time, try to notice if that feeling has any motion."

What in the world? I think to myself, but I consent to try.

The wand resumes its pointless journey back and forth in front of my face, and to my surprise, I realize I can actually perceive the tightness in my chest as a spiraling vortex. It seems to be sucking me in, and I start to feel panicky—like I want to tear the sickening feeling from my chest and chuck it against a wall.

"Can you imagine actually doing that?" Cinda wants to know.

I am shocked to find that I can answer confidently, "No. I can't get to it."

She sets the wand in motion, and I notice heat dropping to my stom-ach and spreading. The light waving back and forth in front of my face briefly conjures up an image of flashing ambulance lights, which I report. I purposely avoid mentioning Caleb's accident. To do so seems overly cliché. Like I'm handing Cinda a psychological gift on a platter.

Now the heat has formed a tight ball high in my chest, and I feel it rising into my face. It feels like pressure in my sinuses and ears and is accompanied by the urge to cry.

"Can you cry?" Cinda wonders, and I tell her, "No. If I start, I'll likely never stop."

I slump back into her soft couch, and my arms fall limply at my sides.

Now, the tightness has returned to my chest, the spiraling vortex sucking me in toward my back. This time, I somehow notice it feels "black."

Cinda asks me an odd question, "What would this blackness say?"

Even more strange is that I automatically know that answer. "It's telling me I have no choice. No control."

Suddenly, I know with an uncanny certainty what's coming next: *rage*.

I'm roiling with anger. There's nothing I can do, nothing I can control. I just have to accept life as it's hurled at me at lightning-fast speeds. Tears begin falling at this perceived injustice as the anger rolls through my body. Cinda tells me to simply notice and feel the anger; when I do, I realize it feels strong. It makes me believe that I do, in fact, have control and a choice.

Suddenly, a warmth starts spreading down my limp arms, and I envision the cornfields ablaze with light. I can almost feel the sun on my face, and I now feel flooded with gratitude. An image flashes through my mind; I'm being carried on white wings over the mountains and then gently placed in my glowing cornfield.

Now, I tell Cinda, the ball in my chest is settled. It is no longer moving or spinning; it's just present. I feel very far away, certainly no longer confined to her basement. It occurs to me that I've gone through a full crisis cycle in minutes—the panic, defeat, helplessness, rage, and tears, and then the eventual relief and gratitude.

Despite the roller coaster of emotions I've just ridden, my insides feel calm, and I feel remarkably restored.

Afterward, I park my car on a side street and pull out the journal I've designated for trauma, separate from my "normal journal." I immediately record the events of my hour-long session. Like a scientist formulating a hypothesis, it seems essential to take careful and precise notes to avoid the twisting, warping, and sensationalizing of my experience over time.

I begin writing about my slumped feeling of defeat, the way my arms flopped uselessly at my sides, and it dawns on me that that was the exact sensation that came over me after Grayson's blood draw and that my depression also started with heaviness in my arms. By the same token, when I realized I *had* control in EMDR, I perceived it was a warmth spreading down my arm, *specifically* down my ring and pinkie fingers, which used to constantly tingle and go numb.

As I write, my gramma's death randomly pops into my mind. I recall it as a historical event confined to the past, one I can no longer experience as if physically present. In contrast, I can still *feel* all my previously listed "traumas" and relive them in real-time.

I find myself pondering this "split" in myself that I have so often observed. Every time, there is the "me" watching from above and the "me" who is actually experiencing the event. This split is interesting, perhaps even a God-given survival mechanism. I find the "watching" part of myself fascinating. In every circumstance, I have a bird's-eye view, always higher in elevation than the actual situation. Curiosity is always involved, but never emotion—like examining Caleb's back wounds in the hospital.

How does this happen? I scribble in my trauma journal. *Why does this split occur?*

My September 10 journal entry reads:

> *Cinda asked me what has changed since Caleb's accident.*
> *Upon reflection, I realize that I carry about a constant sense*
> *of impending doom. If I see police lights, I brace myself to wit-*
> *ness another child's crushed vehicle. When Jacob goes hunting,*
> *I lie in bed waiting for the next "call." If Arin goes four-*
> *wheeling, I know something bad will inevitably happen.*
>
> *Nothing feels right. When Arin's gone, I miss him, and*
> *when he's home, I want to be alone. I eat to my heart's content*
> *then regret it; even food doesn't taste like it should. There is*
> *a constant push/pull of wanting to do something, but then it*
> *never feels like I expect it to.*
>
> *I just can't seem to get comfortable.*

41

Reconnecting

I will sleep no more but arise,
You oceans that have been calm within me! how I feel you,
fathomless, stirring, preparing unprecedented waves and storms.

—WALT WHITMAN, *Leaves of Grass*

September 15—EMDR session 2. "Try to remember that helpless feeling in your arms," says Cinda, waving her magic wand and attempting to resume where our last session left off.

But I don't feel anything—except highly annoyed. The birds outside won't stop chirping, and heat is now rising from my stomach to my chest.

"What would that heat say?" Cinda wonders, and her question grates on me like nails on a chalkboard.

Deciding to answer honestly, I tell her that any answer would be a stretch, a reaching for something not there. Today's not the day for therapy. I can't do it. The stupid birds won't shut up, and I am far too cynical.

"Okay. Just notice your cynicism," Cinda instructs. "What purpose do you think it serves?"

I feel myself relaxing as I observe and then gradually accept this emotion. I even grow slightly defensive, and am surprised to uncover a deep-rooted affinity for my cynicism.

"It protects me," I answer definitively.

"When was the first time you remember feeling this emotion?" Cinda asks.

Strangely, the answer comes to me immediately.

"Back in college, I felt 'impressions' about people," I explain. "Like about their internal struggles or life experiences. One time, I shared such an impression with a friend, and she smirked. Later, one of my favorite psychology professors lectured for a whole hour about how emotions were untrustworthy. I consciously remember choosing to downplay my feelings. They had already embarrassed me once. Cynicism probably emerged from there as a means of self-preservation."

I pause, deliberating, and then open the can of worms I'd been contemplating.

"I've noticed this 'duality' within myself," I tell Cinda. "On one hand, I want to 'absorb' Caleb's pains and passions, but on the other, I want to write him off. Some days, I feel motivated to be patient and tender toward Grayson. Other days, I daydream about getting in my car and driving till I run out of gas. Some mornings, I enjoy sitting in my chair, actively reading and learning. Others, all I want is to zone out and overfill my Amazon cart. The thought of trying to reconcile these dualities feels exhausting."

"Okay, visualize holding each part of yourself like a ball in each hand," Cinda tells me. "What do you feel?"

"Like I want to smash them together. Over the years, I've learned that balance is necessary for self-care. For example, a clean house makes me feel better, so I can't sit around binge-watching Netflix all day. If I let one proverbial ball drop, I have to work four times harder to catch up. I'm so sick of balancing every*thing* and every*one*."

"What emotions are you feeling right now?" Cinda asks, handing me a pie-charted wheel with various emotions.[1]

I look at my available options and flatly reply, "Disillusioned, apathetic, avoidant, bored, hurt, and distant."

"And what do you think of those emotions?" she presses.

"Um, I don't. Mostly, I ignore them; I don't really *let* myself feel these emotions. They imply a lack of gratitude and don't reflect who I want to be."

"Sounds like you've got a bit of judgment affiliated with emotions," Cinda comments. "What would it be like to feel these emotions without judgment? To just notice them? What purpose do you think they serve? Maybe think about these questions throughout the next week."

I fold up Cinda's paper, place it in my trauma journal, and then escape to my car.

Right now, I'm feeling entirely *mistrustful*.

The next morning, I sat in my chair, studying my "wheel of emotions." Its center was divided into seven broad emotions—happy, sad, angry, disgusted, fearful, bad, and surprised—with more specific emotions branching out from each one.

It became readily apparent that I only allowed myself the luxury of feeling two out of seven emotions—only 29 percent. Even within my allowable happy and angry feelings, I repressed many nuanced emotions, such as resentful, distant, critical, proud, and powerful; I'd been taught they were *wrong*.

Impulsively, I copied down the definitions of the first two emotions I'd mentioned to Cinda:

> *Disillusioned—disappointed in someone or something that one discovers to be less good than one had believed*

> *Apathetic—having or showing little or no feeling or emotion: spiritless*

Well, I'd certainly pegged myself with those two words.

In my mind, emotions were either positive or negative, strong or weak, purposeful or pointless. *Historically*, I had avoided all negative, weak, or pointless emotions, and worked very hard to only reside in my two little pie slices of happiness or anger. Yet *realistically*, I had, of course, experienced a wide array of emotions and then punished myself for being alive, being human.

What would happen if I simply noticed and allowed any and all emotions without judgment, like Cinda said? I wondered.

Agreeably, I had wasted a lot of time and energy trying *not* to feel. But by stiff-arming my emotions, had I not somehow exacerbated the very ones I so desperately strived to avoid? Still, I reasoned with myself, if I *permitted* an emotion, wouldn't I inevitably *become* it? Wouldn't apathetic feelings lead to a blasé life? Bitter emotions to a rancorous disposition? Sadness to despair?

I didn't yet understand that honoring my emotions would, in fact, release me from their vice grip, allowing me to pass unfettered through their snares.

As I sat in my chair pondering these things, I also conceded that emotions opened me up to criticism—to being told why I shouldn't feel however I did. They invited unwanted dialogue and debate. Unwanted people in places I worked hard to protect.

When I once opened up to a friend about my painful struggles with Grayson, they "jokingly" retorted, "You should have stopped at three kids."

Then, and in so many other instances, I never felt entitled to my own feelings. Therefore, cynicism became my strong fortress, keeping all unwanted emotions at bay.

For years, I wrote, *I have been unable to find practical help or even validation for my feelings. My "trauma" never seemed big or real enough to be recognized. I'm not a soldier or a rape victim; I'm just a mom with a tough kid. Still, I have felt helpless and defeated. Retreating into myself seemed the only viable option, where the only trustworthy person was me.*

It was then that I remembered the goal of Orthodox Christianity: to become integrated and whole.

Somehow, cowering behind buttressed walls didn't seem conducive to accomplishing such goals.

Around midnight, on September 21, a shrill phone call jolted me from my sleep. The high school principal was wondering whether I would be so kind as to pick up my daughter. Rylee and two of her friends had been caught drinking at the junior homecoming dance. The school resource officer was willing to let them off with a warning if parents would come in for a meeting. Ironically, in a school of approximately 1,500 kids, Rylee and her friends were the only students caught drinking.

Knowing Caleb would still be awake, I called him en route to the dance to pick his brain on how to respond.

"Uh, not like you did with me," he said sarcastically. "Give her some consequences, but don't take away her whole life."

"Well, what would you do if it was your daughter?" I asked him.

He was silent for a moment and then responded seriously, "Maybe say something like, 'I know everyone drinks, and high school is really hard. But you've been making some bad choices over the years. How can we figure out something different to help you?'"

Dumbstruck, I fell silent.

Momentarily, I thanked him for his sound advice; then, before hanging up, I feebly added, "I'm sorry you never got this version of us."

Two days later, our entire family was in Moab, Utah, riding side-by-sides over red dirt and lumpy boulders. Arin had hauled them from Colorado with his truck and a twenty-four-foot trailer while I followed closely behind. Always anticipating our next tragedy, I kept a close watch on the ratchet straps, the trailer brake lights, and whether the side-by-side's tires were inching closer toward the edge of the trailer. By the time we arrived, my hands were exhausted from white-knuckling the steering wheel.

The following day, we pulled up to a gorgeous vacation rental house just ten minutes from Lake Powell, where we planned to spend the remainder of the week.

We rented a speed boat complete with a wakeboard and an oversized tube on our first full day. The kids were still half asleep, and the morning air was far too cool for swimming. Arin maneuvered the boat past the buoys, and then Caleb stepped forward to drive. I subtly shook my head in vehement disagreement, but Arin must not have noticed. Still impulsive, still lacking sound judgment, Caleb rapidly accelerated, and the boat's nose lifted out of the water. I clutched the railing tighter and looked nervously toward Arin. Surely, he would regulate Caleb's speed. Yet my husband and the other children, who had suddenly perked up, seemed to be having the time of their lives. The boat started slamming into the waves. The bow skyrocketed and then dove, and I timidly suggested that Caleb slow down a bit. Seeing my scarred son with a brain injury behind a steering wheel, driving at high speeds, was making my heart race and my throat constrict, but Arin and the kids all laughed and joked about "Mom being a chicken."

Determined not to be a killjoy, I held on to the rail for dear life and then released my mind to journey anywhere besides Lake Powell, Arizona.

As the day heated up, it came time for tubing and wakeboarding. I watched from the boat as necks snapped left and right and bodies went skimming across the water's surface like flat-bottomed rocks. I smiled and laughed appropriately while my clenched jaw throbbed and my insides churned.

After lunch, one of my genius offspring suggested cliff-jumping, and everyone but boring ole Mom enthusiastically agreed. The jumps started small and then increased until my children looked like tiny pinheads on the top of a gigantic sheer-faced stone wall. They flipped and dove into such deep water I feared they'd never emerge, and all the while, I stared so intently at the bottom of the boat that I half expected to see water seeping in through bored-out holes.

The next day, we rented jet skis and rode them down long, furrowing canyons. I felt sure we would get lost and then starve to death or perhaps freeze. Caleb sped out of sight while Jacob and Rylee did doughnuts and soaked each other with their spray. Ridiculously, Arin allowed Grayson to drive. Everywhere I looked, red flags were screaming for my attention.

Still, I had to admit it was nice seeing my family enjoying one another. We laughed that day. A lot. Even me. And when the day was over, every-one jumped on to the wave-runner trailer to hitch a ride back to the jet ski rental shop. But when Arin stretched his leg to step up, there was a loud *RRRIIIIPPP* as the back seam of his swimming trunks split apart. Grayson and I caught quite the eyeful, and the ride back was scattered with erupting snorts and raucous peals of laughter.

To my surprise, I realized that for the first time in a long while, we felt very much like a normal, close-knit family.

Arin wanted to go four-wheeling on the third day, but it was more than my shattered nerves could bear. So Arin took Grayson while our other children lounged and slept by the pool, and I slipped away for quiet time alone, reflecting on this time of healing and undoing family curses. We had all needed this trip to remember who we were.

After lunch, I wandered into a local jewelry shop and bought myself a turquoise ring in commemoration. Arizona had garnered quite a special place in my heart, having first visited the desert monastery, then Anasazi, and now Lake Powell with my family. Next, I wandered into a gift shop where my eyes were magnetically drawn to a fuzzy stuffed rabbit.

Immediately, my mind flashed back to when Caleb and Jacob had led Rylee outside to see a baby bunny while failing to mention it had been squished flat by a car. I had scolded the boys and sent them to their room, yet I had failed to check up on Rylee.

What had my inattentiveness taught Rylee about emotions? I suddenly wondered, absentmindedly stroking the stuffed rabbit. *Don't cry. It's just a bunny.* I imagined myself telling her, had I the presence of mind to say anything at all.

Stunned, I stood frozen at a gift shop rack in Paige, Arizona, considering the long-term implications of my behavior. Without even recognizing my own emotional biases, I had passed them onto my daughter and, most likely, all my children. Each was reticent to speak of their problems because *I had never stopped to listen!*

Hurriedly paying for the stuffed rabbit, I rushed back to the house and asked Rylee to accompany me on a walk along the red cliffs. After a while of meandering small talk, we stopped and sat down. Rocky mesas and blue skies stretched as far as the eye could see.

"Sweetheart," I began, "You just got in trouble for drinking, and you've been making a lot of not-so-good choices lately, right? You're a really sensitive person, and when I think of you, I imagine you wearing a super heavy backpack that contains every sad thing that's ever happened to you. Would you agree?"

She nodded silently while pitching small rocks over the edge.

"What do you think is the earliest memory, the very first sad thing you packed into your imaginary backpack?" I asked her.

Without hesitation, she answered, "When Caleb and Jacob showed me the squished bunny in the street."

My muscles started shaking, as they often do in pristine moments.

"Rylee," I continued, "how would things have been different if I had come into your room and hugged you and then told you I was sorry and helped you bury that baby bunny and give it a funeral?"

A tear dripped off the tip of her nose, turning the red earth into brown clay.

"That would have been really nice," she replied as I unwrapped the stuffed bunny and placed it in her arms.

"I'm so sorry, Rylee," I told her, as a sob caught in my throat. "I'm sorry I wasn't there for you. I'm sorry I missed so many opportunities."

"That's okay, Mama," she said, sniffling.

We sat for a long while atop the red cliffs in silence, Rylee stroking her bunny and me grieving the lost moments that stretched out endlessly as the Arizona vistas and blue skies.

42

Fluctuating

Life is amazing. And then it's awful. And then it's
amazing again. And in between the amazing and awful
it's ordinary and mundane and routine. Breathe in the
amazing, hold on through the awful, and relax and exhale
during the ordinary. That's just living heartbreaking,
soul-healing, amazing, awful, ordinary life.
And it's breathtakingly beautiful.

—ATTRIBUTED TO L. R. KNOST

October 4—EMDR session 4. "Let's talk about the times you've felt out of control," Cinda begins. "You've mentioned the instances with police, your home renovation with Sean, and Grayson's forced hospitalization. Did you feel weak or like you could have done better?"

"No," I confidently reply. "I did the best I could. Those situations were beyond my control."

As we continue delving into past episodes, my legs and back muscles begin shaking, and I start pulling for air.

"Concentrate on those sensations," Cinda tells me, waving her wand.

With a deep inhalation and a slow, forceful exhale, I am pleased to discover that I can make every sensation disappear.

"Where do they go?" Cinda inquires, and I immediately answer, "Back down."

I suddenly realize that, over the years, my emotional suppression has become an acquired skill. I feel what I want when I want. Except for my few meltdowns in front of my priest, therapist, or police officers, historically, I've only released my emotions in the safety of my office—alone and when I felt ready.

It occurs to me that my emotions have been the *one thing* I've been able to control.

"What would happen if you allowed yourself to be out of control?" Cinda wonders.

"I wouldn't," I quickly retort. "I wouldn't *let* myself contribute to the chaos. I *have* to be stable; everyone else is out of control. The only thing I can't seem to control is my eating. It's the one area I give myself freedom, but even then, I feel guilty."

"Would you eat a gallon of ice cream in one sitting? A pint?" asks Cinda.

"No, never," I answer. "Several bites after a meal, or a bowl on extremely rare occasions."

"Have you ever gained fifty pounds in a short amount of time? Twenty-five?" she inquires.

"Definitely not. I never allow myself to gain more than five, and I flat-out refuse to buy bigger clothes. I weigh less now than I did in college," I inform her.

Instantly, Cinda's point becomes crystal clear: I'm regulating even my out-of-control behaviors. Still clawing for order in my uncontrollable world.

❦

On October 7, I wrote in my journal:

> *Caleb moved into his own apartment today, claiming he
> doesn't need any decorative touches because he'll spruce up the
> place with empty vodka bottles. Suddenly second-guessing my
> purpose, everything I've lived for the last eighteen years feels
> like a complete failure and waste of time. I so badly want to
> avoid feeling cynical, but after enough disappointment, you
> stop hoping and settle for reality.*
>
> *Not feeling sadness allowed me to live in denial and left
> room for hope. Nothing makes sense anymore. I guess this is
> the getting-worse-before-getting-better part?*
>
> *I've just sent my son out into nothingness, possessing noth-
> ing. No coping skills except drinking. No financial skills
> except spending. No cooking skills. Just nothing . . .*

Despite the mixed pain of Caleb moving out, the energy at home began
changing. There was new space, I realized, and room to grow.

What would rebuilding look like? I wondered. How could we rewrite
our story and create a new family culture?

"All right, everybody, listen up," I ordered Arin, Rylee, Jacob, and Reagan.
"This Friday, we are having our first official family date night. Caleb is
busy doing his own thing, and Gramma has agreed to babysit Grayson
once a week for as long we choose to do this. I'm going to pick the first
restaurant and activity, and after that, someone else can decide where we're
eating and what we're doing. Attendance is not optional."

Facial expressions ranged from excited to ambivalent to annoyed; even
so, everyone was dressed and ready by 5:00 p.m. that Friday.

Rylee slept the entire way to the fondue restaurant and then refused to
exit the truck. She'd had a terrible day, had a bad headache, and just wanted

to sleep. Yet, before drinks were ordered, she trudged through the door and grumpily plopped her head on the table. And by the time the cheese dip was piping hot, her headache had miraculously disappeared. Little by little, conversational offerings were made. There was talk of cute boys, pretty girls, and horrible teachers. Before long, Jacob, Rylee, and Reagan were all talking over one another, hurling out new stories, and chomping at the bit to share pieces of their day. Arin leaned back in his chair and took it all in through contented, beaming eyes—much like one of the first times I had noticed him in our college cafeteria.

Afterward, we wandered through Old Town Fort Collins into a small chocolatier. We each picked a flavor and then bit and passed each square around the table. Most ended up chewed and spit out in a napkin—neither we nor our children were yet connoisseurs of fine chocolate. Still, we giggled and made fun of one another's writhing faces.

By then, it was time for *Peanut Butter Falcon*, a precious movie about a young Down syndrome man who runs away to fulfill his dream of becoming a professional wrestler. The kids laughed their heads off and were still talking among themselves as we piled into Arin's truck.

There was no tension or fighting on the way home. No one tried to kill anyone. They all said "thank you," and every child asked at least once when our next family date night would be.

I fell asleep in Arin's arms that night, a soft smile lingering on both of our faces.

Five days later, Grayson was screaming bloody murder and clutching his grotesquely angled arm on our front porch. Through torrential tears and cuss words, he told me he had tried to "full-send" a double back flip on the trampoline, which an onlooking Jacob had assured him he could complete. I drove to the hospital left-handed while supporting his limp, dangling arm with my right. X-rays showed his upper arm bone snapped cleanly in half.

One surgery and two long hospital nights later, my mom was back at the house with a drugged-up Grayson, and we were back in Fort Collins for our second anticipated family date night.

Arin selected a seafood restaurant, where he offered everyone fifty dollars each to chug slimy oysters. I immediately opted out while Rylee tipped hers back like a champ. After watching her sister slurp the equivalent of a booger, Reagan decided she didn't really need the cash, and Jacob . . . well, who would have ever known the kid inherited his father's sensitive gag reflex?

The chosen activity on this night was a local escape room where it was all hands on deck. We stooped, crawled, and climbed our way to successfully solving the mystery, ending the night with a city-wide scavenger hunt for the escape room's never-before-found treasure.

Over time, on Fridays, we would find ourselves enjoying steakhouses, go-kart arenas, bowling alleys, and axe-throwing joints together.

And between family date nights, life went on—troubles and accidents included.

Jacob underwent emergency surgery for a strangulated hernia and then proceeded to break two vertebrae in a friendly wrestling match against Grayson. On a later Sunday, I had to leave church to run Caleb to the hospital when he suddenly started vomiting and losing his vision. Surprisingly, I passed Arin on our way home from the hospital, although he was *supposed* to be staying with Grayson. He was heading into the ER himself for a painful encounter with kidney stones. In January, Caleb would get his wisdom teeth removed and then need antibiotics for an infection, and come springtime, Arin would break two vertebrae of his own riding a mule down a mountain.

Amid the chaos, I thought it might be a great time to remodel our backyard, while Arin unexpectedly brought home a new puppy.

Yet, despite everything, we were learning to laugh . . . *together*. Slowly, our family was changing. Old bonds were being strengthened, and new ones were being formed—even with Caleb, whom his siblings had long feared.

Somehow, his brain injury was softening him or perhaps humbling him. Over dinner one night, he repeatedly asked for the "mashed boutines." When everyone died laughing, he didn't get angry but simply joined right in and then innocently asked why we were laughing. When we explained they were called "mashed potatoes," he looked at us like we were nuts.

"That's what I've been calling them!" he exclaimed. "Mashed boutines!"

Another time, Jacob laid out six strips of bacon on the counter and told Caleb to count them.

"One, two, three, four, five, six!" Caleb proudly proclaimed after carefully pointing to each piece with his finger.

"Nope," said Jacob. "There's five. Try again."

For minutes the process continued. Even Rylee and Reagan backed Jacob's assertion—only *five* pieces of bacon.

When Caleb finally realized he was being duped, he and Jacob ended up in a good-natured brotherly tussle on the living room floor.

As good as he was getting at taking a ribbing, Caleb was also growing quite skilled in dishing one out.

"Hey, Grayson," he called one day from the kitchen, "bet you can't touch your feet with a broom in your sleeves."

Always up for a challenge, Grayson accepted.

Caleb threaded a broomstick through one of Grayson's long sleeves, behind his back, and then through the other. In an instant, Caleb yanked Grayson's pants down to his ankles, and Grayson was stuck waddling around the kitchen in his underwear affixed to a broom while Caleb rolled on the floor, heaving with laughter.

Yet in the midst of all the growth, there were still setbacks. One step forward, one step back.

A week of uncovered shoplifting, pornography, lies, hidden phones, sneaking out, drinking, and irrational, angry outbursts, I wrote in my journal. *And it's not the acts themselves; it's the hearts behind them. Everything reflects my failure to love, impart, and inspire. Fathers across the board have historically been absent, and it's been the women, the mothers, who have formed, shaped, and motivated.*

I have grossly neglected to teach my children right from wrong, how to live upright lives, and most importantly, how to love God.

But now I had a new goal: to embody tenderness and become a healing presence.

43

Dying

There is a geological term, isostasy, which is defined as
the tendency of something to rise, once whatever has been
pushing it down is removed. . . . We are liberated from those
relentless downward forces, and our undeniable, inner hidden
wholeness, sensing the promise of freedom, sun, and sky,
breaks ground and bears us upward.

—WAYNE MULLER, *A Life of Being, Having, and Doing Enough*

October 24—EMDR session 6. I begin by telling Cinda about my strange acupuncture experience yesterday. First, the sharp, electrocuting pain in my lower back—in a location where no needle had been placed. Then, a particular spot on my foot—where Lindsay, my acupuncturist, had placed a heater—started feeling extremely hot. I grew terrified of my feet catching on fire—not like a spark leading to an eventual flame, but more like an instant combustion of my lower limbs. I lay there outwardly calm but never managed to shake my internal panic.

When I mentioned this to Lindsay as she was removing my needles, she told me that the painful spot in my back was specifically related to *fear* and the hot spot on my foot was considered an "exit point" of the body.

I feel stupid relaying this to Cinda and imagine how loony I must sound. I also feel ridiculously whiny, catching her up on the details of our last week: Grayson's broken arm, Arin's kidney stones, Caleb's vomiting and loss of vision—all routine events. I wonder why I even feel compelled to share such mundane details and suppose I must be seeking sympathy.

She asks me to name my fears.

Ashamedly, I tell her I am constantly afraid and then begin listing them out loud: dripping water, falling through creaking tile, my bathtub crashing through the floor, flooding basements, unidentified children riding away on bikes, un-locatable screams, my house disintegrating behind the drywall . . .

Why in the world are you in therapy for such absurd fears? I silently question myself.

But Cinda says it's normal to "overreact" to small events when there are layers of "compacted trauma." She says I'm responding not only to dripping water, a broken arm, or kidney stones but to every accumulated occurrence from the past. Therefore, when something "small" occurs, my brain automatically jumps to the worst-case scenario because that's what it's learned to expect.

"This has a name," she tells me. "It's called *catastrophizing.*"

All at once, tears start forming for no apparent reason, and Cinda asks a logical question, "In your mind, do you truly believe a creaking tile will lead to your crashing through the floor?"

"No," I reply, staring at her dumbly.

"What is a logical solution to a creaky tile?" she asks, trying another avenue.

I quickly answer, "Ignore it or have it repaired." I can tell she's driving at something, but I can't yet connect all the dots.

Suddenly, scales begin falling from my eyes, and I finally comprehend Cinda's gently attempted point: *I can fix broken things!* As crazy as it sounds, for the first time, I realize my fears are childlike and irrational. Speaking them out loud somehow detaches me from them, or them from me, and I see for the first time exactly how much I *fear the feeling of fear itself.*

Now, tears are pouring off my face, and I grab tissue after tissue, forgetting another human is present in the room or even on the planet. I cry and cry and cry for reasons unknown to me. Meanwhile, Cinda waits patiently, reverentially. And even as I'm crying, I realize these tears are different. They are not mourning but *purging*, not salty but *pure*. It's as if some internal floodgate has been flung wide open, and the pressure release feels *so amazingly good.* I continue crying and purging until my sobs slow and then stop.

My hour of therapy is finished. I stand to leave and then I take a deep breath. Only then do I notice that the cavity in my chest feels abundantly spacious—like I can inhale for a small eternity without ever reaching my limit.

I feel wholly and wonderfully *released*; I no longer feel afraid.

On November 1, 2019, exactly one week after parting ways with fear, I was awakened by a dream at 2:55 a.m. In this dream, Carol—who was always telling me I needed to write a book—had died. Upon partially waking, I made a groggy commitment: *One day, Carol will die, and when she does, I will write a book dedicated to her memory.* Shaking myself fully awake, I suddenly realized the foolishness of my promise: *If I wait until she's dead, she'll never get to read it.*

With that realization, zero training, and little to no experience, I slipped from my bed into my favorite herringbone chair and began writing.

In fear's absence, a new emotion emerged. It sent me soaring on wings of ecstasy and then plummeting to the depths of despair. It enraged me, made me want to tear the hair from my head, and then slowly supplanted my life with new meaning.

My new companion's name was *longing.*

Writing a book suddenly felt like the most pressing issue in the world. I felt fifty months pregnant and like I'd *die* if I didn't deliver. Suddenly, I started having dreams that I was either expecting or breastfeeding; oddly enough, very few babies (even in utero) were ever mine. Some dreams were morbid—stiff, blue, and dead fetuses I'd forgotten to feed, shrunken breasts, dried-up milk, and starving newborns—while others were frantic. Grayson had been lying in his crib, neglected, while I fed other women's babies and had to rush to tend to him before he failed to thrive. Strangely enough, I *felt* the presence of other mothers and their children in my *heart*—their blurry, wearied faces interposed over my own, their pain comingling with mine.

And so I wrote—terrified, ecstatic, in a spell-bound frenzy.

Seventeen days after starting my book, I woke up enshrouded in a cloud of darkness so suffocating and heavy I could barely function. I felt like there was *something* beyond me I needed to grasp, as if some imperative memo was flitting about the universe just waiting for me to capture it.

I tried to disregard the sensation and bury myself in housework, but the heaviness grew weightier and weightier, until finally, I succumbed.

Plopping down in my chair, I snapped into thin air. "Fine! I'm here. What do you want?"

Nobody answered, so I pulled out my go-to book, *The Impact of God.* Immediately, two quotes jumped out at me: "To come to what you know not, you must go by a way where you know not," and "Night: we cannot stop it, or hasten it; it just comes, and it teaches us every twenty-four hours that we are not in complete control."[1]

Intrigued, I continued reading as if perceiving a message being ghost-written through the words of another. For curiosity's sake, I began copying down every quote that caught my attention:

> It means not cringing submission, but the knowledge that I am part of something bigger than I had ever realised.[2]

He was interpreting his death as a mystery of love. He had written of death like this: "The rivers of love which have long been flowing into the soul swell, bank up, like seas of love as they pour into the ocean." Eternity meant to him love set free. That is where night is leading.[3]

But bridges are for crossing, not just enjoying.[4]

Suddenly, the floating, cosmic message landed in my heart, loud and clear: *You must die so others may live.* At once, I felt confident I would soon die. Simultaneously, skeptical alarms began sounding in my head. What was this? A psychological glitch in the Matrix? A woo-woo pseudo-spiritual omen? A false apparition of my traumatized brain? A justification for my newly felt emotions?

I picked up my phone and dialed Father Evan, whom, after eleven years, I'd grown to deeply trust. Thirty minutes later, I was seated in his office, reading off my listed quotes and explaining my morning.

Interlocking his fingers behind his head, he pensively closed his eyes and then slowly began speaking after a long, silent minute.

"Let me ask you this," he began. "Did this feeling bring you peace?"

"No!" I quickly replied. "It makes me panicky; I don't want to die!"

Another long pause, and then he continued, "I don't think you have anything to worry about. Usually, if people have a true intuition about their death, a sense of peace follows, not angst."

I allowed his words to soothe my troubled soul and then set the experience aside.

In her book *The Writing Life*, Annie Dillard suggests, "Write as if you were dying. At the same time, assume you write for an audience consisting solely of terminal patients. That is, after all, the case. What would you begin writing if you knew you would die soon? What could you say to a dying patient that would not enrage its triviality?"[5]

Soon enough, I would understand the meaning of both my death premonition and Annie Dillard's words. One day, I would attempt to write about Grayson standing outside the railings from the perspective of my floating head, looking down and reporting on the scene. Disgusted by my "trivial" tone, I would fume and delete and delete until, at last, I grew desperate enough to *descend* and allow myself to *truly relive* the experience.

That type of writing came at a great cost. Over time, I became deeply aware of the havoc it wreaked on my body, mind, and soul. Every day required a conscious choice to sit in my chair and force myself to *remember, descend,* and in so many ways, *die a daily death.*

In a roundabout way, my ominous foreboding of death came to pass. For three years, I would fumble through every past traumatic experience, feebly attempt to put them into words, and then visit Lindsay, Cinda, or Father Evan when my burden grew too heavy.

Yet, like St. John of the Cross, I perceived this daily death as a healing river of love that was swelling, banking up, and pouring into the ocean. With every line I wrote, I imagined a specific friend, a struggling mother I'd witnessed in the store, parents of special needs children worldwide, the younger version of myself. I would weep for their pain . . . and mine, their despairing loneliness . . . and mine; and the longer I wrote, the more everyone's faces melded into one bleeding, broken heart—all in the process of being restored.

Daily, I entered an eternal flow as rivers of love were set free.

44

Remembering

Your mind will believe comforting lies while knowing
the painful truths that make those lies necessary. And your
mind will punish you for believing both. "But how do
you fight it?" Conor asked, his voice rough. "How do you fight
all the different stuff inside?" You speak the truth, the
monster said, as you spoke it just now.

—Patrick Ness, *A Monster Calls*

A ttempting to write made me feel again like a toddler learning to walk. I was wobbly and unconfident, and a slightly wrinkled rug could send me sprawling on my face. Therefore, after hesitantly sending out my first chapter to a few close friends and family members, this email response nearly floored me: "I don't read a lot, and when I do, it's usually something that I have a preconception of the basis. I have a short attention span, and if a story doesn't get to its primary point, I get easily sidetracked."

Essentially, this person wanted to know the point of my writing, which, after a brief period of feeling like I'd gotten the wind knocked out of me, I could agree was a fair question.

Truthfully, it was something I'd been wrestling with myself.

In searching for an answer, I—of course—made two lists:

> *Why not write? I'm no good. People who know me will read out of duty; others won't even be interested. I don't have a sensational life and have never done anything extraordinary; I'm just a small-town mom. No one cares.*
>
> *Why write? It's fun. It reminds me of who I am and where I came from. I like words. It leaves a paper trail for my children to follow. It extends "me" past my death. Because for right now, it's the next thing. Because I feel close to God when I write. Because time stops, and I lose myself in another world. Because it suits me, and it's therapeutic. Because I love it.*

Just as longing and my love for writing freely emerged in the absence of fear, so, I quickly discovered, did two other unwelcome emotions I'd long been suppressing.

Suddenly, out of nowhere, I felt overcome by bitterness and resentment. All the unspoken accusations I'd refrained from hurling at Arin began clanging around in my head, desperate to find the same release as my fears: *You don't love me! You don't care about me! You abandoned me when I needed you most! All you care about is work!*

Before, I only knew of two solutions to such feelings—repress them or delicately dance and hint my way around them. I never thought about examining them curiously and honestly, and I certainly never considered stating them bluntly. Doing so might have irreparably hurt the person I loved more than myself.

Yet by naming my fears, I had, in a way, gained dominion over them. Perhaps the same would hold true if I spread my resentful thoughts on a table set for one. Maybe I didn't have to share them with Arin to release them; perhaps it would be sufficient to *admit them to myself.*

The whole process started unraveling (or perhaps coming together) when Cinda asked me to picture Grayson standing outside the railing and then imagine another person standing behind me in support.

"Could it have been Arin?" she wanted to know, and I regretfully told her, "No, it couldn't have been him."

Later, I whispered my most private thoughts to a Dollar Store journal. I very uncharacteristically started writing smack-dab in the middle of the spiral-bound notebook, where my thoughts would be protected on either side by thick layers of wide-ruled paper. The print was so small I can now barely discern it: *What I wanted that day was not someone to help with Grayson, but someone to care for* me. *Someone capable and not crippled by their fears or controlled by their anger. I just wanted to feel cared for, and Arin was not an option.*

In even smaller letters, I wrote an emerging truth: *Even if Arin had been there, it wouldn't have helped. It was easier when he was gone and harder when he was home. I am not very honest about this. I wanted a man who could be counted on in a crisis.*

And in the tiniest letters possible, I wrote my gnarliest, harshest, most naked truth: *Sometimes, I wish I could get a redo. Just walk away from my life and start over.* This *is the truth I keep buried under lock and key. My bitter private resentment. My reason I fear waking up and realizing we're no longer in love. That I'm too much for him. That he's not enough for me. Sometimes, it's more about what's missing, more about what* didn't *happen than what* did. *Fighting against an absence is like punching the air.*

I'd always wondered if a person could unearth themselves if buried alive. After baring my God-honest feelings to the page, I also doubted whether digging myself out from beneath years of stratified pain would ever be possible.

Now, I know the answer to both: You remove one small scoop of dirt and then another by acknowledging one brutal truth at a time.

These secret truths—so dazzling when concealed—appear dull as stones when brought into the light.

Still, they are not without value.

Once acknowledged, my bitter resentment held no more sway over me than my fears. They were no longer invisible powers that bound me but simply curiously conjoined strands of beliefs, thoughts, and feelings. In all honesty, these deep-rooted feelings didn't vanish entirely but still reared their ugly heads—more often at first and then less so—as Arin and I began addressing the parts of our relationship that had taken the hardest hits.

Soon enough, I found the freedom and courage to speak openly of my pain and resentment. Arin listened attentively and then profusely and earnestly apologized. In return, he referenced how I'd hurt, enraged, criticized, and stifled him, and I sought his forgiveness through tears. Even then, the cycle didn't end. We fought and made up and fought and made up; we just always made sure to make amends one more time than we fought.

Eventually our old battle wounds would heal over enough that, just like Caleb's shredded back, we, too, would be able to—first cringingly and then unflinchingly—examine our thick, lumpy scars. In time, we would learn to simply embrace them as part of our life-landscape, as Caleb's scars had become part of his.

In the meantime, admitting my entombed feelings to myself was sufficient, for as I did, an expansive space opened up not just in my chest but, more specifically, in my heart.

I had recently journaled: *In my chronic state of soul-amnesia, I have forgotten my first love. It feels shallow, not substantive, and I wonder—do I just need to settle for what* is? *Still, I want more. I want everything. Yet I look and find nothing. I touch and feel nothing. Am I dead or just buried alive? There is a barrier I can't break through:* self-preservation. *It keeps me from accessing the good memories, the blissful feelings, and the warmth for fear of getting hurt. In this one area, I can't descend from my head to my heart.*

However, once I had spoken my truths, this self-preservation vanished into thin air, for there was nothing left to protect.

Late one night, when Arin was working, I dug out dusty boxes of old love letters and photographs. The man that wrote them was now years older yet, in so many ways, still the same—still exuberant, effusive, and brimming with love for his bride. But his bride had seemingly aged, not just chronologically but deep in her soul. Her weary heart had been broken repeatedly, and she had spent years unintentionally fortifying it to avoid feeling pain. Now she felt ancient, entirely detached from her young, carefree self. And yet . . . and yet . . . she still had her groom. For better or worse, richer or poorer, in sickness and health, they had weathered life's storms. Together. His enduring presence still served as her ever-uniting equator, and the spread of his arms still connected all her severed, disjointed fragments.

I stayed up late that night—hurting, laughing, crying, and *remembering* everything that time had erased.

Shortly after, I sat down to work on my memoir. For once, words tumbled freely onto the page: *For long before the darkness settled, there was light. In the beginning, there was a love story . . .*

We drove a long way down a twisty, snow-covered virgin road that had yet to be littered with tire tracks. The fresh snow creaked and groaned beneath the weight of our car as I directed Arin aloud.

Weeks prior, I'd pressed Arin to describe his dream vacation in great detail and then—from the newly expansive place in my heart—set out to make his dream our reality. Not surprisingly, his ideal getaway was blissfully simplistic: good food, a secluded, rustic cabin, a roaring fire, drifts of snow . . . and me "on a silver platter," as he laughingly—but dead seriously—described it.

The cabin was just as he'd imagined. Small enough to heat with a wood-burning fireplace, it was rustic, cozy, and plush. After traipsing snow across the earthy stone floor to unload bags of groceries and suitcases, at last, we locked the door behind us and didn't once reopen it the length of our stay.

For three days, we cooked every meal together and ate candlelit dinners by the fire. We feasted on filet mignon with herbed butter, crème brûlée, charcuterie boards, and barbacoa street tacos with red pickled onions. Between meals, we napped; we watched movies and the gently falling snow, entangled in each other's embrace. Ice crystals crept up the sides of the windows, courteously shielding us from the world. But by and large, we spent most of our time reading out loud as we once did as newlyweds on my grandparents' farm.

I had recently listened to *A Severe Mercy* by Sheldon Vanauken; it was the only love story I'd ever read that seemingly rivaled our own. As the final chapters unfolded, I had sat frozen on the edge of my bed, dirty laundry clenched in my hand and bawling like a baby as Sheldon's wife, Davy, died an untimely death. After I finally finished crying, I called Arin and *demanded* that we read the book together. I then began searching for the perfect cabin to facilitate our three-day getaway.

We easily slipped into old patterns—Arin would read until he grew tired, and then I'd take over. He started, "We met angrily in the dead of winter. I wanted my money back. Her job was to keep me from getting it. . . . I left it with her and, quite possibly, stalked away."[1] He continued later in Chapter 2, "All the same, though I hadn't said so, she *was* indeed precious to me. The truth is, we were in love almost from the first, falling into love if not fallen on that first night."[2]

I studied Arin as he read, now with glasses, a smattering of gray hair, and a faintly emerging bald spot. Come July, we would celebrate our twenty-first anniversary. Where had the years all gone?

As we handed the book back and forth, we found our own lives overlaid atop Sheldon's and Davy's, the waxing and waning of our own love amid the joys and heartbreaks of life. Therefore, by the end of the book, they had become our newfound friends, and when Davy was diagnosed with cancer, we found ourselves weeping alongside them in her final stages of life.

No longer could we read one chapter before switching. Now, we could barely read a paragraph before passing the book.

Arin reading *A Severe Mercy* out loud at our rented cabin

Through his tears, Arin struggled to read, "At three in the morning, the telephone. I think I knew before my eyes were open. It was the hospital. Davy was dying. Her pulse was slowing. There could be no rally. I asked how long. They thought several hours. It had come at last."[3]

Wiping my eyes, I took over. "There was a long silence, I still stroking her hand. Then she said in a stronger voice: 'Oh God, take me.' I knew then with certainty that she understood that she was dying. I said: 'Go under the Love, dearling. Go under the Mercy.'"[4]

Choking mid-sentence on the lump in my throat, I passed the book back to Arin.

"The hand moved slowly across her," he read haltingly. "It found my face. She touched my brow and hair, then each eye in turn. Then my mouth. Her fingers moved to each corner of my mouth, as we had always done. And I gave her fingers little corner-of-the-mouth kisses, as we had always done. Then her arm fell slowly back. Past seeing and past speaking, with the last of her failing strength, she had said goodbye."[5]

When we finished the book, Arin laid it reverentially on the coffee table. We sat without speaking for a long while; there was nothing to say.

After a while, he crawled from his couch to mine on hands and knees; then we lay together—melded as one—in transcendent silence.

Our last morning at the cabin, I arose when it was still dark, pulled out my journal, and filled its final pages:

> *If ever there has been perfection in days, this was it. Delicious food,* A Severe Mercy, *absolute union and synchronicity. I feel like I have my husband back, and he is remembering who he is and who he was meant to be—or perhaps it is simply I who have remembered.*
>
> *At the end of another journal, I am left undone. God's faithfulness splashed across page after page, a beautiful story being written by Another that is now my privilege to record. It is my testimony to Love incarnate and who I have painstakingly and ever so beautifully learned God to be.*
>
> *"I will not die but live, and will proclaim what the Lord has done."[6]*
>
> *This. This is my "why." This is my reason for writing. To tell of God's goodness and faithfulness. To show that faith, love, and beauty can triumph over darkness.*
>
> *Because this is what I was meant to do . . .*

One month later, I wrote Arin a letter but again failed to share it:

> *My sweet husband,*
>
> *Recalling our past memories without concurrently thinking of the future's limitations is impossible. A life lived so fully as ours does not prepare one to part with the flesh it has spent years becoming one with, even if the separation is*

but temporary. Last night, we sat up late—laughing, crying, remembering our many good times, and falling asleep in each other's arms—satiated and grateful for each and every moment we've shared.

Today, I recall Thoreau's words, which have been a part of me even before you, "I went to the woods because I wished to live deliberately, to front only the essential facts of life, and see if I could not learn what it had to teach, and not, when I came to die, discover that I had not lived. I did not wish to live what was not life, living is so dear; nor did I wish to practise resignation, unless it was quite necessary. I wanted to live deep and suck out all the marrow of life. "[7]

I know this weighs heavily on both of our hearts. How do we live only that which is truly life with our eyes open to the dearness of every day, sucking deeply and savoring the marrow of life? How do we abide in such a state, so that should death come calling unannounced, we would not be found with the acrid taste of regret on our tongue? Rather, we would be able to say, as we always have (though perhaps through torrential tears), "If I died today, I would die a happy man or woman."

Since reading A Severe Mercy, *we have discussed the weighty topic of time in great detail. Historically, it has been depicted as the great enemy, robbing us all of youth, beauty, health, loved ones, and ultimately, our very life. People often speak of slowing time, stopping it, or turning back its hands. Yet I have been wondering, What if our discomfort with time is merely an indication that we are, in fact, created to exist beyond it? Might not our longing for timelessness perhaps be our best evidence that we are, indeed, eternal beings, as the great C. S. Lewis says?*

I've been thinking about these memories we've been reliving—the first time we saw each other, how we met, our first date, etc.—and in each one, the concept of time is mysteriously absent or bizarrely twisted; either the seconds seem eternal or long hours dissipate like a vapor. But no matter how much time passes, such memories are retained with undistorted and unchanging lucidity; I can still see you exactly as you were, yet oddly enough, exactly as you are. Somehow, we are able to meld our past and present-day selves into a sole vantage point, slipping seamlessly between then and now as ageless beings. Regardless of the fact that I am currently forty or the fact that I was but nineteen, in every memory, I exist only as "me" in a singular, ageless form. Upon recollection, I can never perceive my age but only my being.

I have been meditating on these incomprehensible concepts for quite some time now, rolling them around in my head like a sticky ball of wax, only to arrive at more wonderings within my wanderings. What if, in these "timeless" memories, we are experiencing neither the hyperbolic nor the figurative slowing of time, but rather the entrance into its fullness? What if the precious moments of life—a first kiss, a child's birth, the passing of a loved one—do not occur outside of time but rather within its fullness?

What if all these moments are actually holy portals into eternity where we experience, albeit briefly, the undiluted clarity, an etherealness of sorts, that is possible only outside the confines of time? And if this were, in fact, true, could we not learn how to live more frequently within this fullness of time, to "suck the marrow" out of all of life, so that our days simply evolve like stalactites, lengthening and strengthening with the addition of each and every plump, round, and even painful moment?

I have come to believe that this might certainly be a possibility. We recently spent the better part of an afternoon lying together on your sister's porch swing. Normally this would be an opportunity to escape and ramble aimlessly through the endless aisles of my mind, but instead, for whatever reason, I remained not only present but attentive. I became acutely aware of your warm body and breath—both reminders of life and the fact that we had been gifted with yet another day not promised and literally spent in each other's arms. I felt your heart beating within my ear and was carried on the rhythmic rising and falling of your chest. The sun was warm, the breeze was cool, and in that moment, any intruding consciousness of time fell away, and we simply . . . existed. We did not exist for a purpose or a goal, yet our mere existence was not only sufficient but glorious. Perhaps an eternal portal was propped open for an afternoon so we might experience a taste of wholeness and holiness. In that moment, the simple once again became sacred, and time was redeemed.

I vaguely remember drifting off to sleep, full on the marrow of life, deeply and wholeheartedly aware that "if I never wake, I will have died a happy woman."

In hindsight, there is no way of disentangling the good moments from the bad or the happy memories from the painful ones. They have all been intertwined, each pregnant with potential and highly profitable; if even one is removed, the whole tower topples. Without any singular aspect of our life, I cease to be me.

For I am a life constructed of moments—the JoyfulSorrows, the PainfulBeauties—all flip sides of the same coin. In so many ways, I am a walking contradiction.

Although my life is hopefully far from over, after almost twenty-one years of marriage, I can honestly say as you once did, that "I see God" in everything—in you, in every one of our children, in nature, in the ups and the downs, and in each and every bittersweet moment of life.

I'll close with the words of St. Teresa of Avila. Truly, "all the way to Heaven is Heaven."

I remain now and eternally,
Your loving wife

Epilogue

There was once a time when the bottom of my world dropped out, and I tumbled headfirst into deep, dark waters. I was consumed, swallowed whole, and lived for many years like Jonah in the belly of the whale. Black, shallow breaths connected emptiness to more emptiness, and I floated in and out of days like a ghost—partially alive but mostly dead. Like stomach acid, my afflictions corroded my protective callouses, stripped me of my dignity, and left me raw, naked, bleeding, and exposed.

My closest companion was the fear that laid claim to my life. It bound me to itself with tentacled brute force and presumptuously siphoned my life breath as if entitled to half of everything I owned. Unable to escape its crushing embrace, I resigned myself to its presence and simply settled for smaller breaths.

In time, small beams of light began to filter in. They cast a new glow on all that once caused me to shrivel in fear. With newfound confidence, I stretched and righted myself, as humans were meant to stand, and reoriented myself toward the light. I gradually realized that what I had initially perceived as a cavernous belly was, in fact, a sacred womb and the ever-growing light indicative of an impending birth.

Extending my arm toward the light, I beheld my skin. Once raw and festering, it now glowed with the translucence of renewal. It was so glorious I didn't think twice about my naked vulnerability. I felt the womb contract and found myself being pushed forth into the wide world. After years of endless darkness, I reemerged, timid and hesitant, blinking and shielding my eyes from the sun.

Previously blinded by darkness, I now found myself blinded by the light. Yet this light was different. It didn't shine *on* me but rather *through* me. With rays both soft and piercing, it warmed and strengthened me from the inside out.

And so, with a little courage and much determination, I arose.

A singular task still remained. I began the arduous task of freeing myself from my long-term companion, who clung to me still. One tentacled limb at a time, I slashed and peeled and pried. Tears flowed as fear was released, for although it had been burdensome, it had traversed the darkness with me.

Finally free, I sank to the earth. With tearstained cheeks, I lifted my face Heavenward, closed my eyes, and breathed fully, deeply, all the way down to the tips of my toes . . . my first unfettered breath of liberation.

> I don't know how
> But suddenly there is no darkness left at all
> The sun has poured itself inside me
> From a thousand wounds.

—NIKIFOROS VRETTAKOS, "The First Thing of Creation"[1]

As I finish the final version of this memoir, Arin and I are experiencing a second honeymoon of sorts, as we are one year away from being empty nesters. Arin has positioned himself to mainly work from home, and I have found continued healing through psychedelic-assisted therapy. Together, we spend our days reading, hiking, and enjoying good food and each other's company. Reagan is in her senior year of high school and plans to pursue a degree in nursing. Grayson is attending a school in Utah that teaches autistic adults how to live independently. Despite ongoing struggles, he continues to make slow but steady progress and is increasingly learning to embrace his unique neurodiversity. Magic tricks are his newest passion. Jacob is pursuing a psychology degree at a college in northern Colorado. Rylee is living, working, and enjoying the beach in southern Florida, and Caleb is happily guiding fly-fishing river trips in Casper, Wyoming. Personal wounds and broken relationships are being left further and further in the past, as everyone in the family continues to strive toward interpersonal health and wellness.

Acknowledgments

First and foremost, I acknowledge my children: Caleb, Rylee, Jacob, Grayson, and Reagan. Without you, there is no book, no story. As this book evolved, I realized I was writing more for you than anyone. I wanted you to understand your lives and mine; subconsciously, I needed a way to explain your challenges and my shortcomings. Ultimately, I wanted you to know that each one of you is deeply and wholeheartedly seen and loved. This is your story, our story. It's my humble attempt to leave a paper trail that will, God willing, extend beyond my life. I love you all more than words could ever express. You *are* my heart.

Next, I thank my parents, Wayne and Cathi, as well as my sisters and best friends, Jenna and Dani. Dad, you gifted me with your creativity, your eye for beauty, and your sentimentality. Quietly, you taught me to notice what others failed to perceive. Mom, your keen eye for editing and willingness to read anything I've ever written—from elementary school until now—has not gone unappreciated. The security you provided led to my hesitant courage, and your amazing strength and independence paved my way. Jenna and Dani, there is too much. I would be lost without the friendship and all the talks, tears, and laughter.

Sweet Yaya, you have always loved me like a daughter and have cared for our family through thick and thin. You are a tremendous embodiment of unconditional maternal love. Thank you for being you and for raising such an extraordinary son!

Love and friendship go to Jeremy George. You are a beautiful human being, and your loyalty to this family is unmatched. I am so thankful our lives crossed paths.

My undying love and gratitude go to Grayson's incredible village: Drs. Steve and Mary; Dr. Cori; the entire SOAR staff, including Erin P., Michelle P., Sheilah R., Ginette A., Brandon R. (we love you so much!), and Kendra J.; the entire Sierra School staff, including Jennifer S., Jon Paul, Tanner W., Luis C., Emmie S., Ashley H., and Julie; and the Custer County staff, including Carrie D., Ms. CC, and Coach Hal, as well as Chris M. in Utah. I never would have survived without you all; your presence in the world is making a difference!

To *my* beloved village: Suzanne B., Dr. Mary, Lindsay H. K., Cinda, Mother Michaila, Father Tom, Presvytera Pat, Father Evan, Stacy, Father Stephen, and Presvytera Ashley: Each of you has carried the heavy burden of caring for *my* soul in some way, to varying degrees. Father Evan, you've carried the biggest load for the longest and will always hold a special place in my heart. To everyone else: Thank you for helping reassemble my broken pieces. May your loving care be returned to you tenfold!

A huge thank-you goes to all my dear friends and early readers who generously donated their time and encouragement: Emily B., Jean, Nicole B., Anna V., Peder, Kristin, Carly, Tama, Cosette, Michele, Suzanne, Alina, Darrin, Kathryn, Presvytera Ashley, Marge, Pam, and, of course, my family, my children, Carol, and Arin. Your encouragement was like beacons of light shining through the darkness.

Linda Sivertsen, the one and only Book Mama and midwife of stories: I was on my way to pick up the frozen beef from a half-cow (of all things) when I accidentally stumbled upon your *Beautiful Writers Podcast*. I bawled my way through the entire eight-hour drive; I never knew others felt as I did about writing. Thanks to my dear husband, I ended up at your Carmel writing conference, which changed the course of my life. You helped me see my invisible wings and even convinced me I might be capable of flying. From the bottom of my heart, thank you for believing in me.

My sincerest gratitude goes to my writing team: Victoria Savanh, my first editor, who bore the brunt of my grammatical errors (I always looked forward to our chats), and the entire Greenleaf staff—specifically, Benito, Rebecca, Claudia, Kyle, Jenny, Mimi, Laurie, Diana, and Brittany. This whole process has been a joy. Additionally, I would be remiss not to specifically acknowledge Dee Kerr, my first Greenleaf contact. You began sharing your story before even introducing yourself. How often do we moms ever come across another soul who *really gets it*? Thank you for being my cheerleader, my advocate, and now, my friend. You get this book because you've lived it. Blessings to you and yours.

Carol, my sweet *anam cara*, where would I be without you? You've shed the tears I couldn't cry for myself and showed up on my porch with dinner (including a gluten-free dessert for Grayson) when I was at my wits' end. You are my anchor, my heart's twin, my spiritual guide, and my best friend in the whole wide world. I love you more than anything. Thank you for being you.

Finally, to my husband, Arin, the love of my life: I would never have endeavored this project without your steady encouragement. You saw *God* in me when I couldn't find any *good* within; I am who I am because of your unconditional love. Now and always, I offer you my deepest gratitude, respect, admiration, friendship, and love. Indeed, we've created a beautiful life, Mr. Hatfield.

Notes

CHAPTER 2

1. Philippians 4:8 (NIV).

CHAPTER 3

1. Iain Matthew, *The Impact of God: Soundings from St. John of the Cross* (New York: Hodder and Stoughton, 1995), 28.

CHAPTER 5

1. Psalm 127:3, 5 (NIV).

CHAPTER 6

1. Emily Dickinson, "A Word Is Dead," in *The Poems of Emily Dickinson: Reading Edition*, ed. R. W. Franklin (Cambridge, MA: Belknap Press, 2005), 124.

CHAPTER 9

1. John Chryssavgis, *In the Heart of the Desert: The Spirituality of the Desert Fathers and Mothers* (Bloomington, IN: World Wisdom, 2008), 33, 35.
2. Chryssavgis, *In the Heart of the Desert*, 36 (italics added).
3. Chryssavgis, *In the Heart of the Desert*, 45–46.
4. Chryssavgis, *In the Heart of the Desert*, 51.
5. Beldon C. Lane, *The Solace of Fierce Landscapes: Exploring Desert and Mountain Spirituality* (New York: Oxford University Press, 1998), 220.

CHAPTER 11

1. The *Diagnostic and Statistical Manual of Mental Disorders* (*DSM*) is the handbook used by health care professionals in the United States and much of the world as the authoritative guide to the diagnosis of mental disorders.

CHAPTER 17

1. Martin E. P. Seligman, *Learned Optimism: How to Change Your Mind and Your Life* (New York: Vintage, 2006), 15.

CHAPTER 25

1. Brené Brown, *The Gifts of Imperfection* (Center City, MN: Hazelden, 2010), xii–xiii.
2. Brown, *The Gifts of Imperfection*, 1.
3. James 2:15–16 (ESV).

CHAPTER 30

1. John Cassian, *Conferences*, quoted in Olivier Clement, *The Roots of Christian Mysticism* (Hyde Park, NY: New City Press, 2013), 255.

CHAPTER 31

1. Freedom Drilling was the name of Arin's new business.

CHAPTER 34

1. We also read *The Four Seasons of Recovery* by Michael Speakman.

CHAPTER 35

1. Melody Beattie, *Codependent No More: How to Stop Controlling Others and Start Caring for Yourself* (Center City, MN: Hazelden, 1992), 62.
2. Beattie, *Codependent No More*, 75–76.
3. Beattie, *Codependent No More*, 65.
4. These quotations are approximations from various episodes of Dr. Brad Reedy's *Finding You: An Evoke Therapy Podcast*.
5. Beattie, *Codependent No More*, 82.
6. "Bop" is what all the grandkids call my dad.

CHAPTER 36

1. Elitch Gardens is a theme park in Denver, Colorado.
2. Job 13:15 (NKJV).

CHAPTER 39

1. Peter A. Levine, *In an Unspoken Voice: How the Body Releases Trauma and Restores Goodness* (Berkeley, CA: North Atlantic Books, 2010), 181.
2. Levine, *In an Unspoken Voice*, 159.

CHAPTER 40

1. Iain Matthew, *The Impact of God: Soundings from St. John of the Cross* (London: Hodder and Stoughton, 1955), 10.
2. I chose to write these EMDR sections in the present tense because, in so many ways, they happened *outside* of time. They were the culmination of past and present, and it never felt quite right to write about them in past tense.

CHAPTER 41

1. The wheel she had me view is also available at https://feelingswheel.com.

CHAPTER 43

1. Matthew, *The Impact of God*, 51.
2. Matthew, *The Impact of God*, 63.
3. Matthew, *The Impact of God*, 65.
4. Matthew, *The Impact of God*, 65.
5. Annie Dillard, *The Writing Life* (New York: Harper Perennial, 1990), 68.

CHAPTER 44

1. Sheldon Vanauken, *A Severe Mercy: A Story of Faith, Tragedy, and Triumph* (New York: HarperCollins, 1987), 24.
2. Vanauken, *A Severe Mercy*, 28.
3. Vanauken, *A Severe Mercy*, 174.
4. Vanauken, *A Severe Mercy*, 175.
5. Vanauken, *A Severe Mercy*, 176.

6. Psalm 118:17 (NIV).

7. Henry David Thoreau, *Walden and Other Writings of Henry David Thoreau* (New York: Random House, 1950), 81.

EPILOGUE

1. Nikiforos Vrettakos, "The First Thing of Creation," quoted in John Chryssavgis, *Soul Mending: The Art of Spiritual Direction* (Brookline, MA: Holy Cross Orthodox Press, 2000), 48.

About the Author

COREY HATFIELD was born and raised in Colorado. She and her college sweetheart, Arin, have been married for twenty-five years and are the proud parents of five grown children, one of whom is autistic. Through many turbulent, overwhelming years of parenting, Corey encountered beauty to be the great healer of trauma and now feels passionate about sharing her journey with fellow strugglers. Rather than viewing suffering as a curse, she believes it to be a gift, capable of opening humanity to deeper levels of healing and growth. She and her husband now live on eighty peaceful acres in the Wet Mountains of southwestern Colorado.

The Light from a Thousand Wounds is Corey's debut memoir. Readers can connect with her at www.coreyhatfield.com.

Know someone who could benefit from this book?
Send a signed and personalized copy by visiting
www.coreyhatfield.com.

30883709R00236